People, Property, or Pets?

New Directions in the Human-Animal Bond

Alan M. Beck, Series Editor

People, Property, or Pets?

edited by Marc D. Hauser,
Fiery Cushman, and
Matthew Kamen

Purdue University Press/ West Lafayette, Indiana

Printed in the United States of America.

Library of Congress Cataloging-in-Publication Data

People, property, or pets? / edited by Marc D. Hauser, Fiery Cushman, and Matthew Kamen.
p. cm.
Includes bibliographical references and index.
ISBN 1-55753-380-6 (alk. paper)
1. Animals--Law and legislation--United States. 2. Animal rights--United States.
I. Hauser, Marc D. II. Cushman, Fiery. III. Kamen, Matthew.
KF390.5.A5.P46 2005
346.7304'7--dc22

2005012734

Contents

Preface ix

I. Philosophy 1

Ariel Simon
Cows as Chairs: Questioning Categorical Legal Distinctions in a Non-Categorical World 3

Derek Hass
The Case for Animals 9

Neha Jadeja
Why the Status of Animals Should Remain as Property 17

Catie Lowder
The Case for Animals as the Property of Humans 25

Bernard E. Rollin
Animal Ethics and Legal Status 33

II. Law 47

Alex Pollen
Consistency and Rights 49

David Hambrick
A Legal Argument against Animals as Property 55

Ian Tomb
The Legal Perspective on Animal Rights 59

Hélène Landemore
Why Should One Reject the Motion Intending to Remove Animals from the Status of Property? 65

Gary L. Francione
Animals, Property, and Personhood 77

III. Cognitive Science 103

Fiery Cushman
Aping Ethics: Behavioral Homologies and Nonhuman Rights 105

Robbie Silverman
Cognitive Beasts: The Thoughts and Feelings of Animals 119

Justin Jungé
An Argument from Cognitive Science against Increasing Legal Rights for Animals 127

Lewis Petrinovich
Evolved Aspects of Morality Determine Legal Rights of Animals 133

IV. Biomedical Research 143

Frances Chen
A Critical Review of Animal Experimentation: Moral and Practical Problems, Alternatives and Necessary Changes 145

Jonathan Flombaum
Why Animals Should Own Their Genes, and, Therefore, Own Themselves 153

Lisa Guttentag
Nonhuman "Pain" and Animal Rights 159

Virginia Vance
The Importance of Animal Testing in Biomedical Research 165

Andrew N. Rowan
Animal Welfare and Biomedical Research 173

V. Animal Care 181

Matt Kamen
Ethics . . . It's What's for Dinner 183

Rianna Stefanakis
Treating Animals Humanely: Veterinary Medicine's Defense to the Law 191

Allen Yancy
Veterinarians and the Case against Legal Personhood for Animals 197

Temple Grandin
Animals Are Not Things 205

Conclusion 213

Contributors 215

Index 221

Preface

Marc D. Hauser

In the spring of 2002, I offered an undergraduate seminar at Harvard University entitled "Evolutionary Ethics." This book represents the culmination of that seminar, plus more. The essays represent non-technical reflections on a topic with wide ranging implications for law, philosophy, evolution, medicine, psychology, and our own individual lives: how we should think about the legal status of nonhuman animals.

A good seminar is like a good recipe. You need the right ingredients, a good environment, and a bit of luck. I was lucky, and the ingredients fell into place. You can't run a seminar with more than about 20 students. On day one, about 50 showed up, eager to take the class, surprised to be handed an exam. The exam consisted of a moral dilemma. I wanted to see each potential student work through the logic of a question concerning the role of genetics in understanding issues of responsibility. The answers were quite uniformly terrific, but somewhere in the vicinity of 20–25 stood out. I offered these students slots in the course. I ended up with 19 exceptional minds. For the first few meetings of the course, we read parts of a book I was working on, as well as some other general readings. All students in the class had taken a sampling of courses in evolutionary theory, social behavior, cognitive psychology, philosophy, and economics. All were hungry, ready to attack the difficult material that was waiting for them. But there was more. I had recruited the help of friends and colleagues to come and give lectures. The parade of stars included Howard Rachlin, Adele Diamond, Steve Gould, Herb Gintis, Reverend Peter Gomes, David Haig, Daniel Dennett, Dan Gilbert, Steve Pinker, Frank Marlowe, and Alan Dershowitz. Prior to each lecture, we read, discussed, and criticized papers by the lecturer. By the time the lecture was underway, every student was ready, eager to get a word in, challenge, and debate. The seminar was superb. I have never seen student's master material so beautifully, and challenge people far senior to them with grace and intensity. This is all background. My favorite quote from the course came in a discussion with the legal scholar and lawyer Alan Dershowitz. A student had taken apart one of Dershowitz's arguments concerning natural rights, and suggested that it was wrong in at least three ways. The student then asked, "Given these problems, Professor Dershowitz, how can you defend your position?" Dershowitz, after a fairly long silence, said, "My boy, you have no idea how arrogant I am!"

The final exam was a moot court debate. Prior to the debate, each student drew a slip of paper from a hat. On each slip I placed two pieces of information, the student's 1) designated profession and 2) whether they were PRO or CON concerning the target topic of debate. The professions were: lawyer, philosopher, veterinarian, biomedical ethicist, and cognitive scientist. The focal debate question was:

> A proposal has just been presented that, if passed, will be brought in front of the Supreme Court. The motion is to remove animals from the status of property. If such a motion passes, this would eliminate biomedical research on all animals, and would also prevent using animals as sources of food. This motion would also eliminate or at least change how we think about breeding animals either as pets or for medical purposes. As stated, this motion would convert animals from property to a status that is equivalent to children, moral patients who require guardianship from human adults (moral agents). Those arguing for the PRO side should find as much evidence in favor of this motion as possible, while the CON side should find evidence to defeat this motion.

Students were given approximately two weeks to research their positions and then write an essay. Once the essays were in, I revealed the members of the PRO and CON teams. At this point, the teams assembled, went over their notes, and prepared for the debate. The debate went on for three hours, with each side making excellent points and conceding others.

As a teacher, the experience of reading the essays and hearing the discussion was exhilarating. This is what education should be like. I kept telling other faculty about the quality of the seminar and of the essays written for the final exam. It was at this point that I decided that it would be interesting, and educational, to collect the essays and publish them together with invited pieces from distinguished scholars in the areas of animal welfare and rights. This volume represents the culmination of this effort. The student essays represent opinion pieces, the kind of intelligent arguments one expects reading the op-ed section of the *New York Times.*

The invited essays come from experts in each of the target disciplines. Gary Francione, a lawyer who has worked with PETA, has championed the position that is at the core of this book: animals must be removed from their legal status as property. Bernard Rollin, a moral philosopher who early on entered the debates concerning animal welfare, has applied philosophically rigorous arguments to generate suggestions for improving the lives of animals, including most recently issues of euthanasia. Andrew Rowan, a biochemist by training, and currently vice president of the Humane Society of America, has long promoted the rights of animals, focusing on issues of education and alternative biomedical procedures. Temple Grandin, a professor of animal science who is autistic, has used her visually oriented perspective on the world to design animal housing facilities that, due to their sensitivity to an animal's species-typical behavior, greatly reduce stress. Lewis Petrinovich is a comparative psychologist who has worked with captive and wild animals, and has shown how insights from evolutionary theory can be used to dismiss certain untenable positions about animal welfare, while simultaneously supporting other positions.

There are many books on animal welfare. This book is different, not only from other books in the field of animal welfare, but from almost any other book that I know of. Its uniqueness stems from two sources. First, it blends expert critique with intelligent opinion from a non-expert audience or consumer. Second, it provides short, non-technical essays on a topic of utmost importance to the future of biomedical research, diet, legal policy, and our relationship to animals. Although each essay approaches the problem from a different perspective, there is a surprising level of convergence. All of the essays agree that questions concerning the legal status of animals start from questions concerning our obligations to other species. What can we do with and to them? What actions are permissible, forbidden, or obligatory? Answering these questions relies on three sources of knowledge: 1) scientific evidence concerning the thoughts and feelings of animals, 2) legal discussions of property and human rights, and 3) biomedical evidence of human health, including its reliance on animals as food, research subjects, and pets.

Experts in the field should be interested in the student essays, as they represent intelligent opinions on a range of issues related to the legal status of animals; in several cases, they also present interesting ideas for future research, building on some of the latest developments in animal cognition and cognitive neuroscience. Policy makers will find this book of value in that it gives a sense of opinion, of how non-experts think about these important issues, and how they might vote. Educators will find the essays of interest both in terms of their quality, and in terms of thinking about ways to engage students that go beyond multiple choice exams. At one level, teaching represents the transmission of information from an expert to a non-expert. More importantly, I believe, it represents the transmission of questions and challenges from one mind to another. Challenges come in different flavors. This book of essays represents the end product of a long educational journey, including heated discussion among students with different backgrounds, lectures and debates with leading scholars, and critical writings that were edited, edited, and edited. I hope you will enjoy both student and expert essays. They give a sense of what it is like to be in a great seminar. If there is a feeling of quirkiness, then I have done my job. If you have learned something from reading both expert and non-expert, then I have really done my job.

For financial help during the writing of this book, we thank Harvard University, and in particular, the Expository Writing Center for providing us with a small grant. Royalties from this book will be donated to organizations and individuals interested in continuing discussion of these important topics and in promoting animal welfare and conservation.

Section 1—Philosophy

THE PHILOSOPHY OF ANIMAL WELFARE begins with a single question: What is the source of moral value? In this first section, the authors explore a variety of possible answers. Any creature that is able to perceive pain or satisfaction might be owed consideration. Alternatively, higher cognitive abilities might be requisite: self-reflection, rationality, future planning, and language, for instance. Others set the bar still higher, demanding that a being participate in the moral life of a larger community to enjoy the community's protections. And, taking a different approach than the student essays, which typically argue from abstract moral principles, the philosopher Bernard Rollin used his commentary to advocate a more pragmatic source for morality: human intuition.

The problem of locating moral worth shares the limelight in this chapter with the so–called argument from marginal cases, which attempts to prove that animals meet any rational criteria for moral consideration, no matter what those criteria may be. The claim is simply that certain humans—the very young, or severely disabled, for instance—are at least as restricted in all morally relevant capacities as certain animals. This argument interfaces with the assertion that to categorically deny animals moral value is as indefensible as racism, sexism, or other biologically driven distinctions between human classes.

These philosophical essays may leave few issues resolved, but they open the door to diverse inquiries in the chapters that follow, setting the standard for the sorts of arguments—be they legal, scientific, or practical—that will ultimately count in a moral calculus.

Cows as Chairs

Questioning Categorical Legal Distinctions in a Non-Categorical World

Ariel Simon

Introduction

THE AMERICAN MAN'S BEST FRIEND is a delicatessen overseas, but in both cases dogs are classified legally as property. Consequently we fail to recognize the extensive qualitative differences that exist between animals and other forms of property. The crux of this essay is uncomplicated: I will argue that "property," as understood in a western sense, is simply a morally and legally untenable characterization of animal life. I have no pretensions of reclassifying animals in a manner that identifies the full scope of their rights, moral claims, and political standing; rather, I merely aim to show that the categorical barrier that we have erected legally and philosophically to set ourselves apart from nonhumans cannot be justified by the criteria we currently use. I will begin by examining the distinctions we use to justify our treatment of animals. Next, I will discuss the modern conception of "property" and show how it proves completely inadequate when referring to animals. I will conclude by explaining how a change in the moral status of animals would neither demand that we treat them as equals, nor render us incapable of treating various species of animals differently.

The Shortcomings of Existing Distinctions

In 1894, C. Lloyd-Morgan asked whether animals "reason"; centuries earlier, Descartes used "consciousness" as a proxy for delineating human rationality from the lived experiences of mere automata, his classification for "brute animals" (Lloyd-Morgan 1894).[1] Other criteria have been proposed as well: Do animals have emotions? Are they self-reflective? Do they possess a sense of self-ownership? Are they capable of meaningful communication? Is their intelligence different in kind or degree? But despite a number of plausible proposals, none is truly satisfying.

The problem with most attempts at defining the distinction between humans and animals is that they depend on invoking alleged "animal deficits." As a number of academics and animal-rights advocates have convincingly argued, "there is simply no such defect that is possessed by animals that is not also possessed by some group of human beings."[2] Imagine the simplest example: a human with severe, debilitating brain damage is hooked up to a machine that permits others (his children, lawyer, physician, or spouse) to artificially continue his life. In his "natural" condition, he would have died long ago. He lacks consciousness or awareness about his current condition, and has long since stopped interacting with his environment in any meaningful way. In nearly every objective sense, such an individual will never again engage with the environment as richly as a normal chimpanzee, or even a healthy cow. Yet, we would find the proposition that it is appropriate to classify him as property—let alone consume or skin him for hide—morally egregious.

The discord between the rights of animals and humans equivalent in all relevant respects can be reconciled three ways. First, we can accept that consciousness, rationality, and similar cognitive metrics are not coherent moral criteria for the denial of basic rights, and hence cannot be used to classify all animals as morally different in kind from humans. Second, we can maintain that these distinctions are appropriate, accepting that our moral behavior is guided by a species bias. Third, and lastly, we can posit a moral calculus at play that justifies our unequal treatment of otherwise similar human and nonhuman actors.

The first of these alternatives is the only truly acceptable one. We can of course create any number of distinctions to separate our species from others, but whether these distinctions are morally relevant and consistently applied is the question critical to this discussion. I do not wish to ignore or deny gradations in potentially relevant criteria between animals and humans (in terms of intelligence, capacity for the expression of individual preferences, and so on), but as I will suggest later in this essay, these gradations cannot possibly justify the strictly dichotomous classification and treatment of man and animal.[3] First I will address the two alternatives that remain.

The second alternative, which accepts the categorical distinction between humans and animals based on cognitive ability as a matter of acceptable group bias, is simply morally incoherent. While a "speciesist" bias may in fact be a fundamental element of innate human intuitions (possibly even having played a crucial role in our evolutionary past), it is nonetheless an archetype of arbitrary discrimination. This type of group-based discrimination runs counter to nearly every ethical premise of our legal system. It is precisely this sort of intuition that our reason rejects and our laws are designed to protect us from.

The third alternative, which supposes that the violation of animal rights is justified by the consequent human benefits, is at least imaginable; after all, we justify meat eating in a number of ways, such as taste, pleasure, and nutrition. Still, it is very difficult to envision an argument that does not include a conceptual litmus test that justifies categorical differences in treatment or classification. We would never apply similar rules to humans, allowing some to be eaten for the enjoyment of others.

In short, if animals are to hold qualitatively different legal standing from humans, distinctions are needed. But, in the absence of some absolute difference that is legally and morally relevant, these distinctions cannot logically defend categorical lines in how we classify and thus treat animals. We either need new distinctions, or a new way of describing our moral relationship with other creatures.

The Problems with "Property"

The presumption that animals are "property" fails not only because it falsely draws categorical differences where there are none, but also because the category of "property" is one ill-suited to our intuitive and scientific understanding of an animal's own experience of life. It is difficult to imagine that anyone would claim that a pet monkey and an inanimate carbon rod hold equal moral weight. "Property" is a tradable asset—one that can be bartered, used, and abused as an owner sees fit (within limits that do not unduly undermine his or her neighbors' enjoyment of their property). But does anyone truly believe that the well-being of an animal is a tradable commodity?

Robert Nozick, in *Anarchy, State, and Utopia,* offers a brutally direct example of a dilemma that we could not reasonably justify:

> Suppose that I enjoy swinging a baseball bat. It happens that in front of the only place to swing it stands a cow. Swinging the bat unfortunately would involve smashing the cow's head. But I wouldn't get fun from doing *that;* the pleasure comes from exercising my muscles, swinging well, and so on. It's unfortunate that as a side effect (not a means) of my doing this, the animal's skull gets smashed. To be sure, I could forego swinging the bat, and instead bend down and touch my toes or do some other exercise. But this wouldn't be as enjoyable as swinging the bat. . . . So the question is: would it be all right for me to swing the bat in order to get the *extra* pleasure of swinging it as compared to the best available alternative activity that does not involve harming the animal? Suppose that it is not merely a question of foregoing today's special pleasures of bat swinging; suppose that each day the situation arises with a different animal.

"Is there some principle," Nozick rhetorically asks, "that would allow the killing and eating of animals for the additional pleasure this brings, yet would not allow swinging the bat for the extra pleasure it brings?" (Nozick 1974).

Why do we find this a particularly abhorrent scenario? Would it be any different if someone else was doing the swinging for us, and we derived voyeuristic pleasure out of watching him? Or, alternatively, imagine a property owner doing an equivalent thing, except instead of cow heads, he smashes lamps. We might label him a sociopath, but there would probably be nothing immoral about the act. Why? In the previous pages, I voiced skepticism about creating artificial demarcations where there are none—recognizing that, with regard to most capacities, the differences that are generally observed in the animal world (and would be relevant for moral calculations) are differences of degree, rather than of kind. Yet by virtue of what animals can experience—pain, suffering, fear, preference, and so on—they are very different in kind from an unfeeling, senseless carbon rod, a dishwasher, or a car. Property implies that we see an object's value through the context of its owner's welfare, a denial of intrinsic value that seems inappropriate in the case of animals. Do animals really not have some inherent welfare, independent of their owners, that justifies special consideration when we are deciding how to treat them? Given the extent of their similarities, it seems that animals, like humans, deserve not to be subjected to pain, suffering, or fear without consent—these experiences are genuine and carry a greater moral weight than tradable, material property.

Consent, however, is a problematic concept to gauge in the case of creatures generally incapable of complex communication with humans. The limits of human psychology keep us from understanding how an animal would even think about the notion of consent to begin with. We can subject animals to a slew of exams, studying their observed preferences, motivations, and emotional states, but we cannot think like them, and so extrapolating consent from their behavior would be an uncertain endeavor. The appropriate response certainly requires more than assuming that their consent is immaterial. Just as people born deaf and mute lose no rights by their silence, animals' inability to agree to certain forms of treatment does not abrogate their right to self-ownership or their moral standing as creatures with motivations and desires.

The only alternative is to continue to treat animals legally as objects—the means to human ends. Because it denies the intrinsic value of animal lives, this approach fails to capture basic human intuitions. Consider a man who wantonly kills a puppy. In cases such as these, our outrage derives not from the violation of someone else's property (it could be that man's puppy, after all), but from the sense—indeed, the knowledge—that the puppy itself has been wronged. That our legal codes do not recognize the value of animal lives does not mean that we can reasonably group them with armoires under the auspices of the overwhelmingly broad category of "property." Rather, it means that it is time to change the laws.

Thinking in Degrees

Fish are clearly not human beings, and we are rightfully suspicious of any normative world-view that would cast them as moral equivalents. By the same token, cats are clearly not chairs, but we are far less reluctant to classify them under the same legal rubric. When approaching questions of legal status, our inclination is to think in terms of static and easily definable absolutes. I suggest that the animal world is more complicated than that, and, further, that our desire for convenient legal categories does not diminish our ethical obligation to act morally towards other agents who possess moral weight.

It is not as if we lack paradigmatic alternatives. Our legal system recognizes a variety of relationships that defy the labels of "equality" or "property." Children and the mentally ill, for instance, are both recognized as dependents that do not possess the range of skills necessary for full citizenship (they act under what is described as "diminished capacity"), and so are limited from enjoying the entire slate of rights normally afforded to functioning adults. We understand, however, that a categorical denial of rights to these groups would wrongly transform a cognitive difference in degree into a legal difference in kind. Consequently these groups enjoy a set of inalienable legal trump cards—what we call fundamental rights—that cannot be taken away irrespective of their actual emotional, intellectual, and social capabilities.

The same should hold true of animals. While distinctions are precarious when used to create and justify categorical differences in treatment, we can use socially relevant criteria to determine the full scope of empowerment that defines both humans and nonhumans alike. For example, we acknowledge that the cognitive development of children at the age of two leaves them unequipped to vote intelligently, and so they are not extended suffrage. Likewise, there is no reason to believe that reclassifying animals would necessarily entail an egalitarian legal order across species—there should be differences in terms of what kinds of rights they would be extended, as that reflects the non-categorical realities of nature. So, just as we could recognize that certain traits are necessary for the enjoyment of rights in the human political realm, so too would we be able to make distinctions between animals—for instance, recognizing that the pain experienced by a fly is very different from that experienced by horses, and treating them accordingly. An ethical approach to animal rights, in other words, would defy any type of gross generalization, whether it comes in the form of treating animals all as rights-bearing equals or as a morally impoverished form of property. Animals are better understood as dependents—nonhumans with "distinct capacities"—that we are obliged to approach with the same nuanced consideration as we do those with "diminished capacities" within our own species. Nature does not function in terms of categorical boundaries, and it is dangerous and ultimately intellectually disingenuous to force them onto the natural world just because it makes our laws marginally less complex.

Conclusion

In this essay I have argued that not only are categorical distinctions between humans and nonhumans in the legal realm discordant with any coherent system of justice or reflection of the natural world, but that property is a particularly inadequate category under which to group animals. This does not demand that we treat all humans and nonhumans alike, but instead that our legal system better deal with the reality that the natural world exists in shades of gray, rather than categorical reifications of black and white. The exact nature of these distinctions is left open to other legal thinkers, but the fact that such nuanced distinctions should exist in the place of more gross generalizations stands as a compelling argument against treating all animals as mere property. In the end, there is, and should be, a difference between the moral status of cows and chairs.

Notes

1. For a provocative refutation of the Cartesian position towards animal consciousness, see Huxley (1874).
2. For a particularly compelling argument along these lines, see Francione (1996).
3. A similar move was made in the nineteenth century, during the reclassification of slaves to full, rights-bearing citizens. See Lebovitz (2002).

References

Francione, G. L. (1996). "Animals as property." *Animal Law* 2.

Huxley, T. (1874). "On the hypothesis that animals are automata and its history." *Fortnightly Review* 22: 199–245.

Lebovitz, R. M. (2002). "The accordion of the Thirteenth Amendment: Quasi-persons and the right of self-interest." *St. Thomas Law Review* 14.

Lloyd-Morgan, C. (1894). *An introduction to comparative psychology*. London, Walter Scott.

Nozick, R. (1974). *Anarchy, state, and utopia*. New York, Basic Books.

The Case for Animals

Derek Hass

EVERY YEAR IN THE UNITED STATES we kill hundreds of millions of cows, pigs, and sheep, as well as over five billion chickens, for food (Singer 1975). That means each year our country slaughters nearly as many chickens as there are humans on this planet. These astonishing figures do not even include the hundreds of millions of other animals that we hunt or subject to painful and deadly experimentation each year. When one adds the years together, it quickly becomes apparent that humans have killed hundreds of billions and possibly even trillions of our fellow animals, often without much of a second thought.

Historically, this massive slaughter has been easily justified; we have believed that all animals are fundamentally different from humans, and so we have no reason to be concerned about their interests or their moral value. Rarely, if ever, do we eschew this long-held bias and consider if things really are so very different on the other side of the species line. It is not so much that we are scared of what we might realize, but more that the thought never even occurs to us. Having been fed meat from an early age and been taught that humans have used animals throughout the ages, we accept our treatment of animals as part of the natural order of things.

But, if we pause for a moment to contemplate animals' similarities to us, instead of just the differences, perhaps we will arrive at a more sound and reasoned consensus on how we ought to treat animals. Charles Darwin was the first to provide a robust challenge to the longstanding dichotomy between humans and animals. His evolutionary theory led to the inescapable conclusion that animals and humans share a common origin. Robbed of a *scala naturae,* those who have accepted the validity of evolutionary theory have been compelled to postulate specific characteristics delineating man from beast. Many have claimed that animals lack language, that they are not self-conscious, and that they are not aware of their interests. Yet the more we learn about other animals and ourselves, the less sure we can be that any meaningful differences in kind separate us from the rest of the animal kingdom. Philosopher Tom Regan argues in *Defending Animal Rights* that many animals resemble us:

> Like us, they possess a variety of sensory, cognitive, conative, and volitional capacities. They see and hear, believe and desire, remember and anticipate, and plan and intend. Moreover, as is true in our case, what happens to them matters to them. Physical pleasure and pain—these they share with us. But they also share fear and contentment, anger and loneliness, frustration and satisfaction, and cunning and imprudence; these and a host of other psychological states and dispositions collectively help define the mental lives and relative well-being of those humans and animals. (Regan 2001)

Yet, even if we identify some characteristic that the typical member of our species possesses, and the typical member of every other does not, it would be of little help in informing us about how we ought to act. While it may be interesting to examine the similarities and differences across species averages, this group level analysis offers little insight into how we should treat each individual being.

We treat each person as an individual of value when we evaluate his or her moral claims. Rights and interests, like responsibilities, reside in individuals. It is each person's obligation to obey the law, and similarly, each person, assuming he has met the requisite qualifications, has the right to an equal vote. We do not hold all of the members of a group responsible for the crimes of one of its members, nor do we think that when particular members of a group are the victims of a crime that an unharmed member of that group or the group itself has a claim to compensation. Rather, it is the members of that group, who themselves individually suffered, that have the legitimate case. For instance, the German government has provided compensation to Holocaust survivors, but not to all Jews. This is not to say that groups of humans, or similarly species of animals, are purposeless classifications, but rather that from a moral point of view species alone is not the proper level of analysis.

Once we are committed to viewing each individual human or animal on its own, and not as a generic member of its species, it becomes very hard to justify maintaining a dividing wall between all human beings and each and every other animal. As Alan Dershowitz explains in *Shouting Fire*, "There can be no sharp natural line between humans and animals. We are on a continuum. There are some animals closer to the human end of that continuum than some human beings" (Dershowitz 2002). As Dershowitz alludes, although we tend not to view them in this way, many humans are functionally no different from other animals, and some of the time possess even fewer or less developed capacities. Peter Singer points us to the case of massively brain damaged infants that are unable to talk, act, recognize others, or engage in any of the other most basic cognitive behaviors that normal humans exhibit. Many nonhuman animals exhibit these activities to a greater extent than such infants ever will (Dombrowski 1997). If we take any capacity and, as Dershowitz proposes, arrange all living beings on a continuum, many animals would be closer to the "human" end of the scale than many humans would be. We must treat each individual on his or her own accord, and recognize, as Peter Singer makes clear, that for whatever we decide the morally relevant factors are, that we must give equal consideration to each being that has those relevant traits. Thus, while taxonomic classifications may have a good deal of scientific use, they simply have no place in the moral domain.

Many philosophers, such as Carl Cohen, reply that the humans who are unfortunate enough to lack the mental capabilities that most of the rest of us possess should still be considered members of our moral community merely by virtue of our shared humanity (Taylor 1999). While I agree that these humans ought to be legally protected, I do not think that "humanity" itself is the source of those rights. Indeed, in what meaningful way can we say someone is "human" if they are devoid of the intellectual and psychological characteristics that we so closely associate with being human? While they may belong to our species in a biological sense, why does that matter from a moral point of view? Are we more interested in how we group beings by species, or in what goes on inside each of their minds? All humans are entitled to some basic rights; however, there are good reasons for granting them these rights independent of their membership in the human species, which is in and of itself insufficient justification.

It might be replied that we do not place these "marginal" individuals within the moral sphere because of any quality inherent to them, but rather as a practical matter. One consideration, for instance, is that the majority of the population has (or will have, as is the case with children) the as of yet unspecified morally relevant characteristics, and since it is hard for us to identify the few individuals who do not, we err on the safe side and extend the circle of protection to include all people. In this view, the human form becomes a proxy for identifying creatures possessing the requisite capacities for moral worth. This reply falters, though, since it still discriminates on the basis of species, a morally arbitrary characteristic. Applying Singer's equality of consideration principle, the doctrine that all things equal in the relevant regards should be considered equally in a given situation (Singer 1975), we cannot defend a moral system applied overly broadly to humans but narrowly to animals.

It makes no difference that applying the moral system to one group (the marginal humans) more broadly than to another elevates that group above the status that we might otherwise ascribe to it. Imagine that you were a teacher who had just finished grading her class's test. You knew that all of the students in your class who received an "A" were girls, but not all of the girls got an 'A.' Say you were going to give all of the students who received an "A" a piece of candy. However, you did not feel like checking to see which of the students earned an 'A,' so you just give a piece of candy to each of the girls. The boys in the class would be right to complain that if the girls who had not received an "A" still had been given a piece of candy, then they should have gotten one too. The same is true with animals and marginal humans, except that in real life we do not have a limited amount of moral candy to give out. We can continue to protect the marginal humans in the moral community, and still extend a long-overdue invitation to most animals as well.

Expanding the circle of individuals to whom we grant rights is not the only option that is compatible with considering equals equally. As Daniel Dombrowski explains, we could also treat marginal humans as we currently treat animals. Rather than bring members of other species of animals into the community, we would be kicking the marginal humans out. Although logically consistent, this drastic action is hardly an acceptable or justifiable alternative. The ridiculousness of relegating the marginal humans to the status of property does more than merely raise the specter of slavery or genocide, for, in many regards, we currently treat animals far worse than any slave was ever treated. Imagine a society that permitted the hunting of the deficient humans for sport, or one that funded research in which those same individuals were subjected to horrifically painful experimentation.

A more moderate possibility is to reconsider how we view both animals and "marginal" humans. The two groups would be put together into a separate class that is below the rest of humanity, but above those other organisms that do not possess, at a minimum, those relevant characteristics considered necessary for any rights at all (Dombrowski 1997). Yet even this supposed middle ground has rather untoward consequences, regardless of the amount of protection we afford the animals and the marginal humans. History speaks all too clearly on the pernicious effects that come from simply singling out certain groups of people as different or inferior.

Among the possible methods of giving equal consideration to beings with equal capacities—denying rights to some humans, admitting rights to many animals, or applying a set of rights to each that meets part way—the truth is we do not adhere to any. Unfortunately, we cannot simply decide which one of these three alternative worlds seems the most appealing to us. Instead, it is incumbent upon us, the rule makers, to be able to justify the decision to the satisfaction of all parties involved.[1] Our choice is, in large part, determined by the characteristics and abilities we decide are the morally relevant ones. Consequently, we must determine a set of traits, attributes, and capabilities that we believe are necessary in order for their possessor to be treated morally. If we reach a societal consensus that an individual must be able to abide by society's laws and have full use of human language, then we are obviously excluding many humans and all animals. Yet, if we decide that awareness of one's surroundings is the only requisite characteristic for being protected by a scheme of rights, then we would be lowering the bar to include nearly all humans along with many animals.

Due to a number of considerations, it would not be morally defensible to make the cutoff for basic moral consideration a particular level of a cognitive ability. There is no compelling reason why an individual must possess a certain amount of reasoning ability or why he/she must be able to fully use language in order to be granted moral consideration. Why do these, or any similar characteristics, matter when we are trying to decide who has basic legal rights? Is an advanced computer that can speak to and understand us entitled to moral consideration? While these cognitive abilities may be important factors when we are trying to decide whom we can hold responsible for individual actions, or who has additional rights, such as the right to vote, they have no place when we are trying to identify those individuals that ought to receive the basic legal protection of the state. It is instructive to consider how we would feel if we were at the lower end of the spectrum. Imagine some new species came to earth that is more perfect than we in every way. These beings are much more intelligent, more aware, more empathetic, and so forth. Would it be right for them to completely exclude us from moral consideration simply because we do not measure up to them in these cognitive regards? Is there not something about us, and indeed animals as well, that merits attention and respect regardless of how sophisticated our other abilities are?

Peter Singer persuasively maintains that it is incumbent upon us to grant moral consideration to any individual that has an interest, that is, a being about whose desires and interests we can speak intelligently. Applying this standard, we could tell the hypothetical aliens that how we are treated and what we are allowed to do have serious consequences for our well-being and happiness. Singer explains that as long as an individual has interests, his other capacities are not important from a moral point of view:

> We should make it quite clear that the claim to equality does not depend on intelligence, moral capacity, physical strength, or similar matters of fact. Equality is a moral idea, not an assertion of fact. There is no logically compelling reason for assuming that a factual difference in ability between two people justifies any difference in the amount of consideration we give to their needs and interests. (Singer 1975)

So what counts as having an interest? A being has interests if it has affective experiences or, put differently, if what happens to it influences how it feels. A simple way to think about this is to imagine what it would be like to be a certain creature. Based on what we know about animals, if a person suddenly became another animal, that person would still have an interest in a good life. If that same person changed into a flower, however, it would not really be possible to care in a meaningful way what happened to it. While the flower needs water and sunshine in order to grow, it does not feel anything in response to these nutrients. As Bernard Rollin explains, in order to have interests, an individual needs to have things that matter to it (Taylor 1999).

Singer further clarifies that sentience, the capacity for suffering and feeling joy, is both a necessary and a sufficient condition for having interests (Singer 1975). If an individual's well-being can be adversely affected by our actions, what justification do we have for not accounting for that individual's interests when we are deciding how to act? All sentient beings, including humans and the vast majority of animals, ought to be protected by our moral and legal code.

This standard is not as radical as it first appears. It does not change how we consider other humans, but simply extends that same consideration to animals as well. We arrived at this more enlightened position through three simple steps. First we broke down the barriers in our thinking that prevented us from appreciating how similar animals are to us in many respects. Then, based on our newfound understanding, we devised three possible courses of action. We could bring animals into the moral community, exclude marginal humans, or create an intermediate status in which animals and marginal humans are equal. Finally, we considered various criteria for evaluating our three options before we selected having an interest as the most appropriate. This decision necessarily led us to expand our moral domain to include animals. While not revolutionary in theory, our newly refined moral sensibility carries with it important practical consequences.

The first step is to make animals' legal status commensurate with their elevated moral status. This requires changing the legal categorization of animals from that of property to that of legal persons whose interests are protected by the law. It would no longer be permissible for humans to completely disregard animals' interests in the name of science or carnivorous cuisine. It does not matter that the animals themselves are not able to protect their interests from harm in society. Human babies, the very elderly, and severely retarded individuals are no more capable than animals of protecting their interests through the court system, yet with the assistance of legal advisors and guardians these individuals are able to have their interests safeguarded. Nor does it matter that animals are not capable of abiding by society's laws, for neither are many people. An individual can have rights, without having any corresponding duties. Yet, sentience is not always a sufficient condition for the granting of non-fundamental rights; individuals' cognitive abilities do matter a great deal when assessing their duties, or when granting rights beyond the minimum protection of noninterference.

Unquestionably, it will be difficult for many of us to undergo the complete transformation in our daily existences that this conclusion requires of us. Nor will the challenge end there, for we will need to be ever vigilant for our own lapses and for others' infringements. Like a newborn baby, animals will be completely dependent on us for protection of their moral and legal status. However, as we prepare to fulfill our obligations to fellow creatures, we need not see it as an undue burden, for we ought to take heed of Dershowitz's observation that "Those societies that treat animal life with greater respect tend also to treat human life with greater respect" (Dershowitz 2002).

Note

1. While we cannot explain our decision to animals so that they can understand it, we can imagine that the animals had representatives acting on their behalf, whom we would need to convince.

References

Dershowitz, A. M. (2002). *Shouting fire: Civil liberties in a turbulent age*. New York, Little, Brown, and Company

Dombrowski, D. (1997). *Babies and beast*. Urbana, University of Illinois Press.

Regan, T. (2001). *Defending animal rights*. Urbana, University of Illinois Press.

Singer, P. (1975). *Animal liberation: A new ethics for our treatment of animals*. New York, New York Review of Books: Distributed by Random House.

Taylor, A. (1999). *Magpies, monkeys, and morals: What philosophers say about animal liberation*. Peterborough, Broadview Press.

Why the Status of Animals Should Remain as Property

A Philosophical Perspective

Neha Jadeja

IN THE 1970S A PHILOSOPHICAL MOVEMENT BEGAN to challenge the treatment and consideration of animals in modern society (Taylor 1999). Now, a motion has been put forth to legally remove animals from the status of property. If passed, this motion has the potential to drastically alter many facets of modern society. Animals would be given a status similar to children as moral patients, and human adults, as moral agents, would be obligated to respect and guard their rights.

I intend to argue that this proposal is not tenable from a philosophical perspective, and therefore that the moral and legal standing of animals should remain as is. First I will argue that such a change in legal status would lead to morally unjustifiable consequences, such as mandatory vegetarianism and cessation of biomedical research on animals. Second I will argue that regardless of the consequences of this motion, the status of animals cannot change to non-property because animals do not have rights to begin with, and therefore humans cannot be obligated to treat them as non-property.

Consequences of the Motion

Mandatory Vegetarianism

Many sources on human health indicate that a moderate consumption of meat provides essential proteins and is healthier than a completely vegetarian diet (Frey 1987). We may therefore have a moral responsibility to protect ourselves from the health consequences of this proposal. Similarly, an overnight prohibition of eating meat would likely cause massive human death and malnutrition because the current food-production systems could not support the entire human population on a vegetarian diet. Even the most prevalent of animal liberationists, Tom Regan, asserts that death is a greater harm to humans than to animals because it closes more life-paths. Therefore, according to Regan's "worse-off principle," which states that the rights of many can be overridden when a few would be left worse off than any of the many, sacrificing animal lives to save human lives is morally justified (Frey 1987).

In addition, if we allow that even animals raised for slaughter lead satisfactory, though limited, lives and are killed without cruelty, we must conclude that non-existence is less preferable even to a short existence because being alive is a necessary condition for receiving benefits and pleasure. Thus, we may also have a strange responsibility to countless unborn domesticated farm animals to not deprive them of life entirely (Hare 1999).

Elimination of Biomedical Research on Animals

It is undeniable that the health and welfare of mankind has benefited greatly from scientific advances made in the past century that relied on animal research. As Bonnie Steinbock asserts, "freedom from pain and disease is a necessary condition for the exercise of those unique capacities that make possible a fully human life" (Taylor 1999). Thus, to halt this progress in medical knowledge would be to neglect the suffering of humans. It would be immoral to turn our backs on human suffering by abandoning medical research dependent on animal experimentation (McCloskey 1987). Lastly, we can once again use Regan's animal liberationist "worse-off principle" and assert that since death causes more harm to humans than to animals, animal research that undeniably saves countless human lives each year should not be banned.

The Case against Animal Rights

In the above arguments against mandatory vegetarianism and elimination of animal research, the conclusions hold independent of one's personal beliefs about whether or not animals are owed consideration. I now wish to argue from the opposite perspective—one depending not on consequences, but on rights. Irrespective of how untenable the consequences of the motion may be, humans have no obligation to treat nonhuman animals as non-property because animals do not have rights.

Duties towards Animals as Sentient Beings

Before I begin talking about rights exclusively, let me clarify a related issue, namely, the distinction between rights and interests. If we accept the claim of Regan and many other animal liberationists that animals are sentient beings, or that they have the capacity to feel non-trivial pain, then it follows that animals have interests (Dombrowski 1997). "Interests" in this context refers to a creature's preference for what is necessary or good for its own health and survival versus what is not. In this sense, even plants have an interest to obtain water. It is therefore evident that the interests of a shrub, a worm, a monkey, and a human differ categorically. As such, unless we wish to pursue this reasoning to an uninteresting extreme, we must conclude that interests are not the same as rights, and furthermore, that interest alone does not provide a sufficient framework for delineating rights (McCloskey 1983). Thus, while we may accept and even act upon a duty to minimize cruelty and suffering of animals because we recognize that they are sentient beings with valid interests, and perhaps also because we acknowledge that we have a general obligation as moral beings to minimize suffering on the whole, we must at the same time realize that this sense of duty is not and cannot be grounded in rights (Frey 1987). That animals do not warrant such rights will be argued in the remainder of this discussion.

Lack of Autonomy

According to Kantian philosophical thought, it is autonomy and not interests that imparts rights upon a being. Kant's basis for moral obligation in a rights based society, which he terms the categorical imperative, demands that an individual act in accordance with moral rules to govern behavior and not simply respond to desires, or interests, which may be quite contrary to a moral rule. In this view, moral agents possess moral rights because if one moral agent were to infringe upon the rights of another agent, the first agent would be using the second simply as a means to an end, and such an action, incapable of being consistently and rationally universalized to all agents, would violate the categorical imperative. Thus, according to the Kantian perspective, if animals are not autonomous, which is to say they cannot act in any other way then in accordance with their desires, then they are not able to govern their lives on the basis of understanding right and wrong, and therefore are not moral agents deserving of moral rights. Put somewhat differently, they exist outside of the "kingdom of ends," the moral community of autonomous agents bound by universal, reciprocal obligations. Since animals are not moral agents of this kind, humans may use them as means rather than ends without violating the categorical imperative. Therefore animals neither have moral rights nor enjoy corresponding obligations from humans to treat them as non-property.

Counterargument and Rebuttal: Preference Autonomy and the Concept of the Moral Patient

Tom Regan maintains that animals' interests do indeed constitute a form of autonomy, which he calls "preference autonomy." This term captures the idea that individuals are autonomous simply if they have preferences and are able to act on those preferences (Frey 1987). Regan agrees that beings such as animals that have preference autonomy but not the fuller Kantian sense of autonomy cannot be considered as moral agents. As a solution, Regan claims that such beings must be considered as moral beneficiaries, or patients. As moral patients, animals are "subjects-of-a-life" in that they have desires, beliefs, and preferences, and therefore they also have rights, such as the right to life, which moral agents are obligated to respect. However, because animals lack "full" autonomy and cannot make decisions according to an understanding of right and wrong, they do not have reciprocal obligations to other moral agents or beneficiaries (Dombrowski 1997).

Following R. G. Frey, I argue that Regan's concept of preference autonomy is uninteresting and wholly unsatisfying because it does not serve the function that we normally attribute to autonomy, which is to account for the value of a life through the capacity for self-determination. The ability to control desires and make choices is central to autonomy and life value. One can think of autonomy in the following way: all sentient beings have first-order desires or appetites, but the essence of autonomy is to be able to abstract from these appetites and use second-order desires to critically asses, evaluate, and choose between the first-order desires (Frey 1987). Thus, we are not just slaves to our desires, as the preference autonomy view would suggest. Rather, we can choose how to live our lives according to our own conceptions of the good life, and it is precisely this ability to choose and go beyond our first-order desires and preferences that is the fundamental source of meaning, richness, and value in our lives. The concept of preference autonomy is not a useful or satisfying view of autonomy.

Furthermore, even if we were to accept the preference autonomy argument, it still would not follow that animals, as moral patients, would have moral rights. H. J. McCloskey has argued that only moral agents can possess moral rights because the exercise of such rights requires the capacity for moral judgments such as which rights to accept and which to waive, what one can properly demand from another moral agent, and so on. Moral patients lack this moral capacity, and therefore "there can be no moral entitlement, no moral authority, no moral exercise or waiving of a moral right, and hence no moral rights possessed by [animals] that lack moral autonomy" (McCloskey 1987). Once again, we find that animals have no claim to moral rights and therefore humans have no obligation to treat them as non-property.

Counterargument and Rebuttal: The Argument from Marginal Cases

At this point, Regan and several other animal liberationists would turn to what I consider to be their strongest argument, that from marginal cases. The argument from marginal cases (AMC) begins with the observation that infants and severely mentally disabled people are utterly lacking in cognitive faculties, and consequently have no capacity for rationality or morality. The argument goes on to claim that these marginal cases are not autonomous in the full sense described above, and thus cannot be considered as moral agents. The only attributes that these beings do possess are sentience and interests, and yet we assume that infants and severely mentally handicapped people possess moral rights. Activists point out that many animals such as normal, adult mammals have highly developed mental systems, and have at least as much sentience and cognitive and rational capacity as infants and severely mentally disabled people. They harp on the apparent inconsistency of this policy and claim that if we allow marginal cases to have moral rights, we must also admit that some cognitively high-functioning animals possess these rights (Dombrowski 1997).

While the AMC may seem initially compelling, there are several reasons why marginal humans demand greater moral obligations from us than do nonhuman animals, and therefore why the AMC does not really justify animal rights. First, we can summarily exclude infants from the class of marginal cases because even though they do not currently have sufficient rational and moral capacities to warrant moral rights, they have the potential for such mental faculties. Because this potential does not exist in animals, we can say that we have moral obligations towards infants as rights-holders-to-be, but that this does not hold for animals.

Why do we have greater moral obligations toward severely mentally handicapped people than we do toward animals? One argument is that their rights are not based solely upon their possession of sentience, but rather upon their being part of the human species. Animal rights advocates choose sentience as a moral criterion because it is the "lowest common denominator" that marginal cases have in common with normal adult humans, yet even sentience is not "low" enough; such a criteria for moral rights leaves out those afflicted with "congenital universal indifference (or insensitivity) to pain," who cannot sense pain whatsoever, along with those people who are completely anesthetized, hypnotized, or deeply comatose (Fox 1978). Surely we would not want to assert that only these people are left without moral rights. There is simply no attribute that all humans share save for humanity itself, and so what matters in the determination of moral rights are the characteristics typical of a certain class of beings. On the whole, humans have the capacity for rationality, self-awareness, reflection, choice, and several other prerequisites of full autonomy (Fox 1978). Animals are lacking in these respects, and therefore do not possess moral rights.

Speciesism and Moral Consistency

An animal liberationist critic may suggest that the above arguments against the AMC smack of "speciesism," a term which the philosopher Peter Singer has coined to refer to the view that "species is, *in itself*, a reason for giving more weight to the interests of one being than another" (Gray 1991). Singer asserts that this "-ism" is analogous to racism and sexism because it, too, uses an arbitrary difference to justify discrimination and flout basic moral rights (Dombrowski 1997).

The analogy to racism and sexism is flawed primarily because it cannot be proven that animals have rights in the first place, whereas it can be shown that the persecuted groups in racism and sexism are fully autonomous on the whole and are therefore merit moral rights (Fox 1978). Although some animal liberationists will be unconvinced that there is any justification for treating marginal humans and nonhuman animals equivalently, I maintain that even discounting the arguments I have already presented, the assertion that animals do not have moral rights and therefore should remain as property still holds. This position commits me to some challenging and undoubtedly disquieting consequences that must be addressed.

Without the apron of speciesist thinking to hide behind, one must argue, as R. G. Frey does, that severely mentally disabled people have lesser moral rights than do normal adult humans. Because mentally handicapped people lack moral and rational capacities, they are not fully autonomous in the sense that they cannot abstract from their first-order desires and fashion their lives according to their own conception of the good life. This leaves their lives with limited potential for enrichment and thus a lesser value than that of normal adult human lives (Frey 1983). If their lives are of less moral value, then it would not be a violation of Kant's categorical imperative for moral agents to use them as means to ends. Thus, any obligations that moral agents have towards severely mentally disabled people cannot be based on moral rights that the latter possess.

To accept this argument entirely undercuts the usefulness of the AMC to animal liberationists. Even if we assume that some animals with high mental development have the same cognitive capacities, the same degree of sentience, and therefore the same degree of autonomy and life value as severely mentally disabled people, this value is still inferior to the value of normal adult human life. As is the case with mentally handicapped people, any duties that we have toward animals are not grounded in their possessing rights. And if they have no rights, we have no moral obligation to treat them as non-property.

Human Experimentation

If severely mentally disabled people lack moral rights, the door for human experimentation without informed consent is thrown wide open. Still, there are many reasons not to experiment on humans. These include an obligation to family members and all those who would be affected by such an act, the effect of what human experimentation would do to our conception of ourselves as humans, and the slippery slope argument of who might be experimented upon next. None of these practical considerations, however, is grounded in the moral rights of marginal cases.

To permit human experimentation on severely handicapped people will no doubt seem reprehensible to most people, but there are rational explanations for our intuitive abhorrence of the idea, and if we are able to understand these explanations, then perhaps we will be able to abstract from our emotions and think rationally and in a morally consistent manner about the situation. One principle source of our negative intuition is the Rawlsian notion that any one of us could have been born with serious mental deficiencies, and it is only luck that we were not. Therefore, since such a handicap is a morally arbitrary condition, it feels as though those afflicted should have just as many rights as we do.

Regardless of how disturbing the prospect of human experimentation is, we must make moral consistency the priority. Morality cannot, and should not, simply be tailored to our intuitions. We are the only beings in a position to make difficult judgments about who possesses moral agency because we have rationality, self-awareness, and the potential for reflection. These critical abilities should help us abstract from and see beyond our intuitions so that we may live up to our full potential as rational, autonomous beings.

Conclusion

The status of animals should not be changed from property to non-property. Not only would the consequences, such as mandatory vegetarianism and the elimination of biomedical research on animals, be morally untenable, but also there is no sound moral basis for animal rights. Because animals are not fully autonomous beings, their life value is less than that of moral agents, and therefore we, as moral agents, have no obligations to animals based on their possession of moral rights. Therefore, on all accounts this motion is morally and logically unsustainable and should not—indeed, cannot—be passed.

References

Dombrowski, D. (1997). *Babies and beast.* Urbana, University of Illinois Press.

Fox, M. (1978). "Animal liberation: A critique." *Ethics* 88(2): 110.

Frey, R. (1983). *Rights, killing, and suffering*. Oxford, Basil Blackwell Publish, Ltd.

Frey, R. (1987). "Autonomy and the value of animal life." *Monist* 70: 50.

Gray, J. (1991). "In defense of speciesism." In R. M. Baird and S. Rosenbaum (Eds.), *Animal experimentation: The moral issues*. Buffalo, Prometheus Books.

Hare, R. (1999). "Why I am only a demi-vegetarian." In D. Jamieson (Ed.), *Singer and his critics*. Oxford, Blackwell Publishers.

McCloskey, H. (1983). *Ecological ethics and politics*. Totowa, Rowman and Littlefield.

McCloskey, H. (1987). "The moral case for experimentation on animals." *Monist* 70: 67.

Taylor, A. (1999). *Magpies, monkeys, and morals: What philosophers say about animal liberation*. Peterborough, Broadview Press.

The Case for Animals as the Property of Humans

Catie Lowder

PROMPTED BY A GROWING TIDE of literature reporting human-like animal social structures and learning capabilities, people have begun to question the traditional assumptions that confer an inferior, servile status on animals. Singer (1975), for instance, equates assigning a lower status to animals ("speciesism") with the most unjust extremes of racism and sexism. While it is apparent that many mammalian species are so much more than the "automata" of René Descartes (Wilson 2001), it is a similarly fallacious oversimplification to equalize the status of animals with humans and thereby disallow the possibility of keeping animals as property. Animals can rightly be treated as property because of striking differences from the human species—particularly cognitive—that makes their experience of the world incommensurable with a conception of rights as we know them. Furthermore, designating some animals as human property does not have to imply a lack of respect for their status as living, sentient beings, but can be a potentially mutually beneficial arrangement that is justifiable on utilitarian grounds.

Certain fundamental cognitive qualities of human beings delineate our species from others and allow for the complex social interaction and moral sense that are the source of human rights—rights that make very limited sense when they are conferred on other species. Rights are meaningful only in the context of social and societal interactions. They ensure the welfare of individual beings in society when interests are in conflict. Regardless of where we derive rights from (a topic much too complex to begin to broach in this essay), in order to claim moral rights, an agent must be aware of its own agency and have the ability to assess the needs and interests of other agents. Thus, qualities necessary to be subject to rights include reflective awareness of oneself as a mental being and a "theory of mind" faculty capable of generating abstract beliefs about the mental states of others. Animals possess neither of these capacities to a sufficient degree.

A true sense of self requires that one see oneself and one's interests as distinct from others'. Inherent in this conception of the self is the capacity to form intentions to change and control one's future. A sense of self implies an awareness of a coherent identity that exists over time—a recognition of the past through memory of one's experience and the ability to conceive of one's self in the future. Furthermore, a sense of the future motivates decision-making and problem-solving and forms the foundation for extended social interaction.

Staunch supporters of animal rights will cite behavioral evidence of animal consciousness, but the data are generally extremely ambiguous, and the modicum of data supporting self-image in great apes is far more indicative of physical self-image than mental self-image. Either way, the question of whether certain animals are truly self-conscious is extremely difficult—perhaps impossible—to empirically demonstrate. One frequently cited example of proof of self-consciousness is the ability of chimpanzees taught a simplified version of American Sign Language to understand and make use of the signs for "me" and "I". Through signing, such chimps can roughly describe desires and answer extremely simple self-centered questions. There is little semblance of syntax, however, and a great deal of repetition. For example, one language-trained ape, Nim, signed, "Give orange me eat orange give me eat orange give me you" (Leahy 1991). The ability to sign "me" has been cited as proof of self-consciousness, but with the dependence of signing on gestures toward one's body when referencing oneself (Leahy 1991), supposed self-consciousness easily refers to a more primitive recognition of a separate self defined by the body, but not by distinction in interest, feeling, and thought. Along the same lines, the mirror self-recognition test has been presented as a measure of self-recognition and self-awareness. A small number of nonhuman primate species, given time to examine and experiment with a mirror, will eventually determine that the other animal they see—initially approached with hostility—is actually a reflected self image (Leahy 1991). Clearly the chimpanzee is aware of itself as a separate bodily entity, but extrapolating full-blown self-awareness from this visual task is a much too hasty leap forward.

Similar errors plague studies purporting that primates can form complex intentions about the future, another cognitive prerequisite to moral behavior. Examples of some sort of future planning tend to involve food and sex. Goals are immediate and "lack the remote aspirations of human beings" (Leahy 1991). For instance, Jane Goodall describes a subordinate chimp waiting for a dominant chimp to leave so he can get the banana that was concealed on the ground behind him (Leahy 1991). The subordinate chimp planned for the future, kept a banana that was out of his sight present in mind, and then acted as a goal-oriented agent. It is clear, however, that this is a far cry from human inhibitory capabilities and planning. Self-consciousness is not necessary here, only rudimentary memory and physiological cues for hunger, fear, and recognition of dominance.

Admittedly, discounting the possibility for self-consciousness on the grounds of insufficient behavioral evidence is a shaky argument. As the mantra of empirical science goes, absence of evidence is not evidence of absence, and we cannot truly get inside of the head of a chimp any more than we can get inside the head of a human. But a vital difference between humans and nonhumans, and one with vast implications for social behavior and morality, is the unique ability of humans to communicate thoughts and intentions through language. While there are certainly communicative gestures and vocalizations in a host of other animals, nonhuman forms of communication do not have the capacity to cement complex social units together. Perhaps even more critically, human language appears to form an essential cognitive foundation for logic, causative reasoning, and the abstract thoughts about the mental states of others.

Language provides the major foundation for conscious experience as we know it, providing a necessary structure to the complex relationships that need to be understood to solve problems and operate in rule-governed society. Language is not definitively necessary for conscious experience, as evidenced by humans suffering from brain damage in major language areas, but it frames reality such that we can conceptualize the world and our relationships with others in a comprehensible way. For example, Peter Carruthers distinguishes between conscious and nonconscious experience. Using the less attentive perception of the outside world when one is lost in thought or the phenomenon of blindsight as examples of unconscious experience, he defines conscious experiences as those that are available to "higher-order thoughts"—i.e., "a thought that can take as its object another thought" (Wilson 2001). Thus, this capacity for higher order thoughts is necessary for the experience of consciousness.

The question of whether the capacity for higher order thoughts is contingent upon language can hardly be definitively answered, but research into theory of mind makes a convincing case for it. Theory of mind is the "ability to understand the intentions of others; to appreciate that others also have intentions, and that these intentions might be different from (or the same as) their own" (Petrinovich 1999). Dennett describes the probable distinction between animals and humans well: "[We] will grant . . . that Fido wants his supper, and *believes* that his master will give him his supper if he begs in front of his master, but we need not ascribe to Fido the further *belief* that his begging induces a *belief* in his master that he, Fido, wants his supper" (Petrinovich 1999). While children begin to understand that they have different thoughts from others at around age four (first-order beliefs), the ability to hold second-order beliefs (beliefs about the beliefs of others) appears even later. The development of these social abilities occurs in tandem with language, and level of language ability is the best predictor of performance on false belief and theory of mind tasks (Sparrevohn and Howie 1995). Language plays an important role in conceptualizing the attribution of mental states and processing and interpreting information at a much higher level of complexity than any nonhuman animal.

There remains the difficult counterargument: how are these uniquely human qualities to be construed as morally relevant? Is this not just assuming a selfish and anthrocentric view of a species-diverse world? In Peter Singer's utilitarian arguments in favor of "animal liberation," he works from Jeremy Bentham's assertion that "The question is not, Can [animals] reason? nor Can they talk? but, Can they suffer?" (Singer 1975). Singer declares that "The capacity for suffering and enjoyment is a prerequisite for having interests at all" (Singer 1975). Thus, argues Singer, animals clearly have interests. He draws an analogy with racism. Racism is founded on false notions that certain desirable qualities (e.g. intelligence) distribute themselves among humans unevenly and along racial lines, therefore defining one race as superior. But a further fallacy underlies racism—that any single quality can be used to categorically divide a morally worthy group from a morally unworthy group (Singer 1975; Wilson 2001). No matter where the line is drawn between the groups, Singer argues, the choice reflects an arbitrary division. Therefore, the interests of animals need to be considered on an equal level to those of humans.

A major flaw in Singer's argument is his assumption that all differences between animals and humans are a matter of degree, and not of kind. Self-consciousness is certainly debatable in this context, but language is not. There are many forms of animal communication, but nothing remotely as sophisticated as human language; put differently, animals are not less linguistically competent, they are linguistically incompetent. Their capacity for analytic thought is therefore not lesser by degree, but rather, it is lesser by kind. And, as already discussed above, human language carries with it huge implications for an entirely different experience of the world, in the vast possibilities for thought, problem solving, and complex social interactions.

Nor is language an isolated case—animal and human interests are fundamentally different, shaped by the unique experiences of each class. While the suffering of animals needs to be considered, it is of a remarkably different magnitude from that of human suffering. The limitations of memory, of theory of mind, and of a complex sense of the future in animals will both curtail the magnitude of suffering that results from trauma and narrow the events or activities that could cause it, in comparison to humans. For example, a sharp pain in the stomach of a human may be similar to that of a rat, and accompanying stress physiology could be somewhat commensurable. But human cognition will necessarily complicate the experience of it because there could be worry and concern for the source of the pain related to knowledge and fear of the potential for sickness or death, the burden of going or not going to see a doctor, the problem of the social and even economic consequences of pain and sickness. These mental factors do not operate in isolation, but can exacerbate the physical pain itself, introducing an element of suffering. The vast associations of language, memory, and a clear sense of the future that are available to humans necessarily dwarf the magnitude of potential suffering in animals. If animals are capable of mental suffering, it is most likely on a scale incomparable to that of humans.

Of course, by denoting certain characteristics as the essential differences between animals and humans, it becomes essential to address the status of those entities who are biologically and genetically human but lack both self-consciousness and language, such as infants, the severely mentally disabled, and the comatose. Singer (1975) contends that if animals do not have rights on the basis of their relative lack of human qualities, then these "marginal cases" must not either, a conclusion that is intuitively unacceptable. Singer's argument, however, is inherently flawed in its narrowness. These marginal cases are entrenched in a set of social relationships and a society of other humans endowed with a sense of empathy that make them hardly equivalent to animals. Human marginal cases also derive a moral value from their past relationships and their potential for future development. I will return later to the argument from marginal cases which, examined from a more nuanced perspective, may be potentially helpful in establishing what sort of standing animals can have within this context of their necessary distinction from humans and within the framework of property.

To review the argument thus far, nonhuman animals cannot be considered the moral equals of humans because they clearly fall short in critical cognitive domains. The mental deficiencies of nonhuman animals are best described as categorical differences of kind, not gradational deficiencies of degree. This justifies a sharp line dividing human rights from animal welfare.

But a further problem arises when we apply the terminology of property to animals. The word "property" almost inevitably undermines the dignity and status of whatever is owned. The legal status of animals as property means that they "cannot have rights that stand against human owners, and legal regulations regarding animals facilitate the most efficient exploitation by the owner—meaning any animal interest can be overridden if the consequences are sufficiently beneficial to humans" (Petrinovich 1999). Critics argue that this is an inappropriate classification for animals that denies necessary welfare protections.

Quite to the contrary, there are many reasons to think that the consequences of treating animals as property are morally acceptable and, at times, in the best interest of the animals themselves. While some may compare the use of animals in labor to a form of slavery, their lack of self-awareness protects them from the knowledge that they are property, removing the especially insidious psychological component of human slavery—the recognition of self as slave, as the property of someone else, and as an inferior.

Furthermore, humans benefit greatly from the ownership and companionship of animals. If the institution of animals as property were to be eliminated, there could be potentially catastrophic economic and environmental consequences. Our dependence on animals is great, the number of domesticated animals set free could have detrimental effects on ecosystems, and some domesticated animals may not be able to survive without the care of humans. Although efforts could be made to make the transition gradual enough that economic and ecological costs would be minimized, it is morally questionable to cause domesticated animals to artificially go extinct—caring for them until death, but preventing reproduction. Animal rights may appear beneficial in the abstract, but turn out to be a tremendous burden to humans and nonhumans alike.

The concept of property, on the other hand, has the potential to encourage better treatment of animals, especially if we recognize the possibility of placing limits on the treatment and use of such living property. Property is more than just the designation of belonging and ownership. It is a relationship between owner and property that allows for a sense of responsibility and value. It also serves an essential social function by drawing practical boundaries to prevent dispute or confusion, ensuring that each animal under the guardianship of humans generally is associated with an individual human specifically.

Opponents of animals' property status focus on a narrow definition of property that takes no account of the legal protections against the abuse of animals. Power over property is not absolute, nor does ownership deny any inherent value in property. For example, we are the owners of our own bodies first and foremost. As Locke would have it, all notions of property derive from this very fact (Munzer 1989). While we are ultimately in possession of our bodies, the government can still intervene in what we may do with them. For example, laws against prostitution and against the use of drugs both define limits for our use of our bodily property. Similarly, the government can limit what a landowner can do with or to his land, or require a person to renovate a building according to certain safety specifications. Within the rubric of human ownership, limitations and specifications can be imposed on how animals are housed, treated, and killed; indeed, such limitations are already in place. Such limitations not only decrease the suffering of animals, but also take into account the fact that cruelty to animals could potentially undermine respect for human life.

Establishing the appropriate legal protections of animals is not a simple matter, and it is instructive to return to the marginal case of human children as a representation of how one's level of moral status can rightfully vary with the capacity for self-awareness and theory of mind. Like animals, young children have few rights. They are under the complete control and responsibility of their parents and lack a high degree of self-awareness and have little language ability until the age of two or three. In this case, Petrinovich makes the distinction between moral agents, who have the capacity to understand and take responsibility for their actions, and moral patients, who "lack abilities that make them accountable for the outcomes of their actions" (Petrinovich 1999). Children and animals are both moral patients to whom moral agents have moral obligations, although children are distinguished by their potential to become fully developed adults. When a child turns 18 in the U.S.—an arbitrary cutoff—he/she becomes a full citizen, gaining full autonomy and rights. There is no absolute equivalence between the marginal cases and animals, but just as children occupy an intermediate position in reference to their abilities, their rights, and their autonomy, animals can occupy a similar middle ground.

At times animals are eerily human-like in their behavior, yet upon closer examination there is a fundamental difference in how an animal experiences the world. As reasoning, planning, communicating humans, however, it is impossible to truly understand it; our tendency as humans is to anthropomorphize everything, and our lack of words to succinctly and precisely describe the actual behavior of nonhuman animals reveals a major obstacle in discussing the status and nature of animals. Our use of language both distinguishes us from animals, yet makes us feel some sense of empathy towards them. This tension inevitably pushes the issue closer to a middle ground that recognizes both an inherently lower level of cognition that requires a different moral status and the importance of the humane treatment of animals.

References

Leahy, M. P. (1991). *Against liberation.* New York, Routledge.

Munzer, S. R. (1989). "Property, incorporation, and projection." *Nous* 23(3): 291–306.

Petrinovich, L. (1999). *Darwinian dominion.* Cambridge, MIT Press.

Singer, P. (1975). *Animal liberation: A new ethics for our treatment of animals.* New York, New York Review of Books: Distributed by Random House.

Sparrevohn, R., and P. M. Howie (1995). "Theory of mind in children with autistic disorder: Evidence of developmental progression and the role of verbal ability." *Journal of Child Psychology and Psychiatry* 36(2): 249–63.

Wilson, S. (2001). "Animals and ethics." The Internet Encyclopedia of Philosophy, http://www.utm.edu/research/iep/a/anim-eth.html.

Animal Ethics and Legal Status

Bernard E. Rollin

THOUGH THE ESSAYS IN THIS VOLUME speak to many salient arguments across the field of animal rights the issue remains unavoidably too broad for a complete view. I will therefore begin by exploring other, related issues in the field to which I have dedicated my work. The first systematic modern analysis of the moral status of animals is Peter Singer's *Animal Liberation,* published in 1976. This book has had an incalculable influence on how an entire generation looks at animals by forcing an awareness that animals have interests of their own and thus their treatment cannot simply be taken for granted, but is in fact morally problematic in every social use of animals, from agriculture to zoos, and including animal research, the testing of drugs and consumables on animals, hunting, fishing, trapping, animals used in entertainment, wildlife management, animals used in education, and even the human ownership, training, and breeding of companion animals. Singer's book will forever be acknowledged as moving animal treatment from ground to figure, and for shining a clear moral searchlight on practices humans have historically taken for granted.

However clear Singer's book was as a moral wake-up call, it was not a manual for effecting change in a highly diverse, pluralistic, and variegated democratic society. It is, after all, one thing to affirm that hurting animals in research for human benefit is morally highly suspect, and quite another to turn that insight into policy that will create moral progress. My book *Animal Rights and Human Morality*, generally recognized as the second major book on animal issues, appeared in 1981, and reflected not only my training as a philosopher but, equally importantly, my professional involvement with researchers, veterinarians, agriculturalists, and others whose careers depended on exploiting animals for the benefit of society. Effecting change in the sociocultural arena is far more complex than simply clearly enunciating philosophically consistent and coherent moral principles. Diverse philosophies, cultural biases, and vested interests must be reconciled. One cannot simply affirm that animals suffer and thereby deductively extract inexorable changes in social behavior. The historical discrepancy between our society's clear proclamation of principles of universal human suffrage in the 18th century and our failure to even approximate this ideal in practice over two centuries is clear proof that much more is needed.

We can learn from Kant that *ought* implies *can;* in other words, that our moral theory must be constrained by what is pragmatically achievable in our actual sociocultural, psychological milieu. (This is not exactly what Kant intended to teach!) Henry Spira, whom Singer eulogized in a biography as the most successful animal activist of the twentieth century, often stressed both in his writings and in personal conversations that moral theory must be actualizable in practice, else it is "philosophy-fiction," and that all ethical revolutions in U.S. history have been incremental, given the enormous numbers of conflicting interests and vectors operative in U.S. society. Success in such an arena involves moral psychology as well as moral philosophy, and a sound grasp of the empirical grounding of the moral issues raised in such specific areas as animal research.

My own 1981 book, and my subsequent work, therefore, were perhaps less an exercise in original moral theory than an attempt to articulate the following five points: First, I wished to provide good reason to believe that society was in fact moving in the direction of greater social concern about animal treatment, and the reasons for such a move. Second, I wished to make people aware of the fact that in our society there is clearly a consensus social ethic for humans, which pervades our thinking and which is to a great extent, represented in our legal system. Such an ethic would be predictably augmented to the benefit of animals if social concern for animals reached a certain threshold. Third, I wanted to show that whatever theoretical differences between ethical approaches separated moral philosophers who may be utilitarian, deontological, Platonist, Marxist or whatever, a social consensus ethic is very much operative in our culture, and is fertile ground for ethical change. Fourth, I wanted to show that if society was indeed becoming increasingly concerned about animal treatment in research, agriculture or whatever, change could be most plausibly effected via the legal system reflecting the consensus ethic. My own issue of concern from 1976 to 1985 was creating federal legislation guaranteeing better treatment of research animals. It seemed clear to me from my own experience with animal research that we were nowhere near doing the best we could by animals even within a research context. For example, animal care was slipshod and capricious, which not only hurt the animals but also adversely affected variables relevant to the scientific investigations for which the animals were utilized. Even more egregious, there was virtually no literature on, or use of, analgesia in animal research, and the scientific community was thoroughly agnostic about animal pain, distress, discomfort, suffering, etc.

Fifth, I believed people knowledgeable about animal abuse in research and about animal ethics could direct burgeoning public concern about animal treatment to support practicable legislation; a goal we in fact accomplished in 1985 with the passage of two federal laws protecting research animals.

It is in fact for the above constellation of reasons that I focused on *animal rights* in my 1981 book. I was far less interested in the venerable philosophical problem of natural rights than I was in plugging increasing social concern for animal treatment into our social ethic and its primary engine of change—the legal system—and creating legal protection for animals which would encode at least minimal protections for their interests and natures. My approach received succor from the fact that significant elements of the medical research community violently opposed legislation, presumably on the grounds that once animals enjoyed legal protection, such "rights" could not be evaded or avoided.

Despite this undeniably practical orientation, I did present a moral ideal in the 1981 book. I argued that if animals' moral status were to be fully recognized in our social ethic, animals' legal status would need to be changed from that of simply property. Indeed, legal history in classical times and in the pre-Civil War U.S. had seen the attempt made to reconcile humans' moral status with the institution of slavery by referring to slaves as "property with a soul" and by stipulating that slave murder was, in principle, a capital offense. In the early 1980s, I wrote a brief for the Canadian Law Reform Commission arguing this point, as the Commission was eager to move animals beyond simply enjoying property status.

In *Animal Rights and Human Morality,* I argued that since municipalities, ships, and corporations enjoyed legal personhood, it would not be absurd to confer a similar status on animals, making them analogous to children, who had historically moved beyond property status. I articulated this argument as follows:

What would it mean to grant legal rights to animals? Very simply, this would mean that the law would recognize animals as enjoying legal standing in themselves, not as property. As such they could institute legal action, or more accurately, have legal action instituted on *their* behalf (rather than to their owner), have injuries to *them* legally considered (rather than to their owner), and have legal relief run directly to their benefit. The relevant legal analogy here is the case of children. Although children cannot press legal claims on their own behalf, they still enjoy legal rights. They are not the property of their parents. Their rights can be pressed by others, by social welfare agencies, police, courts, guardians, etc.; so granting rights to entities that cannot themselves speak for those rights is far from unprecedented. It is not difficult to imagine those who might serve to press claims for the animals; the most plausible candidates are of course members of humane societies and veterinarians.

There are two major ways in which rights could be established for animals. In the first place, we can speak of *extending* existing rights to animals, even as constitutional rights were extended by arguments stressing the absence of relevant moral difference from native-born, white, adult, male, property owners to corporations, naturalized citizens, non-property owners, blacks, Orientals, children and women.

The argument that only human persons can have such rights is easily trumped by the fact that corporations have enjoyed such legal standing since the early nineteenth century, as have ships, trusts, cities, and nation-states. Obviously it is far more difficult to defend legal rights for such non-living things than for animals, given our earlier argument connecting legal and moral rights. It is hard to defend the notion that a ship or corporation is a direct object of moral concern, yet corporations have legal rights. It is, as we have seen, almost impossible rationally to deny that animals are direct objects of moral concern, so it is quite easy in this light to demand legal standing for them.

How might such an extension be accomplished? Let us imagine a bold, daring test case that would force these issues to the forefront of legal discussion. Let us recall that we have shown in detail that rationality and capacity for language are strictly irrelevant to something being a direct object of moral concern. Nonetheless, the intuitions of ordinary people and historical precedent both militate against ready acceptance of this position. Most people are still committed to the idea that speech is somehow of pivotal moral significance. One of my colleagues for example, who has no interest whatever in animals rights, concedes that he would be greatly interested in these questions if we found an animal that could speak. Very well, let us milk this essentially indefensible intuition. Most of the public is at least passingly familiar with recent work done on teaching language (or something seen as language by most people) to higher primates. Though many theoretical linguists, most notably Noam Chomsky, would decline to speak of these animals as linguistic beings for a number of technical reasons, our intuitions push in the other direction. After all, these animals do put signs together in new ways, even to the point of insulting the researchers. Since language is, philosophically speaking, morally irrelevant anyway, what counts is not whether this is or is not language, but that many people who *think* language *is* morally relevant see these animals as having language.

Now consider an ape who has learned to communicate with humans using some system *seen by most people as linguistic*. The experiment is terminated, and the animal is no longer of use. What can be done with it? The animal is, as has actually happened, turned over to a zoo. Could we not press the claim that the animal is suffering cruel and unusual punishment and has been denied due process? By current standards, the animal has measurable intelligence; in fact, one such creature scored an 85 on a standard I.Q. test—many humans score a good deal lower. In fact, the animal lies, swears, and equivocates—sure marks of intelligence. In any case, could one not press a plausible case on the grounds that the animal's civil rights had been violated? I am envisioning a new "monkey trial" at least as spectacular in its implications as the Scopes trial, which tested the Tennessee law against the teaching of evolution. Such a trial would be extraordinarily beneficial in just the same sense.

The Scopes trial forced a public airing of our scientific, conceptual, and educational commitments as well as a dialectical examination of the roles of science and religion. This trial would force an examination of our moral commitments and illuminate areas too long left in the dark. Eventually, and incrementally, by a process of legal and moral argument stressing the absence of relevant differences, one can envision the judicial extension of some rights to all animals.

The second way of establishing legal rights for animals involves not judicial extension but rather legislative *conferral*. Laws governing the treatment of animals must be written in the language of rights, with animals seen as objects of moral concern, and with human utilitarian interests relegated to the background. This, as we have argued, is the force of all talk of "rights." Probably, in the long run, this route is more plausible than judicial extension. But the question remains as to *which* rights need to be legally established, by whatever means. There are innumerable areas in which this question ramifies—animal experimentation, factory or intensive farming, horse and dog racing, pet ownership, zoos, etc. In our next section we shall discuss in depth the role of such laws in animal experimentation. In the following chapter, we shall discuss pet animals—perhaps the most psychologically acceptable candidates for legal standing in the minds of most people, who can compare these animals to children. Suffice it to say that the basic content of such laws has already been established in our earlier discussion of the moral status of animals and of the rights that accrue to them in virtue of that status. Fundamentally, the right to life, the right to be protected from suffering, and the right to live life according to their *telos* or nature are basic rights that should be legally codified for animals.

Some of this analysis has indeed been instantiated in the twenty-plus years since I wrote *Animal Rights and Human Morality*. Most notably, some jurisdictions, like Boulder and San Francisco, have declared that companion animals are not property, and that the people with whom they reside are not their owners but their guardians, and not entitled to dispose of them as they see fit. Noble in intention as these ordinances may be, I do not believe that they could stand up to constitutional challenge, since there is no constitutional basis for personhood for animals. Ultimately, then, the possibility of legal personhood for animals would require a constitutional amendment to be realized.

In the meantime, raising animal status has been furthered by such activities as the Great Ape Project, which stresses the proximity of these animals to humans, and attempts to forestall such activities as using them for invasive research, and by laws extending their economic value beyond market value, as we shall shortly discuss.

Though people of good faith can argue about how much of a conceptual difference the laboratory animal laws have made in addressing the ultimate and purely moral issue of whether it is or is not morally legitimate to use animals in invasive research for human benefit, few can deny that it is far better to be an animal used in research after these laws went into effect than before. For example, from finding no papers on pain control by analgesia in laboratory animals when I did a literature search in 1982, we have gone to literally thousands of such papers. More important, the widespread ideological denial of pain and other feelings in animals, which I called "scientific common sense," has been significantly eroded if not yet totally vanquished. And, perhaps most importantly, most scientists can now at least see the moral questions surrounding research animal use.

The debate about animals' status in the legal system, around which the current volume centers, is thus a paradigmatic example of what I hoped to achieve with my discussion of "animals rights," and, even more importantly, is a sound indicator of the fact that society is moving in the direction I anticipated. Even portions of the student essays opposing "rights" for animals still accept the reasonableness of increased protection for animal interests. Whereas when my book was published, the major conceptual issue in this area revolved around convincing skeptics that animals belonged in the moral arena at all, i.e. deserved full moral considerability, these essays show that the focus of the debate has changed and that the current issue is centered around what form that moral status should take, though some of the arguments against animals' having rights advanced in this book utilize the old arguments about the limitations of animal consciousness and cognition, which were previously used to deny moral status altogether!

In any case, raising the legal status of animals is no longer an odd social concept. The *New York Times* referred to the 1988 Swedish law abolishing confinement agriculture as a "Bill of Rights for farm animals." Books and articles by legal scholars like Steven Wise, Gary Francione, Joyce Tischler, and David Favre regularly address strategies for raising animals' legal status, as do the highly publicized Great Ape Project, which argues for augmented legal status for the higher primates and which has resulted in some countries' banning invasive research on these animals, and the guardian ordinances mentioned earlier. Even more significantly, laws protecting animals continue to proliferate. A recent California law makes shipping horses for slaughter a felony, and is currently being pressed at the federal level. In 1998, I was told by the executive director of the American Quarter Horse Association, the largest equine group in the U.S., that the organization's single largest expenditure was paying a research group to keep track of U.S. equine welfare bills, summaries of which, in 1998, filled a volume as thick as the Manhattan phone book!

What, then, should we say about elevating the legal status of animals today, twenty years after my initial musings?

In my view, while the movement to elevate the legal status of animals is far more plausible and well-supported today than it was twenty years ago, momentum will continue to gather in two distinct ways, depending on the function of the animal in human society. I believe that the movement from human ownership of animals as simple property to something like guardianship will continue to grow with regard to companion animals. This is the case for a number of reasons.

In the first place, surveys have repeatedly shown that well over 90 percent of the U.S. pet-owning public affirms that they see their animals as "members of the family." Attorneys specializing in divorce relate that oftentimes the most hotly contested aspect of a divorce concerns who will receive custody of the pet!

After World War II and the Dustbowl, there was a massive exodus from farm areas to the cities. Economic dependence on animals declined, and their major social role became that of companion. Life in the cities, as opposed to life in farm and rural communities, became a matter of *gesellschaft*, not *gemeinschaft*. People didn't know their neighbors and didn't care to. One could live for years in an apartment building and never speak to—let alone get to know—the people in neighboring apartments, let alone neighboring buildings. Privacy lay in lack of social intercourse. If one saw a person fall on the street, one stepped over or around him/her. "Don't get involved," became the urban dwellers' mantra. "Don't talk to strangers; don't even make eye contact, lest it be taken as a challenge." At the same time, the security of the nuclear family began to crumble with more than half of the marriages recorded ending in divorce.

In such a world, it is not easy to make friends, nor is it possible to seek succor from the natural world, for the little nature that exists in massive cities is contrived, not natural. I recall meeting a black child from Harlem, perhaps ten years old, who firmly believed that concrete grew wild and that grass and trees had to be artificially placed. If one believes that people need both friends who provide love and companionship, and some contact with nonhuman nature, one can readily see why dogs and cats would start to fill that lacuna in the human soul. Companion animals became family, nature, excuses to exercise, protectors, and friends.

Even more dramatically, companion animals, particularly dogs, became lubricants for social interaction. An entire culture made up of "dog people" taking their dogs for exercise to the parks sprung up, with people interacting in virtue of their common interest in their pets. Oftentimes people met daily in virtue of dog-walking and struck up relationships with other "dog people" without even knowing their names, identifying them only as "Fifi's mom" or "Red's dad." Even more bizarrely, they began to care for each other through their animals. When Red's owner went into the hospital for major surgery, we all took turns walking Red, a huge German shepherd, passing the key around. When I was devastated by asthma and threatened with a long hospital stay, Red's owner brought me an envelope in the park. "What's that?" I asked. "The key to my cabin in Thunder Bay and a map showing how to get there. Go there for a few weeks and breathe some clean air."

My own dog, a 160-pound Great Dane, loved all people. Children climbed on her back; old people hugged her. As a graduate student, I kept odd hours, often walking the dog late at night for miles. Most moving, I remember the prostitutes in the theater district running over to hug and kiss the dog and buying her donuts; she was the only living creature they could shower with genuine love.

New York City may represent an extreme, but we have lost *gemeinschaft* in most communities, and our animals are sources of unconditional love. They play with and protect children, and, as Dr. Leo Bustad recognized when he forced through Congress federal legislation allowing elderly people to keep animals in federally funded housing projects, they give old people a reason to keep living.

The public views the mass euthanasia of healthy dogs and cats as a tragedy, and for this reason "no-kill" shelters have proliferated.

In a world where people value companion animals' lives as unique and irreplaceable and their untimely deaths as tragedies; where people may spend six-figure sums on animal health; where veterinary specialties have proliferated to assure companion animal health; where animals are valued for more than their market value, it is plausible to move to change the legal status of such animals away from property. And this is indeed recurring in many ways beyond the "guardian" ordinances mentioned earlier.

Some states have legislated that companion animals can be economically valued well beyond their market worth. Tennessee now allows recovery of up to $4,000 for the negligent or wrongful death of a companion animal. Illinois allows up to $25,000 for punitive damages, and recovery for psychological damage to an owner, as well as veterinary bills if an animal is harmed or killed through cruelty or malpractice. Similar laws have been introduced in Rhode Island, Maryland, California, and Michigan. Such laws attest to a growing social tendency to view companion animals as possessing value beyond market value, certainly a step towards independent legal status.

For non-companion animals, particularly for farm animals or laboratory animals, the companion animal move we have just described is incoherent, since these animals are not produced to "give and receive love," as one court said of companion animals, but to serve as food or experimental subjects. More importantly, their death is socially presupposed, not mourned, and not seen as tragedy or outrage. Thus a move towards valuing their lives beyond market value, or moving them closer to persons possessed of non-utilitarian value, is conceptually ill-formed. On the other hand, society has clearly displayed concern for their pain, suffering, and distress while they are alive, as evidenced by the proliferation of laws covering all aspects of animal use. So while the status of this class of animals is unlikely to be moved closer to personhood and away from property, we will see an elevation in their legal status in terms of increasing legally mandated restrictions on how they are used. As we have already mentioned, this has already occurred with regard to laboratory animals and farm animals in various parts of the world. Though their lives are accepted as being at our disposal, how they live is increasingly being removed from the purview of their owners. And this will surely continue to proliferate, as will constraints on how they are killed to assure absence of suffering. As socially imposed mandates slowly preempt owners' prerogative to treat animals as they see fit, it is appropriate to see this as a different form of elevated legal status. As we will discuss shortly, a bill of rights for animals makes perfect sense to assure consistency in mandating treatment and accommodations for non-companion animals consumed for human benefit and destined to die.

In the end, then, whether we are talking about companion animals who garner new status approaching personhood (or intrinsic value), or animals whose value is utilitarian, the law will continue to move in the direction of raising their moral status.

II

Without nitpicking at any of the excellent papers in this volume, and recognizing that the authors are not experts, it is nonetheless necessary to mention some pervasive arguments appearing therein that need correction. The papers opposing changing the legal status of animals seem to assume that the current status of animals as property is fully compatible with the pervasive social desire to raise their moral status. A similar position has been expressed by Jerold Tannenbaum and others, who have argued that increased moral status for animals compatible with their being legally property can be achieved simply by strengthening the anti-cruelty statutes, since such and other laws historically limit the absolute rights of owners over their animal property. Such a view, I believe, is misguided, for reasons I will briefly sketch.

The anti-cruelty laws, going back to the Bible, rest on two distinct moral concerns. One, known in the rabbinical tradition as "tsaar baalai chaim," essentially expresses the view that suffering of all living things is inherently evil and needs to be regulated. The other, largely emphasized by Thomas Aquinas, focuses on the psychological insight that those who would hurt animals frivolously, if allowed to do so unchecked, will graduate to abusing people. (Aquinas took such a view and not the other since Catholicism does not allow a direct moral status for animals, who lack an immortal soul.) Western society, including our own, has been dominated by the latter view. This view, expressed in many statutes and supported by psychological research of the last two decades, reiterates Thomas's position that those who are permitted to abuse animals "intentionally," "sadistically," or "willfully" in deviant ways, as the anti-cruelty laws usually say, will tend to abuse defenseless people. This has been shown to be true of wife and child abusers, serial killers, violent offenders incarcerated in Leavenworth federal prison, and many of the young schoolchildren who have rampaged and shot their peers. Further, these laws specifically exclude from their purview anything accepted as standard practice in any industry "ministering to the necessities of man." Thus, no standard agricultural practice, however painful or offensive to normal moral sensibilities, can be prosecuted under the cruelty laws, nor could any "scientific" experiments, however absurd or useless. (One scientist determined the LD50 for distilled water, i.e. the dose that kills 50 percent of the experimental animals to whom a substance is administered. Since distilled water is nontoxic, he evaluated the dose that caused internal bursting of water-logged organs!) Thus, neither hot-iron branding of cattle nor confinement of veal calves is, or could be, by definition, legally cruel! In other words, the purpose of the cruelty laws is to seek out deviant and sadistic behavior towards animals that might identify sadists and psychopaths, who are a danger to people, *not* to minimize animal pain and suffering. And since the vast majority of animal suffering is not the result of "willful, deliberate, intentional, sadistic, deviant behavior" but rather comes from perfectly normal decent motives such as curing disease or producing cheap food or protecting the public from toxic substances or understanding disease processes, the vast majority of animal suffering is invisible to the anti-cruelty laws and ethics.

Thus, while the cruelty laws can and will change as society does (hence a New York State judge declared the USDA guilty of cruelty when, in 1982, it mandated hot iron face branding of cattle it bought in a massive attempt to shrink the U.S. dairy herd, because it had not considered less patently invasive methods), they are still largely directed against human deviance, not against animal suffering, and are thus conceptually ill-suited to express emerging social and moral concern about animal treatment. Thus the cruelty laws, as limitations on how one can deal with one's own property, fail to capture burgeoning social-ethical concerns about the animals themselves experiencing suffering occasioned by sources other than cruelty, indeed by perfectly decent motives.

Thus to retain the "animals as property" concept, modulated only by the prohibition against deviant sadism, is to lower the river, rather than raise the bridge, and indeed is a non sequitur. Augmenting the cruelty concept totally ignores the direct concern for animals themselves, reflected in burgeoning social thought about animal use in all areas. Even if we could demonstrate that hurting animals in research has never made any researcher more socially dangerous, people still want that hurting controlled, for the animals' sake.

This point was well-appreciated by a group I addressed in 1980 representing all the Canadian ministries associated with animal use in society—the Ministry of Oceans and Fisheries, the Ministry of Agriculture, the Ministry of the Environment, etc. I gave a half-day seminar on emerging social ethics for animals and we enjoyed an extensive discussion. These people astutely recognized that the cruelty concept was totally inadequate to emerging social ethics, and that some overriding principles were needed to make coherent and consistent legislation addressed to various animal issues—research, agriculture, hunting, etc. They wisely suggested something like an overarching bill of rights for all animals used by humans. Such a bill or charter would be couched in general terms, but all legislation would need to be consistent with it. For example, such a law might mandate that animals used by us in any activity must be housed in accommodations compatible with their physical and psychological needs and natures—their *telos,* as I call it. Such a mandate exists in the Swedish law for farm animals, and to a lesser extent in 1985 U.S. laboratory animal laws mandating environments for primates that "enhance their psychological well-being." But the point is that a general bill of rights would cover both of these cases, as well as zoos, circuses, and other domestic animal uses. As we mentioned, there is some precedent for such limitation on property use in ancient and U.S. slave law, which acknowledged human slaves as property, but "property with a soul." Such overarching principles erected within the current property classification might be easier to achieve in the short run than moving animals from property to some sort of quasi-personhood, though, as we saw, precedent exists in the legal system making corporations, municipalities, and ships into "legal persons."

Most likely, social ethics will slowly chip away at the rights of owners to hurt animals for legitimate reasons, as well as out of cruelty, and will not confront the legal status of animals directly.

To otherwise achieve personhood for animals would be extraordinarily difficult in the current legal system, and would seem to require a constitutional amendment (or Supreme Court decision for a lesser conceptual change). These sorts of changes are currently unimaginable, though much can be done—and is being done—to dispose the public towards that direction. For example, Eugene Linden has written of a chimpanzee brought up in a household like a human child and taught sign language. When the funding ran out, the researchers turned the animal over to a toxicology lab for invasive research. One caretaker at the lab, observing repeated frantic signing by the animal, called the researcher in. The animal was saying "want to go home"!

One can easily imagine the profound emotional/moral effect (moral psychology again!) of such an animal allowed to testify before a sympathetic judge on grounds of denial of due process or cruel and unusual punishment! Such a "monkey trial," well-covered by the media, could well accelerate public support for greater animal protection beyond the property status.

In short, I believe that the property status of animals will be eroded not by a frontal legal theoretical attack on it, but by ever-increasing social and moral concern for animals, which will ramify in a proliferation of laws constraining animal use in a multitude of areas. Without something like our previously mentioned overarching bill of rights for animals these laws will be a patchwork crazy quilt of contradictions but will still move animal morality forward. (For example, there are rules currently mandating humane euthanasia of laboratory mice but not house mice.) Theorizing about animal ethics can help render such laws more coherent than they would be without it.

I have a number of other concerns about some of the arguments in the student papers opposing rights. In particular, I am troubled by the weak but pervasive Cartesian arguments against animal mentation, which are then used to diminish the value of animals. Too many philosophers accept the old Kantian saw about moral agents being of inestimably greater moral value than mere moral patients, with only the former being "ends in themselves" or having "intrinsic value." I have never seen any persuasive defenses of this claim that are close to justifying it, however widely accepted it may be. Indeed, the only sense that I can make of "intrinsic value" is that a being can itself value what happens to it, in which case animals surely have intrinsic value if they are conscious as common sense believes them to be.

Nor have I seen persuasive defenses of the related claim that animals lack any strong sense of self-awareness. For example, I have argued in my *Unheeded Cry: Animals Consciousness, Animal Pain and Science,* that if Kant's arguments in favor of a unity of consciousness or apperception work for humans, the same arguments must work for animals as well. The argument that since humans have "ectypal" intellects that receive disjointed Humean impressions from "outside" but emerge with a unity and flow of objective experience, they must have a unity of consciousness, applies equally to animals, as simple observation of animal behavior attests—they perceive unity of objects and causation just as we do! This is evident in cats waiting outside of mouse holes for mice, lions intercepting gazelles, dogs standing at their dishes to be fed, etc.

The arguments of Gordon Gallup from mirror recognition and particularly those of Peter Carruthers invoked in one of these papers are equally without substance. As I again argued at length in *The Unheeded Cry*, the failure of animals to heed their reflection does not prove that they lack sense of self—Gallup himself admits that other behavior suffices to vouch for self-awareness—e.g., deception. I have seen my own dog feign a limp when being reprimanded for running away, after having been coddled when she did have a limp. And to arguments that such stories are "anecdotal," I have no problem with anecdotes evaluated critically, as I discuss in *The Unheeded Cry* and elsewhere. Even Darwin saw anecdotes as providing vital access to natural animal behavior. And the Carruthers arguments are even weaker. To go from a deviant, pathological, and rare condition in humans—blindsight (seeing without being aware that one is seeing)—to the assertion that all animal "awareness" *could* be of that form and therefore *is*, does not represent serious grounds for denying morally relevant states of consciousness to animals, in the face of almost universal common experience that solidly affirms it. Certainly common sense reigns here in the context of seeing animal behavior as worthy of moral attention.

These sorts of arguments are, in my view, the last vestiges of a moribund ideology that captured science for three hundred years. Particularly noteworthy in this regard are arguments about pain in animals, especially the argument that since animals lack a sense of future, they cannot suffer the way we do. Since the human suffering created by a visit to the dentist involves, it is alleged, fear of the visit for days ahead of time, anxiety that the dentist might have had a fight with his wife, be angry with me, or be a Nazi torturer (à la *Marathon Man*)—all modes of consciousness animals lack—we suffer because of the experience worse than an animal can. As I and many others have pointed out, this neglects the fact that with human temporal consciousness comes awareness that the dentist visit will be over soon, that I can get up and leave, or hope that the dentist will smile on me. If animals lack anticipation and hope, they *are* their pain, their whole world is pain, they cannot foresee its end, which is terrible indeed.

Some scholars of pain like Ralph Kitchell have argued that since the pain experience contains two components, one affective and motivational, the other cognitive and ratiocinative, and animals are weak in the latter, an animal's pain may hurt *more,* since that is what motivates the animal's escape from the source of pain.

In summary, scientific ideology about animal consciousness dies hard. The International Society for the Study of Pain still outrageously makes the possession of language a necessary condition for experiencing pain in its official definition of pain. Such bad philosophy contains the seeds of its own undoing—if animals don't feel pain, how can they be used as research models for pain in humans? But such bad philosophy must be exposed to the light to be vaporized. And the sorts of discussions these student papers present are admirable and paradigmatic examples of careful analysis of what was, until recently, assumed without defense or critical discussion.

Section 2—Law

THIS SECTION SQUARELY ADDRESSES THE QUESTION that frames *People, Property, or Pets:* Should animals be granted the legal rights that accompany personhood? Most of the authors divided this question into two parts, first asking if animals are owed rights in principle, and then asking if legal rights are the only practical means to achieve animal welfare.

It is not immediately obvious what legal rights accompany personhood. Clearly, animal rights of any variety ought not include the right to vote, granted by the U.S. constitution, or the right to paid vacation, granted by the UN Declaration of Human Rights. These essays propose a number of versions of animal legal rights, ranging from the right to have their interests considered, to the right to legal standing in court, to the right not to be treated as property. Yet another step removed are the real-world consequences of abstract rights. Does the right to have one's interests considered preclude biomedical experimentation? Can non-property be eaten?

Gary Francione, one of the leading proponents of the view that animals be removed from the legal category of property, emphasizes that the law plays the role of bridging the gap between our philosophical commitments and our day-to-day lives. Although the essays in this chapter disagree profoundly on the specific protections that animals are owed, all agree that lawmakers bear the responsibility to regulate the ethical treatment of animals, and that animal welfare is a matter not just of personal virtue, but of public policy.

Consistency and Rights

Alex Pollen

FOR MANY, THE TERM "ANIMAL RIGHTS" evokes an image of overly sentimental and often naïve activists protesting issues without much regard for the consequences of their demands. This stereotype reveals an unfortunate misapprehension: that animal welfare is a matter of weighing consequences rather than respecting rights. The utilitarian argument frequently brandished against animal rights, however, runs strongly against the grain of the American legal system, the cornerstone of which is a system of universal rights. Human rights originate from the faculties displayed by our species, not from the simple boundary that the category "human species" presents. Indeed, arbitrary boundaries have been abused in human history, justifying war, discrimination, and slavery by marginalizing the rights-holding status of certain groups. Defining a concrete basis for rights that includes all humans ensures protection against arbitrary discrimination. To be effective, however, these universal minimal standards necessarily expand the scope of right-deserving status beyond our species. I will argue that, at a very minimum, animals have the right to be considered—to have their interests taken into account.

Anglo-American jurisprudence has traditionally honored human rights over utilitarian calculations. Rights, the principle legal protection conferred by the Constitution, are inalienable protections and guarantees. We would intuitively be wary of accepting a system of law allowing the violation of individual rights for the common good, and the courts have interpreted the law in a manner consistent with this intuition. Among the best-known examples—a classic in first-year law courses—is the 19th-century British case *Queen v. Dudley and Stephens.* The defendants, two men lost at sea for eighteen days more than a thousand miles from shore, killed a young boy aboard their raft in order to save themselves and a third sailor aboard the raft. By feeding on the flesh of one, three lives were saved, and but for the extra meal all four sailors would have died. The court regarded utility as "no legal justification," and pronounced Dudley and Stephens guilty. "[S]uch a principle," wrote the judges of the defendants' utilitarian claim, "might be made the legal cloak for unbridled passion and atrocious crime." A similar case in the United States, in which sailors threw their compatriots off sinking life rafts to save the rest of those aboard, also prompted a guilty verdict. These examples illustrate dramatically the general principle of Anglo-American justice: utility and economics cannot justify the violation of fundamental rights.

The rights of humans in our legal tradition are universal and inalienable, extending even to individuals with the most limited cognitive capacities. In the case of a permanently comatose girl, the Supreme Court of Massachusetts ruled that "Cognitive ability is not a prerequisite for enjoying basic liberties," and the girl was "entitled to the same respect, dignity, and freedom of choice as competent people" (Wise 2000). Rulings in other marginal cases all uphold individual rights, even when the individual is incapable of independent decision-making. Some individuals are able to survive many decades while never developing mental capacities beyond those of an eighteen-month-old child. Legally state courts have repeatedly upheld the basic rights of these people (Wise 2000). The rights of these individuals cannot be violated in any way, even one that confers an obvious societal benefit.

As an example, consider the case brought before the Massachusetts high court of a sixty-year-old man suffering from acute leukemia. The man suffered congenital disabilities capping his mental capacity below that of a three-year-old child. In short, he was capable of only expressing the most basic preferences. Overall economic advantage would dictate that the man be allowed to die naturally, or perhaps that he be a subject for cutting-edge experimental treatments, which he might even have volunteered for, were he able to understand the choice. One could argue that such treatments would save future lives, and bring satisfaction to the man's family members. These considerations, however, are secondary to the man's own rights. In this case, and similar cases around the country, the courts have ruled in favor of the rights of the individual, even when the individual is incapable of expressing his/her preferences (Wise 2000). The standard legal position towards humans operating below the mental capacity of a normal adult is that they have the right to have their interests taken into account.

Animals must merit this same right to consideration for the simple reason that there is no characteristic—be it an ability to express interests, the capacity for pain, or intelligence—possessed by all rights-holding humans and no animals. Therefore, no matter what the requisite criterion for moral consideration may be, it is met by at least some nonhuman animals. A great many animals display cognitive capabilities greater than, for instance, an encephalitic baby, born with large brain regions missing, permanently unconscious, and absent of the indicators of pain or suffering for the few months of its life. If an absolute standard exists to protect these human individuals, some animals will invariably merit protection as well.

There are two alternatives to granting rights based upon some concrete standard that invariably includes animals. The first is to allow morally aware humans to revoke the rights of those marginal human cases who appear to not merit or deserve rights by cognitive standards. In this case, humans would be equally justified in denying rights to animals. The second alternative is to define rights as exclusive to the human species, or even by some absolute quality of humanness. In this manner, rights could be denied to animals, while conceivably still granted to all humans.

Regarding the first option, history shows that drawing boundaries between the rights of humans has allowed for some of humankind's darkest moments. Slavery in America continued for several centuries based upon a boundary; slaves were simply considered subhuman. The Holocaust left six million Jews murdered, again because Jews were considered subhuman. Atrocities and genocides continue today, and arbitrary boundaries continue to propagate rather than prevent these tragedies. Additionally, these atrocities have occurred and continue to occur within nations that have institutions to protect rights. To once again draw an arbitrary line dividing humans into those deserving rights and those not seems to beg for another moral tragedy. Imposing a uniform standard for rights applicable to all, if nothing else, serves as an insurance policy against future human atrocities.

As for the second option, even if "humanness" were considered an absolute quality from which rights could be derived, the standard would still fail to capture the essence of our intuition about what sorts of creatures deserve rights. Consider a thought experiment in which a group of Martians land on earth tomorrow. Despite being entirely comprisedof foreign molecules and sharing no physical component whatsoever with humans, these hypothetical creatures still behave morally, still feel pain, and still demonstrate preferences. Have we any moral obligation to these creatures? Or may we buy, sell, trade, experiment, eat, and own such organisms? Rights defined by boundary and rights defined by humanness fail to protect such creatures. Only the application of a concrete standard for rights recognizes that the faculties these creatures display merit rights.

Consider another hypothetical case, that of transgenic creatures. Does a chimpanzee merit rights on its own? Imagine inserting more and more human genes into a chimp. Is there a number of genes at which the hybrid creature is protected by human rights? Alternatively, how many animal genes may be inserted into a person before the person loses human rights status? These questions, becoming distinct possibilities with modern technology, again show that rights cannot be derived from simply a "human species" boundary.

To review the argument thus far, I have shown that rights are fundamental to Anglo-American jurisprudence in a way that precludes the exploitation of rights-holders for maximum utility. Furthermore, in applying an absolute standard that protects the rights of all humans, the rights of some animals must also be protected.

But it is important to recognize that the use of low-functioning humans to justify the basic rights of any organism does not imply that all creatures falling above the minimum human standard deserve equivalent rights. Our society denies children the right to vote, removes the mentally ill from public life, and allows for lifetime guardianship of the mentally challenged. Analogous limitations would presumably apply to animals; the significant difference is that, for the first time, the right to be considered would be granted to animals. Consideration of an animal's interests is a right that is fundamentally beyond that afforded to any item of property. And it is just this—the consideration of interests—that courts have always extended to all humans.

There is nothing trivial about determining how best to give due consideration to the interests of nonhuman animals, but a good place to start is with the contractualist theory of John Rawls. Rawls rightly received a great deal of attention for a simple idea: the rules governing a society should be constructed in a way that everybody would agree to before knowing their specific identity. This perspective, from behind what Rawls called the "veil of ignorance," is referred to in philosophical jargon as *ex ante*—literally, "from before."

An *ex ante* thought experiment shows how this universal animal right to consideration may be thought of, and how subsequent rights can be rationally derived. Imagine your position from behind a veil of ignorance so complete that you could not even predict your eventual species: you might end up as an amoeba, a bird, a chimpanzee, or any animal. As an amoeba you would receive few inputs from the outside world, demonstrate few preferences, lack any kind of computational anatomy, and have no concept of the future. In designing a system of basic rights, few rights seem relevant to the amoeba's situation beyond that to exist. However, for a chimpanzee who demonstrates a richness in interacting with the world, forms complex relationships, and exceeds the mental capacity of some marginal humans, many more rights must be considered. Put somewhat differently, many humans might accept a few extra headaches in exchange for the right against being a biomedical research subject in the hypothetical future.

The thought experiment is not such a leap from the traditional Rawlsian view. Already, you could imagine being born as a terminally ill baby, or a child missing large brain regions. Under the Rawlsian veil of ignorance, the inherent situation of such humans must still be considered. Importantly, the theory of animal rights presented here is not deduced or dependent upon Rawlsian ideals. The *ex ante* thought experiment merely shows how the right to consideration could operate.

Here I present animal rights as a product of a necessary absolute standard for right-holding status. Rights defined by boundary are not enough to protect all humans and they overlook the essential origin of rights. By necessity, and to be consistent with our legal tradition, this concrete standard must protect all humans. Consequently some species of animals will merit rights as well. Legally, no argument of utility justifies a rights violation. The relevant question for animal rights then becomes: What morals and rights ought to be afforded an organism demonstrating a certain mental capacity and understanding of the world? Extending the scope of the Rawlsian veil of ignorance may help explore the answers to this question. This does not impose a hierarchy of rights, but instead is representative of our recognition that many human rights are irrelevant vis-à-vis other organisms' different needs and preferences, but a few basic rights must be inalienable, first among these, the right to be considered.

Reference

Wise, S. M. (2000). *Rattling the cage: Toward legal rights for animals.* Cambridge, Mass., Perseus Books.

A Legal Argument against Animals as Property

David Hambrick

I ADDRESS THIS ESSAY TO ANYONE WHO AGREES that animal welfare is important—anyone who believes that an animal's interests, including life, freedom from torture, and basic comforts, should count for something in the way that we treat it. No matter how much you think an animal's interests should count, as long as you think that interests should count for something, then you should support removing animals from the legal category of property and granting them rights.

A society that wants to take an animal's interests into account and still considers them to be property deprives itself of one of the most effective tools that the law offers for protecting interests—rights. Legal rights allow their holders (1) to take legal action for injury done to them, (2) to have a court recognize and take account of that injury, and (3) to receive legal relief that benefits them (paraphrased from Stone 1996). In this way, rights guarantee that the law recognizes and protects the rights-holder's interests.

Relegating animals to the status of property contradicts a widespread consensus that their interests are owed consideration. We hold up animal welfare as a worthwhile goal and claim that it is important to treat animals humanely. Many countries have "animal welfare laws" to this effect, acknowledging that animals have certain interests and that we sufficiently value these interests to protect them legally. On the other hand, these animal welfare laws continue to treat animals as property, a status that prevents animal interests from being recognized as interests in any legally meaningful way. This contradiction is exemplified by New Zealand's amendment to its animal welfare act, legislation that leaves to bureaucrats, not courts, the question of when a great ape has been treated in a way inconsistent with its welfare. If we are truly concerned with protecting animals' interests, why not grant them certain rights to protect those interests? Why not move questions about what constitutes mistreatment of animals and what an animal's interests are into the courts?

One possible answer is that these questions are too difficult, perhaps irresolvable. Intelligent people will disagree about what an animal's interests are—when and how much an animal suffers, whether or not it is even meaningful to speak of an animal "suffering," which cages an animal is comfortable in, and so on. The worry is that granting animals rights is like putting the cart before the horse; since animals cannot communicate their interests to us, how can we grant rights protecting those interests?

This objection assumes that in other legal situations interests are explicit, but nothing could be further from the truth. Interests are often not fully or clearly expressed and the court must act on what is observed and implied, or what it believes to be in the interests of the rights-holder. For example, corporations, infants, estates, municipalities, and universities all hold rights, yet none express their interests directly. Instead, these entities rely on executives, guardians, spokespeople, or elected officials to bring their rights to the attention of the courts. In such cases, interests are often not objective facts; rather, they are nothing more than constructions imposed by experience and estimation. Likewise, our inability to "really" know what an animal's interests are should not stop us from debating the matter and making the best choices we can. Indeed, the very act of estimating interests has a value. It may be the case that we will never know with much certainty what a fish or a monkey feels, but to carefully consider what counts as suffering, for instance, in these and other animals encourages reflection and debate, and animals' interests are better served when we make it a practice to try to take them into consideration.

Another objection to granting animals rights is that it legally binds us to a radical position, but there is much confusion about what granting animals rights would mean. For instance, it is often claimed that granting animals rights would mean treating them too much like humans, especially if we were to grant animals the same rights as humans. But removing animals from the legal category of "property" and granting them rights just means granting them the type of protection implicit in the concept of a right—access to legal action, consideration before a court, and the possibility of compensatory relief. The specific content of the rights, and therefore the nature of the protection, remains unspecified. Furthermore, even if animals were granted some of the same rights as humans, this does not necessarily entail an identical interpretation of these rights. The same rights are already interpreted differently for different kinds of rights-holders. For instance, the U.S. Supreme Court has interpreted the Fourteenth Amendment right to equal protection under the law to apply more strictly in cases of racism than in cases of ageism. "Having rights" does not mean "being human" nor even "being treated like a human." "Having rights" means being recognized by and afforded protection under the law. For instance, a court could order that a great ape, too old and unhealthy to live comfortably and too expensive to support, should be destroyed. This would be perfectly compatible with the ape's rights so long as it was compensated somehow—by a safe habitat, enough food, or even a painless death. My point here is that granting animals rights does not dictate a specific content, but rather a specific form—one designed to guarantee that their interests are taken into account.

So, how would a rights-based approach to animal welfare play out? Let's consider the following hypothetical case: Suppose that the United States wants to follow New Zealand's example in protecting great apes, but decides to do so by granting apes rights instead of amending its animal welfare act. The U.S. government drafts a "Great Apes Bill of Rights" that allows animals (1) to take legal action for injury done to them, (2) to have a court recognize and take account of that injury, and (3) to receive legal relief that benefits them.

In this hypothetical case, both New Zealand and the U.S. agree that great apes should not be subject to research, testing, etc.—they share a common notion of what counts as "humane" treatment of animals (at least regarding great apes). However, each has employed a different strategy. New Zealand has opted to enforce its notion of "humane" treatment of great apes without changing their legal status as property. The important difference is that in the U.S. it is the courts that decide when an infraction has occurred, not a guardian or spokesperson. In the U.S., any organization or person can bring a lawsuit on behalf of a great ape, and the courts must consider whether or not the ape's rights have been violated. In New Zealand, great apes are beholden to a government official, who decides what constitutes a violation of the ape's interests. Furthermore, when the court determines that an injury has occurred, it has an obligation to relieve the right-holder in a way that benefits it. Contrast this with the situation in New Zealand, where the court would only have to punish the lawbreaker or take steps to prevent future infractions.

My argument is simply based on the way rights function in the legal system. As I have described them, rights are procedural tools for giving the rights-holder a way of accessing the legal system. They do not guarantee any specific ends. Rights simply guarantee uniform access to the law. If we have some criteria for the "humane" treatment of animals that we want to debate, then this debate should occur with animals being given every procedural advantage possible. Even if we do not hold animals and animal welfare on a par with humans and human welfare, these issues deserve to be debated on equal legal ground.

Reference

Stone, C. D. (1996). *Should trees have standing? and other essays on law, morals, and the environment.* New York, Oceana Publications.

The Legal Perspective on Animal Rights

Ian Tomb

TWO POSSIBLE ARGUMENTS CAN BE MADE for increasing the rights of animals (Dershowitz 2002), and in this essay, both of these arguments shall be examined and dismissed in turn. First, one could argue that animals deserve increased rights because humans should not be forced to live in a society in which animals are treated as property. By this reasoning, animals should not be treated as property simply because humans would be too offended by this position. However, this argument may be passed over simply by noting the immense popular support for the status quo. The second possibility is that animals deserve increased rights because their own species-typical qualities are sufficient for moral consideration. But a close examination of the differences between humans and animals reveals that humans, the only organisms that live in a moral community, are the only creatures that deserve legal personhood.

The argument that animals should not be classed as property because it would be offensive to other humans depends on the power of communities to disallow certain activities simply on the basis of moral indignation. That is, communities at the state and local levels have the power to ban any activity they deem immoral, as long as that activity is not specifically protected by a constitutional amendment. Indeed, this reasoning has been effective in banning sodomy, an activity that has no victims and, when done in private, is not viewed by others. In the landmark case *Bowers v. Hardwick*,[1] Supreme Court judges upheld a Georgia statute prohibiting sodomy based on the community's moral condemnation of the act. Likewise, one could imagine that, given a local or state community that viewed using animals as property as immoral, a similar decision could be made.

This type of argument, however, is not able to support the reclassification of animals from the category of property. First of all, the vast majority of communities and, in most cases, the vast majority of people in each community, support the status quo regarding the use of animals (Guither 1998). Indeed, groups supporting increased rights for animals, such as the People for the Ethical Treatment of Animals (PETA), are commonly viewed as radical, outside elements of society (Guither 1998). Thus, the general moral outrage necessary to ban the treatment of animals as property would not be possible, given the present insufficient public support.

Given the overwhelming popular support for the classification of animals as property, a legal case against the status quo based on the moral outrage of a community is rendered impotent. The remaining argument in favor of increased animal rights, however, is more challenging. According to many animal rights activists, the intrinsic properties of animals are sufficient to place them in a class that is separate from property. It is clear that such a suggestion runs quite contrary to current law. Mention of animals is absent from the Constitution, and thus any specific laws involving animals are statutory. However, no legal rights have been granted to animals. Instead, the United States and most other countries have established a system of legal welfarism, in which a balance is struck between human and animal interests in order to prevent cruelty to animals (Francione 1995).

One of the earliest modern laws concerning animal cruelty was the Humane Slaughter Act, a particularly high-profile proposal voted into law in 1958. This law required that animals slaughtered for food be killed by only one sharp blow, gunshot, or some other rapid means of butchery. In this case, the animals' suffering, even suffering necessary for the purpose of slaughtering the animal, was regulated. Another landmark law regarding animal welfare, the Laboratory Animal Welfare Act of 1966, was originally intended simply to prevent theft of pets that would later be sold for research purposes. However, numerous successive amendments instituted provisions for laboratory animals, including restrictions on minimum cage size, the introduction of institutional review boards for animal research, and the regulation of pain-relieving drugs (Bekoff 1998). Once again, although the suffering of animals is clearly the focus of the law, animals are still treated as property; their potential for suffering, however, entitles them to special protection.

These examples of legal welfarism are simultaneously encouraging and discouraging to the animal rights activist. Clearly, they are designed to decrease the suffering of animals, which is of utmost importance to the animal rights cause. However, these laws still validate the categorization of animals as property. The categorical split between property and person depends on the longstanding divide between human and animal, one loaded with historical and philosophical baggage (Regan 1982). Thus, any legal case in favor of changing current laws such that animals are not viewed as property rests critically on the distinction between human and animal.

The lines of reasoning used to divide humans from animals vary greatly. However, the main divide lies in a utilitarian versus a deontological approach to morality. A utilitarian account generally involves a weighing of the pains and pleasures of individuals in order to determine if a certain act (or a certain law) is moral. The deontological, or rights-based, approach rejects this kind of "moral calculus," arguing that certain moral absolutes form impermeable boundaries that must be upheld regardless of the pleasure and pain involved.

Though many individuals on both sides of the animal rights debate have used utilitarian arguments to support their points of view, these arguments may not be suited to the legal distinction between human and animal. For example, "painism" and other utilitarian theories argue that animals should have increased rights based solely on the fact that they can suffer (Bekoff 1998). That is, because the moral value of humans as well as all animals is determined by pleasure and pain according to utilitarian theory, there should be no dividing line between species. On the other side of the debate, activists for the status quo argue that research that greatly benefits human society by saving millions of lives would cease to exist without the use of animals as experimental subjects (Fox 1986). Again, this is utilitarian in that it places importance solely on the pleasure and pain of society in general. However, United States law and, in particular, the Supreme Court have traditionally been wary of utilitarian arguments. For example, in *Gregg v. Georgia*, an important Supreme Court decision upholding the death penalty, the Court agreed that an argument for the death penalty is more appropriately justified by retribution than deterrence, and that the death penalty is a necessary step that a legal system is forced to take given the moral rules of a community:

> Indeed, the decision that capital punishment may be the appropriate sanction in extreme cases is an expression of the community's belief that certain crimes are themselves so grievous an affront to humanity that the only adequate response may be the penalty of death.[2]

Not only is utilitarian reasoning generally disfavored in American jurisprudence, it falls especially short when attempting to justify animal rights. As the philosophers Carl Cohen and Tom Regan (2001) have pointed out, there is a major distinction between human obligations towards animals and animal rights. It can be agreed that utilitarian arguments, including the acknowledgment of animal suffering, obligate humans to restrict their treatment of animals. Indeed, an acknowledgment of animal suffering is the main impetus behind animal welfare laws, such as the Humane Slaughter Act and the Laboratory Animal Welfare Act. From this admission of obligation towards animals, however, it does not necessarily follow that humans must grant animals the status of personhood or its associated rights.

Therefore, I will approach the argument against personhood from a deontological perspective, appealing to the rights-based logic familiar to the American legal tradition. One question then is, Upon what basis is this difference established in United States law? Clearly, an argument from the Book of Genesis giving man dominion over all animals (Wise 2000), as is cited by many proponents of the status quo, must be rejected out of hand, given separation of church and state in the United States. A secular perspective of humans and animals grounded in evolutionary theory cannot identify any categorical "silver bullet" that clearly distinguishes humans from animals. Instead, such a distinction must come from an analysis of the moral abilities of humans, and the lack thereof in animals.

First, the considerable cognitive abilities of animals should be mentioned. It is clear that animals are quite different from other forms of property. For example, it is a common assumption of scientific fields such as behavioral neuroscience that animals, including chimpanzees, monkeys, and even rats, can experience emotions in a way that may be analogous to humans (Kim and Meyers 2001). Moreover, whether animals may have a "mental life" that is similar to what humans experience, including some form of consciousness, remains a lively debate (Wise 2000).

Nonetheless, no matter how sophisticated, these possible similarities between human and animal cognition are not sufficient to support an argument for animal rights. No matter where the line between mental (hence moral) worth is drawn, the argument will fail. To choose a dramatic illustration, consider the case of individuals whose mental faculties fade in and out during a severe sickness, or even fully normal humans who go to sleep for the night. Clearly, in neither case do the humans lose the right to moral consideration though they do in fact lose consciousness. A system of rights based entirely on mental abilities would be completely unwieldy, for exactly this reason.

An argument for rights, and an explanation of why humans are entitled to them while animals are not, depends on the human capacity to reason morally. While moral reasoning does depend in part on general cognitive abilities, it remains a separate realm of thought that humans alone possess. Humans are the sole possessors of moral reasoning because they have created, and exist in, a moral society: a unique and crucial trait. Rights can only exist in a moral community, which is something only found in human society (Regan and Cohen 2001); a right cannot exist without proper moral context. A right is an agreement between an individual and the surrounding moral community: essentially, a right is a valid claim of an individual demanding the protection of society (Law.com 2001). Thus, an individual must be a member of a moral community or society in order to make a claim upon that society. It is implausible that animals should be considered members of the United States, and hence its moral community, given that they are unable to make contributions to the society in the ways humans can. Other philosophers have even taken this point one step further, arguing that a right not only ceases to exist for an individual who is not a contributing member of society, but that there can be no concept of a right without a surrounding moral community (Regan and Cohen 2001).

Animals lack the fundamental ability to reason about complex moral issues, and thus lack perhaps the most fundamental capacity required of a member of a moral community. Although it is acknowledged that some animals possess remarkable cognitive abilities, and may even own a sense of self and consciousness (Wise 2000), it is self-evident that no non-human animal is able to reason about complex moral issues, such as hypothetical moral situations. The sort of abstract reasoning necessary has simply never been found in even the best candidate species. Because of their internal moral deficit, animals remain unable to recognize the concepts of right and wrong (both for other individuals and for themselves), and thus are unable to participate in a moral society.

Opponents of this viewpoint argue that there are certain examples of human beings who do not possess concepts of right and wrong. For example, individuals in coma states are unable to reason morally and yet are granted rights by society. But many of these individuals may have the chance to be aided towards normal functioning at some point in the future, and the law takes this possibility into account when granting rights to all humans. In addition, people who are not able to reason morally—such as individuals in coma states, suffering from mental retardation, or in early childhood—should be granted normal human rights due to the complex emotional ties that bind humans together. That is, although Children or coma victims may not be able to reason in an adult, moral way at a particular time, the bonds between them and their loved ones are reason enough to grant them rights.

Finally, any proposal to move animals outside of the realm of property would necessarily run into an intractable legal problem with no clear, defendable answer: Which non-human creatures deserve rights? Animal rights activists have proposed many criteria for distinguishing deserving animals from non-deserving ones, but all of such criteria are problematic. For example, Steven Wise (2000) has created a ranked scale upon which to place animals, with a fraction of the animals at the top end of the scale deserving rights. This system is inherently arbitrary, and, like all other attempts to decide which organisms deserve rights, is based on unclear criteria. Others have argued that there is not a natural dividing line between animals and plants, and that it may be impossible to deny plants the same consideration as animals simply on the basis that plants are inherently less "human" (Silverstein 1996).

Arguments to release animals from the status of property fail to give a satisfying account of why animals deserve increased rights. It is clear that current law fails to grant animals any semblance of personhood, a situation which appropriately reflects the fact that animals remain separate from the human moral community. Although individuals concerned with animal rights may hope for change within the framework of more powerful animal welfare laws, the divide between human and animal is too great to grant animals personhood.

Notes

1. (1986). *Bowers v. Hardwick.* 478 U.S. 186, United States Supreme Court.
2. (1976). *Gregg v. Georgia.* 428 U.S. 53, United States Supreme Court.

References

Bekoff, M. (1998). *Encyclopedia of animal rights and animal welfare.* Westport, Greenwood Press.

Dershowitz, A. M. (2002). *Shouting fire: Civil liberties in a turbulent age.* New York, Little, Brown, and Company.

Fox, M. (1986). *The case for animal experimentation: An evolutionary and ethical perspective.* Los Angeles, University of California Press.

Francione, G. L. (1995). *Animals, property, and the law.* Philadelphia, Temple University Press.

Guither, H. D. (1998). *Animal rights: History and scope of a radical social movement.* Carbondale, Southern Illinois University Press.

Kim, J., and K. M. Meyers (2001). "Fear: Psychological and neural aspects." In N. J. Smelser and P. B. Baltes (Eds.), *International encyclopedia of the social and behavioral sciences.* Amsterdam, Elsevier.

Law.com (2001). Real life dictionary of the law.

Regan, T. (1982). *All that dwell therein: Animal rights and environmental ethics.* Los Angeles, University of California Press.

Regan, T., and C. Cohen (2001). *The animal rights debate.* New York, Rowman and Littlefield Publishers.

Silverstein, H. (1996). *Unleashing rights: Law, meaning and the animal rights movement.* Ann Arbor, University of Michigan Press.

Wise, S. M. (2000). *Rattling the cage: Toward legal rights for animals.* Cambridge, Mass., Perseus Books.

Why Should One Reject the Motion Intending to Remove Animals from the Status of Property?

Hélène Landemore

ALTHOUGH I SYMPATHIZE WITH MANY OF THE INTENTIONS behind the animal rights movement, I believe that it is a mistake to reason from these appealing motivations to the far more radical conclusion that animals merit legal personhood, a step taken by Stephen Wise, among others. To be sure, we owe animals consideration and have strong moral obligations to protect their welfare—obligations that may extend as far as protecting pets as well as wild animals from unnecessary cruelty, or even promoting vegetarianism as an ethically superior way of life. The appropriate way to ensure the proper treatment of animals, however, is not to grant them legal personhood and the associated legal rights, but rather to extend a different, limited set of rights while maintaining their status as property.

I will show that the two main lines of argument that justify the removal of animals from the status of property are flawed and therefore fail to be convincing. The first one, which analogizes animals to cognitively impaired humans, jumps from acceptable premises to a false conclusion. The argument is that if fetuses, the disabled, or even dead people are recognized as rights holders, then so, too, should animals. This analogy is sustainable only if one accepts the implicit theory of rights that underlies it. I will offer an alternative theory of rights that is at least as convincing and remains immune to animal rightists' claims. The second line of argument is purely practical, maintaining not that animals have an absolute right to legal personhood, but rather that to extend such a right is the only available means of ensuring their proper treatment. I will show that, quite to the contrary, property is the only status that allows for their maximum protection.

Before I start to present and discuss the arguments of animal rightists, let me make a few preliminary remarks about the notion of a "right." First of all, I want to make clear that, as a lawyer, I will only deal with legal rights, and not with moral rights. I leave it to the philosopher whether there is a necessary or logical connection between the two. That way, my argument against legal rights of animal has no bearing against the moral obligations we may individually have towards animals. Following Ronald Dworkin and, after him, Steven Wise, I define legal rights as "trump cards" that individuals can play against appeals to the society, that is, "side-constraints" or "limits or vetoes." In this perspective, as Dworkin puts it, "a right that does not stick in the spokes of someone's wheel is no right at all" (Dworkin 1977). Later in the essay, I develop a distinction between *active* and *passive* rights which I think is consistent with the Dworkinian definition.[1]

Secondly, regarding the relationship between rights and personhood, I adopt two different positions. In the first half of this essay, in which I argue against the notion that personhood must be extended to animals because they are owed certain rights, I follow Wise's lead and accept that rights are contingent upon personhood (Wise 2000). I take this approach for the sake of providing the strongest argument against animal rightists by refuting the heart of their claim, that animals are owed rights, rather than attacking the more superficial association between rights and personhood. However, in the second part of my argument, where my point is simply to deny that personhood is necessary to the adequate protection of animals, I allow that the notions of right and personhood can be disconnected; I thus argue that animals can be property and at the same time rights-holders. Nevertheless, the rights to which animals are entitled are essentially distinct from the active rights of human beings. They are passive rights and are best expressed as a correlative or mirror image of human duties. The critical point is that in both versions of my argument—one in which animals have no legal rights and one in which they have some specific ones—there is no need to remove them from the status of property.

The position of animal rightists I intend to discuss is not the caricature often denounced by its opponents. Most animal rightists do not deem animals equal to human beings in every respect, nor do they mean to grant animals all the kinds of rights that human beings enjoy. Rather, they advocate a limited set of rights for animals. For example, Peter Singer,[2] who advocates rights for all sentient beings and criticizes "speciesism" as an unjustified prejudice in favor of one's species analogous to racism or sexism,[3] acknowledges that "a rejection of speciesism does not imply that all lives are of equal worth" and that "a life of a self-aware being, capable of abstract thought, of planning for the future, of complex acts of communication, and so on, is more valuable than the life of a being without those capacities" (Singer 1975). Tom Regan, another eminent animal rightist, proposes an even less universal criterion to the entitlement of rights. In his perspective, rights should be acknowledged only in "mentally normal mammals of a year or more," that is, animals that meet his "subject-of-a-life-criterion" (Regan 1983). More recently, Steven Wise demanded legal personhood for only two species of mammals, namely chimpanzees and bonobos (Wise 2000). While he calls for the destruction of the legal wall that separates human animals from non-human animals and therefore deprives chimpanzees and bonobos from legal rights, he agrees that, of the more than one million extant species of animals, "many of them, say bees and ants, should never have these rights" (Wise 2000). To borrow a metaphor of Wise's, the objective of animal rights activists is simply to rebuild the legal wall separating rights-holders from non-rights-holders in a more inclusive way.

Beneath the appealing moderation of these claims, however, lurks a fatal inconsistency. If Singer, Reagan, and Wise follow their own arguments to their natural conclusions, they would be cornered into a far more radical position. The main inconsistency in Peter Singer's position is his commitment to the idea of equal rights for all animals on behalf of their sensitivity *and* the idea of a different right to life proportionate to mental complexity. The compatibility of those two principles is not self-evident. As Rod Peerce illustrates with the example of a dog in a medical experiment, you cannot consistently argue that nothing, not even the suffering of human beings, legitimates the suffering of the dog, but that on the other hand it is perfectly legitimate to (painlessly) kill the dog if human life is at stake. What if the suffering of the dog would save a human's life? Peter Singer seems to assume that it is better for the animal to be dead than to suffer, but this sounds plausible only in the case of excruciating or chronic pain. There may well be cases in which the dog suffers only a little, saves a human life and lives happily ever after. In those cases, it may seem preposterous to advocate the idea that one should let the person die unless she can be saved by killing the dog. Peter Singer's idea that mental complexity does not affect equal consideration in the case of suffering, but overcomes equal consideration in the case of the value of life, seems unsustainable. Either all sentient animals have equal rights, or rights are proportionate to mental complexity, but you cannot have it both ways. More importantly, the distinction Peter Singer makes between these two types of rights sneaks through the back door exactly the kind of "speciesist" bias he condemns in others. If the mental capacity of humans accords a preferential right to life, isn't it because, implicitly, Peter Singer acknowledges a differentiation of rights according to a hierarchy of species?

In Regan and Wise, the problem is one of "drawing the line." Whether you draw the line between human and non-human mammals, or between human, chimpanzees, and bonobos on the one hand, and all other animals on the other hand, the decision is in both cases hard to justify. In fact, once you admit that there is only a difference in degree between human beings and animals, the decision to rank mammals higher than insects or chimpanzees higher than mice is just as arbitrary as the decision to entitle humans alone with rights. If there is no categorical difference in kind between species, then rights must slide down a slippery slope of degree until mosquitoes and snakes are accorded the same extensive rights as humans.[4]

These radical conclusions are implicit in the universal and egalitarian rights favored by animal rightists. What I want to criticize here, however, is not the lack of courage in animal rightists who fail to draw the logical conclusions of their radical assumptions. In fact, animal rightists tend to be more and more radical, endorsing with ever greater confidence the extreme conclusions they first denied. Instead, I intend to address what is the most seductive argument in favor of the radical animal rights position, namely the "argument from marginal cases." In one form or another, this argument is at the core of Peter Singer's, Tom Regan's and Steven Wise's defenses of animal rights.

The argument from marginal cases requires two steps. First, all the reasonable candidates for the criteria of moral worth are listed. Sentience, awareness, complex cognitive abilities and the capacity to create and develop affective bonds with other creatures are criteria often identified as morally significant and, among others, are held by animal rightists to be the properties defining the capacity to hold rights. The second step of the argument relies on the intuition that human fetuses, children, mentally retarded individuals, senile adults, and even dead individuals retain some rights. But one cannot possibly acknowledge these so-called "marginal cases" as rights-holders without being logically compelled to entitle at least a certain category of animals to the exact same rights; and conversely, one excludes animals only at the peril of being logically forced to exclude human claimants as well. To illustrate this point, compare normal mature dolphins, or apes, with pre-natal, senile or mentally retarded people. In terms of cognitive capacities, autonomy or self-awareness, dolphins and apes score higher than any of those human marginal cases. In fact, if you push the logic of this type of comparison to the extreme, even a bacterium scores higher in all these respects than a dead person. Although probably no animal rightist goes as far as claiming rights for bacteria,[5] there is something problematic in the slippery tendency of the argument from marginal cases.[6]

The flaw in this superficially logical argument is that it works if and only if one accepts the sort of theory of rights that makes relevant the comparison between human beings and apes, and between dolphins and bacteria. Otherwise, the analogy becomes meaningless and the argument is no longer compelling. The theory of rights that is to be found behind the analogy can be identified as both "univalent" and "internalist." According to Loren Lomasky, "[a] theory is univalent if it attempts to ground all ascription of moral status to beings on their possession of some one property" (Lomasky 1987). It is internalist because it assumes that rights "lie in and depend on something internal to the rights holder rather than in a relation to something external." On the contrary, a multivalent and externalist theory "incorporates more avenues than one by way of which a being can be accorded moral status" and considers rights not as native but as conferred by a given community. To put it briefly, a theory of rights is univalent if only one property or set of properties is enough to entitle its bearer to rights and it is internalist if this property is rooted in the nature of the person itself.

Lomasky identifies two ways in which animal rightists employ a univalent and internalist theory of rights. Adherents to the "radical" approach choose a criterion for rights such as sentience, reflective self-awareness, or the capacity to entertain and act on behalf of desires. Although they may sometimes propose several criteria, they generally pick one as key.[7] On the other hand, representatives of the "conservative" approach are agnostic regarding the nature and number of properties defining the rights-holder. They simply show that, whatever this ground is—a single natural property or several—one cannot exclude animals without being logically compelled to exclude human claimants as well. Like the radicals, the conservatives implicitly assume a univalent position: all beings that have rights do so for essentially the same reason or set of reasons, whatever they might be. Both approaches are thus internalist and univalent.

Against those assumptions Lomasky proposes a multivalent and externalist theory of rights denying that there is any one feature or group of features requisite to rights and that the source of rights is internal to the individual rather than external. According to Lomasky, the possession of rights rests on two conditions. The first one is the criterion of "project pursuit," which she defines as the long-term commitment to certain ends. Lomasky calls *projects* ends "which reach indefinitely into the future, play a central role within the ongoing endeavors of the individual, and provide a significant degree of structural stability to an individual's life" (Lomasky 1987).[8] The second condition is inclusion in a moral community whose members traditionally are or develop into project pursuers. It is important to note that the second condition comes as a necessary complement to the first one—no project pursuer can be granted rights or, more precisely, be recognized as a project pursuer, unless included in a moral community—but this condition also functions as a unique requirement where project pursuit is clearly inapplicable, as in the case of senile or dead people.

At this point, one may object that the criterion of "being a project pursuing individual" is in fact an internal property typical of what I just denounced as univalent and internalist. This is not the case. First, if Lomasky's theory were univalent, it would hold that only those beings that are project pursuers are rights-holders. Yet, Lomasky recognizes that certain beings that do not pursue projects (e.g., fetuses, children, and dead persons) are also rights holders. Second, according to Lomasky's theory, rights do not stem from any of the several internal characteristics that make an individual a project pursuer, but from an external source, namely a moral community. Rights are external properties conferred in and by the intersubjective community of rights-holders. Outside of this moral community—exclusively human so far but potentially open to any creature acknowledged by the moral community as belonging to a project pursuing class—the notion of rights doesn't even make sense.[9] Since rights do not stem from the internal characteristics that make an individual a project pursuer, but from an external source, it should be clear that Lomasky's theory of rights is neither univalent nor internalist.

The strength of such a multivalent and externalist theory of rights is that it avoids much of the difficulty in "drawing the line" between those who hold rights and those who do not. For one thing, the project pursuit criteria is tailored more narrowly than the principle alternatives, such as the possession of sentience or rationality. Only human beings are, according to Lomasky, aptly characterized as project pursuers. Second, this theory allows including children, fetuses, disabled and even dead people in the category of rights holders, along with project pursuers, without having to include animals at the same time. Although they cannot be said to be project pursuers, children, fetuses, disabled and dead people enjoy the status of rights-holders by virtue of the social relations to project pursuers in which they stand. Children and fetuses,[10] Lomasky argues, are entitled to rights as prospective project pursuers. Symmetrically, dead persons are considered erstwhile project pursuers and are entitled to rights in the name of the significant interests they leave behind. Lastly, mentally disabled humans, although they might be unable ever to pursue projects, are also granted rights because they are "embedded in networks of social relationships with others of their kind" (Lomasky 1987). In this latter case, the absence of project pursuit is entirely supplanted by inclusion in a moral community of project pursuers. As to animals, contrary to what the argument of marginal case suggests, they do not qualify for membership into the moral community defined by Lomasky's criteria. Animals cannot be considered "project pursuers," be it prospective, erstwhile or by virtue of belonging to a class of beings that ordinarily develop into project pursuers. Since animals fulfill none of the criteria of a multivalent and externalist theory of rights, there is no convincing reason to consider them as "persons" and to remove them from the status of property.

There are undeniable difficulties in Lomasky's position. Among other things, it is not clear why she shies away from a fully fledged externalist theory by clinging to the criterion of project pursuit. Although this criterion does not make for an internal theory, it still seems to be the ambiguous residue of a belief in the necessity to find some "natural" ground for rights and personhood. As a matter of fact, I would personally subscribe to a fully fledged externalist theory relying only on inclusion in a moral community. According to a purely externalist theory, a "person" is simply whomever the law deems to be so,[11] in which case there are simply obvious practical reasons, to which I shall turn soon, why animals should be excluded. The main point of the argument that precedes is thus not so much to replace one theory of rights with another, but rather to show that the battle over the status of animals is not to be won or lost on the uncertain ground of a theory of rights. As an alternative to the animal rightists' position, Lomasky's theory may be no more plausible, but it is certainly no less. At the very least, it makes the power of the marginal case an open question.

If both sides draw a tie on the level of theoretical arguments, let us turn to the more practical considerations.[12] According to Wise's argument, removing animals from the status of property is a necessary step towards the improvement of their living conditions. I will argue, however, that the status of property is no obstacle to our moral obligations towards animals, and that what is denounced by animal rightists as our "dominion" over animals may be ultimately the best hope for their proper treatment.

As a preliminary remark, one may argue that to cause suffering is wrong whether or not it violates a right,[13] in which case the question of whether or not animals are persons or have rights is a secondary issue. We may indeed have obligations towards animals that do not emanate from their status as legal rights-holders. The simple fact that animals are able to suffer or to have desires and needs should be sufficient to impose moral or even legal obligations on human beings. In fact, both animal rightists and their opponents agree on the moral necessity to preserve animals from unnecessary suffering and to provide them with a minimal level of protection, even though they disagree on the definition of "unnecessary suffering" and the exact level of desired protection. The acknowledgment of human obligations towards animals need not, however, correspond to the acknowledgment of rights in animals. Although most animal rightists take for granted the correlativity of rights and duties, the latter is a very controversial issue.[14] To conclude from the existence of duties in humans towards animals that there are "rights" in animals might be in fact mere fallacy, a fallacy we might call *the fallacy of semantic symmetry*.[15] From that point of view, indeed, "animal rights" are nothing more than a convenient though misleading name for the mirror image of humane duties.

As to the status of "property" itself, so much criticized by animal rightists, it is no obstacle to the moral consideration of animals. First, it is legally possible to impose duties on human beings regarding animals and other types of "property" without raising the latter to the status of persons. Even if one subscribes to the idea that to a right held by one agent always corresponds a duty for another, human duties and obligations towards animals can simply be derivative of other *human* rights. For instance, I can have an obligation not to pollute a river without the river having a right not to be polluted. My duty is simply derivative from other human beings' rights to live in a clean, healthy environment. Similarly, I may have an obligation not to torture an animal because of somebody else's right not to be exposed to shocking manifestations of cruelty and malevolence. To put it otherwise, my obligation not to torture animals is not an obligation to animals, but to other human beings, *regarding* animals.[16]

Second, the status of property is not an obstacle to the recognition of animal legal rights.[17] If one accepts that the notions of personhood and rights can be disconnected, it becomes possible to acknowledge rights in "property."[18] Animal rightists themselves recognize this point. Arguing against the use of animals by farmers, Tom Regan, for example, insists that "property rights are not absolute," so that "if . . . animals have basic moral rights, then these rights ought to be recognized as imposing strict constraints on what any farmer may be allowed to do to them in the name of exercising his 'property rights'" (Regan 1983). Relying implicitly on the correlativity of right and duty thesis, Regan suggests that the legal constraints imposed on the farmer naturally translate into legal rights on the animal side. Yet, granted the correlativity thesis and Regan's conclusion that animals have or should have legal rights, it does not follow still that animals ought to be acknowledged as persons. This is the main point I want to make: Animals can have the status both of legal rights bearer *and* property.

There is another reason why the debate about animal rights is wrongly focused on the issue of "legal personhood." There is indeed something quite hypocritical in the criticism of our "dominion" over animals when even Steven Wise's regime of animal rights calls for human jurisdiction—i.e., dominion—over animals. According to Wise, courts should adopt a legal fiction that the animal is "autonomous" and, therefore, a "person," as it does in the case of legally incompetent humans. In practice, courts would be charged with resolving animal conflicts by determining what the animal would wish if it were capable of speaking for itself. However, one can hardly see how the best interest of animals is to be objectively determined. Who, if not man, is going to set up the hierarchy of rights between the different species? The fiction of "legal personhood" would not change the fact that human beings ultimately decide for animals, according to the needs and wants they grant animals and according to a hierarchy of beings that they entirely set up. The true fiction is to suppose that the limits a democratic society imposes on itself in its dealing with animals stem from any source other than human will.

The proposition to remove animals from the status of property raises interesting issues regarding the nature and meaning of the concept of "property" itself. Acknowledging our moral responsibilities and obligations towards animals should entitle them to a status that clearly distinguishes them from *things*, without necessarily raising them to the status of *persons*.[19] By the word "property," Locke, for example, meant not only real estate and the product of one's labor, but also bodily integrity and life, which obviously are more than "things." If humans were to accept a responsibility to nature similar to their self-directed responsibility for bodily integrity, it would certainly be possible to protect animals, and even the entirety of nature, without resorting to the extension of full-blown personhood, maybe even without appealing to any kind of "animal" rights. An approach to animal protection grounded in the recognition of responsibilities towards some classes of property requires talking about "animal rights" only if we endorse the thesis of the correlativity of duty and right. In the latter case, however, it then seems necessary to draw a distinction between *active* and *passive* rights.[20] Active rights are the rights which right-bearers are themselves responsible to enforce on other people, through the intermediary of laws and the political sphere. Clearly only human beings (probably not even all of them) qualify for this type of rights. Passive rights, on the contrary, are characterized by the fact that it does not fall upon their bearers to enforce them; this task is left to a specific legislative setup organized by the active right-bearers. Passive rights thus merely reflect the existence of duties in the bearers of active rights. They can apply to a number of human and non-human creatures, possibly even things.[21] Because they derive from the existence of duties in active rights-bearers, passive rights are simply the semantic mirror image of the latter. The rights of animals (and maybe also babies, dead people and the other embarrassing "marginal cases" we confronted above) should certainly be conceptualized as such passive "rights." The advantage of this approach, by contrast with that proposed by Wise and the other animal rightists, is that it does not require the removal of animals from the status of property in order to achieve a satisfactory level of protection of animals' interests.

Of course, this approach to animal protection in terms of passive rights is unlikely to satisfy the most extreme animal rightists, in particular because it seems to preserve the speciesist dichotomy between man and animal, i.e., between the species which creates rights and that which can at best benefit from them. This dichotomy potentially leaves the door open for the further utilization of animals by man. On the other hand, the nature of our duties towards animals might well imply to defend vegetarianism as the most *efficient* way to protect animals' interests and fulfill our moral duties towards them, given the difficulties of treating them well while raising them in farms and then killing them painlessly.[22] Similarly, there is nothing incompatible here with the call for a ban or at least for strong restrictions on animal experimentation. In that sense, a theory of passive rights theoretically allows for the maximal protection of animals without granting them legal personhood. The suffering inflicted on sensitive beings should in itself appeal to our moral obligations and incite us to revise our laws on animal property.

There is no necessary logical bridge from the premise that animals are beings endowed with many of the qualities of humane rights-holders to the conclusion that the law should consider animals as persons entitled with rights. In fact, all the criteria proposed by animal rightists to establish the existence of legal rights in animals fail to be convincing as soon as one refuses the univalent and internalist theory of rights that underlies the analogy. A multivalent and externalist theory of rights makes no room for such an analogy and thus defeats the crux of animal advocates' main argument.

Another mistake is to assume that the status of property is an obstacle to the protection of animals, and that only the status of personhood is sufficient to achieve this protection. The category of property is broad enough to make room for a particular status of animals in it, a status that restricts the allowable treatments of animals by human beings. In fact, if one disconnects the notion of person from that of rights, one may even concede to animal rightists the possibility of legal rights for animals. Those rights—conceptualized as passive rights derived from our moral duties towards animals—would be precisely the restrictions which Peter Singer, Tom Regan and Steven Wise have been calling for from, in my view, the wrong perspective.

Notes

In the writing of this essay, I owe a lot to the following persons: Marc Hauser, first, for leading one of the most exciting classes I took during my year as a Visiting Fellow at Harvard, and for including me in the whole project; the editors of the book, in particular Fiery Cushman for his wonderful work on my English prose (originally closer to, at best, poetry) as well as innumerable comments and suggestions that considerably helped reshape the original draft; Richard Tuck for valuable remarks (acknowledged in my notes) and in particular for convincing me of the superiority of a fully externalist, Hobbesian approach to rights; and Andrews Williams for helpful comments and a meritorious though unrewarded attempt at reasoning me, once, over a Chinese dinner, into vegetarianism.

1. Rights on a Dworkinian account are guarantees and there are no reasons why we could not guarantee passive rights (e.g., protection from cruelty) to the same degree as active rights (e.g., free speech).
2. I am aware that given his utilitarian suspicion regarding the vocabulary of rights, Peter Singer should more appropriately be qualified an "animal liberationist." He is committed, however, to positions common with those of self-proclaimed animal rightists like Tom Regan and Steven Wise. Since I only intend to discuss those assumptions, I will consider Peter Singer an animal rightist in the loose sense of someone who considers that if human beings have rights, then animals, which possess the quality in virtue of which human beings are rights-holders, should also have rights.
3. Resorting to Bentham's criterion: "can they suffer?" (Bentham, Burns, et al. (1996). In that respect, if an animal feels no pain, it has no rights.
4. Cf., for example, Michael W. Fox, who states that "all life is equal. It is unethical to value any one life over any other" and sees "humans and other animals as coequal, morally equivalent" (Fox 1990).
5. Bernard Rollin, who grounds rights in the sole possession of "interests" and any sort of "mental life" and is one of the most extreme animal rightists, "only" goes down "to insects, worms, and perhaps planaria" (Rollin 1992).
6. I do not think that the "slippery slope" argument I resort to here falls prey to the fallacy of assuming that the lack of an obvious stopping point along a continuum renders imprecise the point that is ultimately chosen. I am not saying that the line proposed by animal rightists is imprecise—it is on the contrary very precise (though varying from one author to the other)—nor am I suggesting that going down that route would necessarily lead us to endow bacteria with rights. Rather, I am criticizing the lack of convincing justification for any line and the consequent necessity to approach the problem of animal rights from an altogether different point of view.
7. For example, Tom Regan's "subject-of-a-life criterion."

8. Examples of "projects" are: "raising one's children to be responsible adults, striving to bring about the dictatorship of the proletariat, serving God, serving Mammon, following the shifting fortunes of the New York Yankees come what may, bringing relief to starving persons in Africa, writing the great American Novel, promoting White supremacy, and doing philosophy" (Lomasky 1987).
9. To come back to Wise's proposal, even if science could prove that chimpanzees and bonobos qualify as project pursuers there would still remain the obstacle of acknowledgement by the moral community. Some authors, like Wise, anticipate this challenge and attempt to convince us to include chimpanzees and bonobos in the moral community.
10. I concede that the issue here is debatable. If fetuses can be considered prospective project pursuers, why not as well the combination of egg and sperm that precedes them?
11. This type of hard-core externalist theory is illustrated by Hobbes, as Richard Tuck pointed out to me. In the *Elements of Law,* Hobbes thus takes a strong stance against any kind of expertise on who qualifies as a human being. "Upon the occasion of some strange and deformed birth, it shall not be decided by Aristotle, or the philosophers, whether the same be a man or no, but by the laws" (II, 29, 8, p. 181).
12. I will not tackle here the problem of whether or not these practical reasons obtain for human marginal cases as well. I suspect that they do and that this fact renders debatable the status of rights-holders of a number of human marginal cases. Whatever the answer to that latter question, however, it is entirely independent from the conclusion reached on the status of animals.
13. "To do what is right and to do what is demanded by rights should not be conflated" (Lomasky, 1989).
14. Cf. in particular Lyons 1970 or Hart 1984.
15. I admit that it is going a bit far to say that "semantic symmetry" is a fallacy. As I hope I show later in the essay, as long as we are clear about the correlativity thesis, nothing should follow from the ascription of passive rights to animals except the ascription of a corresponding duty on human beings. The problem is that animal rightists do try to derive something additional from what might otherwise be more charitably called the illusion of semantic symmetry. They derive legal personhood in animals, which I deny. This is where, I think, the illusion produces a fallacy. Thanks to Richard Tuck for commenting on this point.
16. I am playing devil's advocate—Kant's advocate, in fact!—in order to undermine the traditional defense of animals' or nature's "rights." Although I do not share Kant's indirect duty view of rights (as exposed for example in his Lectures on Ethics, in the section entitled "Duties towards animals and spirits"), I also find unconvincing arguments that derive rights in animals from the existence of human duties regarding animals.
17. These are precisely the type of limited rights that U.S. law acknowledges in animals, like the right to be protected from their owners' cruel treatment (correlative of the first anti-cruelty law among the United States, enacted in 1828 by the New York State Legislature).

18. Note that in that case the notion of legal rights can be extended not only to animals but also to valuable (i.e., morally significant) inanimate objects, such as nature as a whole, or, in another sphere, works of art.
19. In fact, this is exactly and all of what Bentham suggests in the footnote to *An Introduction to the Principles of Morals and Legislation*, which is usually cited to make Bentham the first animal rightist (Bentham, Burns, et al. 1996). In this footnote, entitled "Interests of the inferior animals improperly neglected in legislation by the insensibility of ancients jurists," far from demanding extensive legal rights, let alone personhood, for animals, Bentham is simply bemoaning in the corresponding passage the fact that jurists have "degraded" the animal realm "into the class of *things*." Although Bentham believed that animals were entitled to legislative protection from cruelty, he still thought that they should be eaten.
20. This distinction was suggested to me by Richard Tuck.
21. Why not indeed argue, from my duty to respect an old tree, in favor of a right of the tree not to be cut down?
22. Note, however, that this would imply to impose vegetarianism on lions and any carnivorous animal besides man, probably leading to the extinction of many species. This raises moral issues that animal rightists rarely address. I owe the latter two remarks to Richard Tuck.

References

Bentham, J., J. H. Burns, et al. (1996). *An introduction to the principles of morals and legislation*. Oxford, Clarendon Press.

Dworkin, R. (1977). *Taking rights seriously*. Cambridge, Harvard University Press.

Fox, M. W. (1990). *Inhumane society: The American way of exploiting animals*. New York, St. Martin's Press.

Hart, H. L. (1984). "Are there any natural rights?" In J. Waldron (Ed.), *Theories of rights*. Oxford, Oxford University Press.

Hobbes, T., and J. C. A. Gaskin (1994). *The elements of law, natural and politic*. Part I, *Human nature*, part II, *De corpore politico; with three lives*. Oxford, Oxford University Press.

Lomasky, L. E. (1987). *Persons, rights, and the moral community*. New York, Oxford University Press.

Lyons, D. (1970). "Correlativity of rights and duties." *Nous* 46(4): 45–55.

Regan, T. (1983). *The case for animal rights*. Berkeley, University of California Press.

Rollin, B. E. (1992). *Animal rights & human morality*. Buffalo, N.Y., Prometheus Books.

Singer, P. (1975). *Animal liberation: A new ethics for our treatment of animals*. New York, New York Review of Books: Distributed by Random House.

Wise, S. M. (2000). *Rattling the cage: Toward legal rights for animals*. Cambridge, Mass., Perseus Books.

Animals, Property, and Personhood

Gary L. Francione

THE ESSAYS ON LEGAL TOPICS are interesting and creative, raising two issues that I will explore further: the property status of animals and the meaning of "animal rights." The first issue matters because any consideration of the moral status of animals must take into consideration that animals are our property—they are things that we own. When we consider our moral obligations to animals without first addressing the status of animals as property, we tend to confine our discussion to ways in which we might exploit animals more "humanely" rather than to ask whether our exploitation—however "humane"—is morally justifiable. The second issue matters because a great deal of confusion surrounds public discourse on the moral status of animals. For example, the animal rights position is often understood—including by some animal advocates—as maintaining that animals should have many of the legal rights enjoyed by humans.

In this essay, I will address these two issues. First, I argue that although we claim to take animal interests seriously, the property status of animals means that their interests will virtually always be ignored whenever it will benefit humans and despite the many laws that supposedly protect animals. Second, I argue that if we are to take animal interests seriously, then we must accord animals one right: the right not to be treated as our property. Our recognition of this one right would result in the abolition of animal exploitation, just as our acceptance that humans had the right not to be treated as property resulted in the abolition of slavery. Although this is an ostensibly radical conclusion, it necessarily follows from certain moral notions that we already claim to accept. In conclusion, I will argue that our recognition of this right would not preclude our choosing humans over animals in situations of genuine conflict.

I. Animals as Property

We claim to take animals seriously and to reject the notion that animals are merely things without any morally significant interests and to whom we owe no moral obligations.[1] Virtually everyone would agree with what we may call the humane treatment principle, which says that we ought to treat animals "humanely" and that we have an obligation not to inflict "unnecessary" suffering on animals.[2] We take the humane treatment principle so seriously that we enshrine it in animal welfare laws that purport to provide for the protection of animals. These laws are of two kinds: general and specific. General animal welfare laws, such as anticruelty laws, prohibit cruelty or the infliction of suffering on animals without distinguishing between various uses of animals. For example, New York law imposes a criminal sanction on any person who "overdrives, overloads, tortures or cruelly beats or unjustifiably injures, maims, mutilates or kills any animal."[3] Delaware law prohibits cruelty and defines as cruel "every act or omission to act whereby unnecessary or unjustifiable physical pain or suffering is caused or permitted," and includes "mistreatment of any animal or neglect of any animal under the care and control of the neglector, whereby unnecessary or unjustifiable physical pain or suffering is caused."[4] In Britain, the Protection of Animals Act of 1911 makes it a criminal offense to "cruelly beat, kick, ill-treat, over-ride, over-drive, over-load, torture, infuriate, or terrify any animal" or to impose "unnecessary suffering" on animals.[5] Specific animal welfare laws purport to apply the humane treatment principle to a particular animal use. For example, the American Animal Welfare Act, enacted in 1966 and amended on numerous occasions,[6] the British Cruelty to Animals Act, enacted in 1876,[7] and the British Animals (Scientific Procedures) Act of 1986[8] concern the treatment of animals used in experiments. The American Humane Slaughter Act, originally enacted in 1958, regulates the killing of animals used for food.[9]

The operation of these animal welfare laws purports to require that we balance the interests of animals against our interests to determine whether animal suffering is necessary.[10] To balance interests means to assess the relative strengths of conflicting interests. If our suffering in not using animals outweighs the animal suffering involved, then our interests prevail and the animal suffering is regarded as necessary. If no justifiable human interests are at stake, then the infliction of suffering on animals must be regarded as unnecessary. For example, the British law regulating the use of animals in experiments requires, before any experiment is approved, a balancing of "the likely adverse effects on the animals concerned against the benefit likely to accrue."[11]

In sum, the humane treatment principle assumes that we may use animals when it is necessary to do so—when we are faced with a conflict between animal and human interests—and that we should impose only the minimum amount of pain and suffering necessary for our purpose. If a prohibition against unnecessary suffering of animals is to have any meaningful content, it must preclude the infliction of suffering on animals merely for our pleasure, amusement, or convenience. If there is a feasible alternative to our use of animals in a particular situation, then the principle would seem to proscribe such use.

Although we express disapproval of the unnecessary suffering of animals, nearly all of our animal use can be justified *only* by habit, convention, amusement, convenience, or pleasure.[12] To put the matter another way, most of the suffering that we impose on animals is completely unnecessary. For example, the uses of animals in entertainment, such as in films, circuses, rodeos, and for sport hunting, cannot, by definition, be considered necessary. Nevertheless, laws that supposedly prohibit the infliction of unnecessary suffering on animals protect these activities. It is certainly not necessary for us to wear fur coats, or to use animals to test duplicative household products, or to have yet another brand of lipstick or aftershave lotion.

More important in terms of numbers of animals used, however, is the animal agriculture industry, in which more than 8 billion animals are killed for food annually in the United States alone. These animals are raised under horrendous intensive conditions known as "factory farming," mutilated in various ways without pain relief, transported long distances in cramped, filthy containers, and finally slaughtered amid the stench, noise, and squalor of the abattoir. No one maintains that it is necessary for reasons of health to eat meat or animal products; indeed, an increasing number of mainstream health care professionals claim that these foods may be detrimental to human health. Moreover, respected environmental scientists have pointed out the tremendous inefficiencies and resulting environmental costs to the planet of animal agriculture. For example, animals consume more protein than they produce. For every kilogram (2.2 pounds) of animal protein produced, animals consume an average of almost six kilograms, or over thirteen pounds, of plant protein from grains and forage. It takes more than 100,000 liters of water to produce one kilogram of beef, and approximately 900 liters to produce one kilogram of wheat. In any event, our only justification for the pain, suffering, and death inflicted on these billions of farm animals is that we enjoy the taste of their flesh.[13]

Many of us regard the use of animals in experiments as involving a genuine conflict of human and animal interests, but the necessity of animal use for this purpose is open to serious question as well. Considerable empirical evidence challenges the notion that animal experiments are necessary to ensure human health and indicates that, in many instances, reliance on animal models has actually been counterproductive.[14]

In short, we suffer from what might be regarded as moral schizophrenia as far as nonhuman animals are concerned. We claim to accept a moral and legal obligation not to inflict unnecessary suffering on animals, but we routinely disregard that obligation and we impose unnecessary suffering on billions of animals. The explanation for this disparity between what we say and what we do concerns the status of animals as our property.[15] Animals are commodities that we own and that have no value other than that which we as property owners choose to give them. Under the law, "animals are owned in the same way as inanimate objects such as cars and furniture."[16] They "are by law treated as any other form of movable property and may be the subject of absolute, *i.e.*, complete ownership . . . [and] the owner has at his command all the protection that the law provides in respect of absolute ownership."[17] The owner is entitled to exclusive physical possession of the animal, the use of the animal for economic and other gain, and the right to make contracts with respect to the animal or to use the animal as collateral for a loan. The owner is under a duty to ensure that her animal property does not harm other humans or their property, but she can sell or bequeath the animal, give the animal away, or have the animal taken from her as part of the execution of a legal judgment against her. She can also kill the animal. Wild animals are generally regarded as owned by the state and held in trust for the benefit of the people, but they can be made the property of particular humans through hunting or by taming and confining them.

The property status of animals renders meaningless any balancing that is supposedly required under the humane treatment principle or animal welfare laws, because what we really balance are the interests of property owners against the interests of their animal property. It is, of course, absurd to suggest that we can balance human interests, which are protected by claims of right in general and of a right to own property in particular, against the interests of property, which exists only as a means to the ends of humans. Although we claim to recognize that we may prefer animal interests over human interests only when there is a conflict of interests, there is always a conflict between the interests of property owners who want to use their property and the interests of their animal property. The human property interest will almost always prevail. The animal in question is always a pet or a laboratory animal, or a game animal, or a food animal, or a rodeo animal, or some other form of animal property that exists solely for our use and has no value except that which we give it. There is really no choice to be made between the human and the animal interest because the choice has already been predetermined by the property status of the animal; the "suffering" of property owners who cannot use their property as they wish counts more than animal suffering. We are allowed to impose any suffering required to use our animal property for a particular purpose—even if that purpose is our mere amusement or pleasure. As long as we use our animal property to generate an economic benefit, there is no effective limit on our use or treatment of animals.[18]

There are several specific ways in which animal welfare laws ensure that there will never be a meaningful balance of human and animal interests. First, many of these laws explicitly exempt most forms of institutionalized property use, which account for the largest number of animals that we use. The most frequent exemptions from state anticruelty statutes involve scientific experiments, agricultural practices, and hunting.[19] The Animal Welfare Act, the primary federal law that regulates the use of animals in biomedical experiments, does not even apply to most of the animals used in experiments—rats and mice—and imposes no meaningful limits on the amount of pain and suffering that may be inflicted on animals in the conduct of experiments.[20]

Second, even if anticruelty statutes do not do so explicitly, courts have effectively exempted our common uses of animals from scrutiny by interpreting these statutes as not prohibiting the infliction of even extreme suffering if it is incidental to an accepted use of animals and a customary practice on the part of animal owners.[21] An act "which inflicts pain, even the great pain of mutilation, and which is cruel in the ordinary sense of the word" is not prohibited "[w]henever the purpose for which the act is done is to make the animal more serviceable for the use of man."[22] For example, courts have held consistently that animals used for food may be mutilated in ways that unquestionably cause severe pain and suffering and that would normally be regarded as cruel or even as torture. These practices are permitted, however, because animal agriculture is an accepted institutionalized animal use, and those in the meat industry regard the practices as normal and necessary to facilitate that use. The law presumes that animal owners will act in their best economic interests and will not intentionally inflict more suffering than is necessary on an animal because to do so would diminish the monetary value of the animal.[23] For example, in *Callaghan v. Society for the Prevention of Cruelty to Animals*, the court held that the painful act of dehorning cattle did not constitute unnecessary abuse because farmers would not perform this procedure if it were not necessary. The self-interest of the farmer would prevent the infliction of "useless pain or torture," which "would necessarily reduce the condition of the animal; and, unless they very soon recovered, the farmer would lose in the sale."[24]

Third, anticruelty laws are generally criminal laws. Criminal laws require the state to prove beyond a reasonable doubt that a defendant engaged in an unlawful act with a culpable state of mind. The problem is that if a defendant is inflicting pain or suffering on an animal as part of an accepted institutionalized use of animals, it is difficult to prove that she acted with the requisite mental state to justify criminal liability.[25] For example, in *Regalado v. United States*,[26] Regalado was convicted of violating the anticruelty statute of the District of Columbia for beating a puppy. Regalado appealed, claiming that he did not intend to harm the puppy and inflicted the beating only for disciplinary purposes. The court held that anticruelty statutes were "not intended to place unreasonable restrictions on the infliction of such pain as may be necessary for the training or discipline of an animal" and that the statute only prohibited acts done with malice or a cruel disposition.[27] Although the court affirmed Regalado's conviction, it recognized that "proof of malice will usually be circumstantial, and the line between discipline and cruelty will often be difficult to draw."[28]

Fourth, many animal welfare laws have wholly inadequate penalty provisions and we are reluctant, in any event, to impose the stigma of criminal liability on animal owners for what they do with their property.[29] Moreover, those without an ownership interest generally do not have standing to bring legal challenges to the use or treatment of animals by their owners.[30]

As the foregoing makes clear, because animals are property, we do not balance interests to determine whether it is necessary to use animals at all for particular purposes. We simply assume that it is appropriate to use animals for food, recreation, entertainment, clothing, or experiments—the primary ways in which we use animals as commodities to generate social wealth and most of which cannot be described as involving any plausible conflict of human and animal interests. Animal welfare laws do not even apply to many of these uses. To the extent that we do ask whether the imposition of pain and suffering is necessary, the inquiry is limited to whether particular treatment is in compliance with the customs and practices of property owners who, we assume, will not inflict more pain and suffering on their animal property than is required for the purpose. The only way to characterize the process is as a "balancing" of the property owner's interest in using animal property against the interest of an animal in not being used in ways that fail to comply with those customs and practices. Although animal welfare laws are intended to protect the interests of animals without reference to their being property, animal interests are protected only insofar as they serve the goal of rational property use.[31]

Our infliction of suffering on animals raises a legal question only when it does not conform to the customs and practices of accepted uses—when we inflict suffering in ways that do not maximize social wealth, or where the only explanation for the behavior can be characterized as "the gratification of a malignant or vindictive temper."[32] For example, in *State v. Tweedie,*[33] the defendant was found to have violated the anticruelty law by killing a cat in a microwave oven. *In re William G.*[34] upheld a cruelty conviction where a minor kicked a dog and set her on fire because she would not mate with his dog. In *Motes v. State,*[35] the defendant was found guilty of violating the anticruelty statute when he set fire to a dog merely because the dog was barking. In *Tuck v. United States,*[36] a pet shop owner was convicted of cruelty when he placed animals in an unventilated display window and refused to remove a rabbit whose body temperature registered as high as the thermometer was calibrated—110 degrees Fahrenheit. In *People v. Voelker,*[37] the court held that cutting off the heads of three live, conscious iguanas "without justification" could constitute a violation of the anticruelty law. In *LaRue v. State,*[38] a cruelty conviction was upheld because the defendant collected a large number of stray dogs and failed to provide them with veterinary care; the dogs suffered from mange, blindness, dehydration, pneumonia, and distemper, and had to be killed. In *State v Schott,*[39] Schott was convicted of cruelty to animals when police found dozens of cows and pigs dead or dying from malnutrition and dehydration on Schott's farm. Schott's defense was that bad weather prevented him from caring for his livestock. The jury found Schott guilty of cruelty and neglect, and the appellate court affirmed. These are, however, unusual cases and constitute a minuscule fraction of the instances in which we inflict suffering on animals.

Moreover, the very same act may be either protected or prohibited depending only on whether it is part of an accepted institution of animal exploitation. If someone kills a cat in a microwave, sets a dog on fire, allows the body temperature of a rabbit to rise to the point of heat stroke, severs the heads of conscious animals, or allows animals to suffer untreated serious illnesses, the conduct may violate the anticruelty laws. But if a researcher engages in the exact same conduct as part of an experiment (and a number of researchers have killed animals or inflicted pain on them in the same and similar ways) the conduct is protected by the law because the researcher is supposedly using the animal to generate a benefit. A farmer may run afoul of the anticruelty law if she neglects her animals and allows them to suffer from malnutrition or dehydration for no reason, but she may mutilate her animals and raise them in conditions of severe confinement and deprivation. The permitted actions cause as much if not more distress to animals as does neglecting them, but they are considered part of normal animal husbandry and are, therefore, protected under the law.

Thus, because animals are our property, the law will generally require their interests to be observed only to the extent that it facilitates the exploitation of the animal. This observation holds true even in countries where there is arguably a greater moral concern about animals. Britain, for instance, has more restrictions on animal use than does the United States, but the differences in permitted animal treatment are more formal than substantive. In discussing British animal welfare laws, one commentator has noted that "much of the animal welfare agenda has been obstructed and it is difficult to think of legislation improving the welfare of animals that has seriously damaged the interests of the animal users."[40] The law may in theory impose regulations that go beyond the minimum level of care required to exploit animals, yet it has rarely done so, for there are significant economic and other obstacles involved.[41] Voluntary changes in industry standards of animal welfare generally occur only when animal users regard these changes as cost-effective.[42]

The status of animals as property renders meaningless our claim that we reject the status of animals as things. We treat animals as the moral equivalent of inanimate objects with no morally significant interests. We bring billions of animals into existence annually simply for the purpose of killing them. Animals have market prices. Dogs and cats are sold in pet stores like compact discs; financial markets trade in futures for pork bellies and cattle. Any interest that an animal has is nothing more than an economic commodity that may be bought and sold to maximize overall social wealth and has no intrinsic value in our assessments. That is what it means to be property.

II. Animal Rights

The humane treatment principle holds that we may prefer humans over animals when necessary, but we have a moral obligation not to inflict unnecessary suffering on animals. The problem is that we use animals in ways that cannot be described as involving any conflict of human and animal interests, and we inflict extreme pain and suffering on them in the process. Even if we treated animals better, that would still leave open the question of our moral justification for imposing any suffering at all if animal use is not necessary. We may, of course, decide to discard the humane treatment principle, and acknowledge that we regard animals as nothing more than things without any morally significant interests. This option would at least spare us the need for thinking about our moral obligations to animals: we would not have any.

Alternatively, if we are to take animal interests seriously, then we can do so in only one way: by applying the principle of equal consideration—the rule that we ought to treat like cases alike unless there is a good reason not to do so—to animals.[43] The principle of equal consideration is a necessary component of every moral theory. Any theory that maintains that it is permissible to treat similar cases in a dissimilar manner would fail to qualify as an acceptable moral theory for that reason alone. Although there may be differences between humans and animals, we recognize that we have a shared capacity to suffer and an interest in not suffering.[44] In this sense, humans and nonhumans are similar to each other and different from everything else in the universe that is not sentient. If our supposed prohibition on the infliction of unnecessary suffering on animals is to have any meaning at all, then we must give equal consideration to animal interests in not suffering.

The suggestion that animal interests should receive equal consideration is not as radical as it may appear at first if we consider that the humane treatment principle incorporates the principle of equal consideration. We are to weigh our suffering in not using animals against animal interests in avoiding suffering. If there is a conflict between human and animal interests and the human interest weighs more, then the animal suffering is justifiable. If there is no conflict, or if there is a conflict of interests but the animal interest weighs more, then we are not justified in using the animal. And if there is a conflict of interests but the interests at stake are similar, then we should presumably treat those interests in the same way and impose suffering on neither or both unless there is some non-arbitrary reason that justifies differential treatment. But, as we have seen, there can be no meaningful balancing of interests if animals are property. The property status of animals is a two-edged sword wielded against their interests. First, it acts as blinders that effectively block even our perception of their interests as similar to ours because our "suffering" is understood as any detriment to the property owner. Second, in those instances in which human and animal interests are recognized as similar, animal interests will fail in the balancing because the property status of animals is always good reason not to accord similar treatment unless to do so would benefit us.

The application of the principle of equal consideration similarly failed in the context of North American slavery, which allowed some humans to treat others as property.[45] The institution of human slavery was structurally identical to the institution of animal ownership. Because a human slave was regarded as property, the slave owner was able to disregard all of the slave's interests if it was economically beneficial to do so, and the law generally deferred to the slave owner's judgment as to the value of the slave. As chattel property, slaves could be sold, willed, insured, mortgaged, and seized in payment of the owner's debts. Slave owners could inflict severe punishments on slaves for virtually any reason. Those who intentionally or negligently injured another's slave were liable to the owner in an action for damage to property. As a general rule, slaves could not enter into contracts, own property, sue or be sued, or live as free persons with basic rights and duties.

It was generally acknowledged that slaves had an interest in not suffering: slaves "are not rational beings. No, but they are the creatures of God, sentient beings, capable of suffering and enjoyment, and entitled to enjoy according to the measure of their capacities. Does not the voice of nature inform everyone, that he is guilty of wrong when he inflicts on them pain without necessity or object?"[46] Although there were laws that ostensibly regulated the use and treatment of slaves, they failed completely to protect slave interests. The law often contained exceptions that eviscerated any protection for the slaves. For example, North Carolina law provided that the punishment for the murder of a slave should be the same as for the murder of a free person, but the law "did not apply to an outlawed slave, nor to a slave 'in the act of resistance to his lawful owner,' nor to a slave 'dying under moderate correction.'"[47] A law that prohibits the murder of slaves but permits three general and easily satisfied exceptions, combined with a general prohibition against the testimony of slaves against free persons, cannot effectively deter the murder of slaves. That the law refused to protect the interests of slaves against slave owners is underscored in *State v. Mann*, in which the court held that even the "cruel and unreasonable battery" of one's own slave is not indictable: courts cannot "allow the right of the master to be brought into discussion in the courts of justice. The slave, to remain a slave, must be made sensible that there is no appeal from his master."[48] To the extent that the law regulated the conduct of slave owners, it had nothing to do with concern for the interests of the slaves. For example, in *Commonwealth v. Turner*, the court determined that it had no jurisdiction to try the defendant slave owner, who beat his slave with "rods, whips and sticks," and held that even if the beating was administered "wilfully and maliciously, violently, cruelly, immoderately, and excessively," the court was not empowered to act as long as the slave did not die.[49] The court distinguished private beatings from public chastisement; the latter might subject the master to liability "not because it was a slave who was beaten, nor because the act was unprovoked or cruel; but, because ipso facto it disturbed the harmony of society; was offensive to public decency, and directly tended to a breach of the peace. The same would be the law, if a horse had been so beaten."[50]

Slave welfare laws failed for precisely the same reason that animal welfare laws fail to establish any meaningful limit on our use of animal property: the owner's property interest in the slave always trumped any interest of the slave that was ostensibly protected under the law. The interests of slaves were observed only when it provided an economic benefit for the owners or served their whim. Alan Watson has noted that "[a]t most places at most times a reasonably economic owner would be conscious of the chattel value of slaves and thus would ensure some care in their treatment."[51] Any legal limitations on the cruelty of slave owners reflected the concern they should not use their property in unproductive ways; as expressed by the Roman jurist Justinian, "'it is to the advantage of the state that no one use his property badly.'"[52] Although some slave owners were more "humane" than others and some even treated slaves as family members, any kind treatment was a matter of the master's charity not of the slave's right, and slavery as a legal institution had the inevitable effect of treating humans as nothing more than commodities. The principle of equal consideration had no meaningful application to the interests of a human whose only value was as a resource of others. Slaves were rarely considered to have any interests similar to slave owners or other free persons; in those instances in which interests were recognized as similar, the property status of the slave was always a good reason not to accord similar treatment unless to do so would benefit the owner.

We eventually recognized that if humans were to have any morally significant interests, they could not be the resources of others, and that race was not a sufficient reason to treat certain humans as property.[53] Although we tolerate varying degrees of exploitation, and we may disagree about what constitutes equal treatment, we do not regard it as legitimate to treat any humans, irrespective of their particular characteristics, as the property of others. Indeed, in a world deeply divided on many moral issues, one of the few norms steadfastly endorsed by the international community is the prohibition of human slavery. It matters not whether the particular form of slavery is "humane" or not; we condemn all human slavery. Although more brutal forms of slavery are worse than less brutal forms, we prohibit human slavery in general because all forms of slavery more or less allow the interests of slaves to be ignored if it provides a benefit to slave owners, and humans have an interest in not suffering the deprivation of their fundamental interests merely because it benefits someone else, however "humanely" they are treated. It would, of course, be incorrect to say that human slavery has been eliminated from the planet. But the preemptory norms in international law—those few, select rules regarded as of such significance that they admit of no derogation by any nation—include the prohibition of slavery, which humanity deems so odious that no civilized nation can bear its existence.

The interest of a human in not being the property of others is protected by a right. When an interest is protected by a right, the interest may not be ignored or violated simply because it will benefit others. Rights are "moral notions that grow out of respect for the individual. They build protective fences around the individual. They establish areas where the individual is entitled to be protected against the state and the majority *even where a price is paid by the general welfare*."[54] If we are going to recognize and protect the interest of humans in not being treated as property, then we must use a right to do so; if we do not, then those humans who do not have this protection will be treated merely as commodities whenever it will benefit others. Therefore, the interest in not being treated as property must be protected against being traded away even if a price is paid by the general welfare.

The right not to be treated as the property of others is basic, and different from any other rights we might have because it is the grounding for those other rights; it is a pre-legal right that serves as the precondition for the possession of morally significant interests. The basic right is the right to the equal consideration of one's fundamental interests; it recognizes that if some humans have value only as resources, then the principle of equal consideration will have no meaningful application to their interests. Therefore, the basic right must be understood as prohibiting human slavery, or any other institutional arrangement that treats humans *exclusively* as means to ends of others and not as ends in themselves.[55]

The protection afforded by the basic right not to treated as property is limited. The basic right does not guarantee equal treatment in all respects or protect humans from all suffering, but it protects all humans, irrespective of their particular characteristics, from suffering any deprivation of interests as the result of being used exclusively as the resources of others and thereby provides essential protections: we may not enslave humans; nor, for that matter, may we exert total control over their bodies by using them as we do laboratory animals, or as forced organ donors, or as raw materials for shoes, or as objects to be hunted for sport or tortured, irrespective of whether we claim to treat them "humanely" in the process.[56] An employer may treat her employees instrumentally and disregard their interest in a mid-morning coffee break, or even their interest in health care, in the name of profit. But there are limits. She cannot force her employees to work without compensation. Pharmaceutical companies cannot test new drugs on employees who have not consented. Food processing plants cannot make hot dogs or luncheon meats out of workers. To possess the basic right not to be treated as property is a minimal prerequisite to being a moral and legal *person*; it does not specify what other rights the person may have. Indeed, the rejection of slavery is required by any moral theory that purports to accord moral significance to the interests of all humans even if the particular theory otherwise rejects rights.[57]

Animals, like humans, have an interest in not suffering; but, as we have seen, the principle of equal consideration has no meaningful application to animal interests if they are the property of others just as it had no meaningful application to the interests of slaves. The interests of animals as property will almost always count for less than do the interests of their owners. Some owners may choose to treat their animals well, or even as members of their families as some do with their pets, but the law will not protect animals against their owners. Animal ownership as a legal institution inevitably has the effect of treating animals as commodities. Moreover, animals, like humans, have an interest in not suffering at all from the ways in which we use them, however "humane" that use may be. To the extent that we protect humans from being used in these ways and we do not extend the same protection to animals, we fail to accord equal consideration to animal interests in not suffering.

If we are going to take animal interests seriously, we must extend to animals the one right that we extend to all humans irrespective of their particular characteristics. To do so would not mean that animals would be protected from all suffering: animals in the wild may be injured, or become diseased, or may be attacked by other animals. But it would mean that animals could no longer be used as the resources of humans and would, therefore, be protected from suffering at all from such uses. Is there a morally sound reason not to extend to animals the right not to be treated as property, and thereby recognize that our obligation not to impose unnecessary suffering on them is really an obligation not to treat them as property? Or, to ask the question in another way: why do we deem it acceptable to eat animals, hunt them, confine and display them in circuses and zoos, use them in experiments or rodeos, or otherwise to treat them in ways in which we would never think it appropriate to treat any human irrespective of how "humanely" we were to do so?

The usual response claims that some empirical difference between humans and animals constitutes a good reason for not according to animals the one right we accord to all humans.[58] According to this view, there is some qualitative distinction between humans and animals (all species considered as a single group) that purportedly justifies our treating animals as our resources. This distinction has almost always concerned some difference between human and animal minds; we have some mental characteristic that animals lack, or are capable of certain actions of which animals are incapable as a result of our purportedly superior cognitive abilities. The list of characteristics that are posited as possessed only by humans includes self-consciousness, reason, abstract thought, emotion, the ability to communicate, and the capacity for moral action.

The proposition that humans have mental characteristics wholly absent in animals is inconsistent with the theory of evolution. Darwin maintained that there are no uniquely human characteristics: "the difference in mind between man and the higher animals, great as it is, is certainly one of degree and not of kind."[59] Animals are able to think, and possess many of the same emotional responses as do humans: "the senses and intuitions, the various emotions and faculties, such as love, memory, attention, curiosity, imitation, reason, &c., of which man boasts, may be found in an incipient, or even sometimes in a well-developed condition, in the lower animals."[60] Darwin noted that "associated animals have a feeling of love for each other" and that animals "certainly sympathise with each other's distress or danger."[61]

It is, indeed, difficult to defend the existence of a qualitative distinction between humans and other animals. Perhaps the most important difference offered to justify treating animals as resources is that animals lack self-consciousness or self-awareness.[62] Even if we cannot know the precise nature of animal self-awareness, it appears that any being that is aware on a perceptual level must be self-aware. Biologist Donald Griffin has observed that if animals are conscious of anything, "the animal's own body and its own actions must fall within the scope of its perceptual consciousness."[63] Yet we deny animals self-awareness because we maintain that they cannot "think such thoughts as 'It is *I* who am running, or climbing this tree, or chasing that moth.'"[64] Griffin maintains that "when an animal consciously perceives the running, climbing, or moth-chasing of another animal, it must also be aware of who is doing these things. And if the animal is perceptually conscious of its own body, it is difficult to rule out similar recognition that it, itself, is doing the running, climbing, or chasing."[65] Griffin concludes that "[i]f animals are capable of perceptual awareness, denying them some level of self-awareness would seem to be an arbitrary and unjustified restriction."[66] Griffin's reasoning can be applied in the context of sentience: any sentient being must have some level of self-awareness. To be sentient means to be the sort of being who recognizes that it is *that* being, and not some other, who is experiencing pain or distress. When a dog experiences pain, the dog necessarily has a mental experience that tells her "this pain is happening to me." In order for pain to exist, some consciousness—some*one*—must perceive it as happening to her and must prefer not to experience it.

Antonio Damasio, a neurologist who works with humans who have suffered strokes, seizures, and conditions that cause brain damage, maintains that such humans have what he calls "core consciousness." Core consciousness, which does not depend on memory, language, or reasoning, "provides the organism with a sense of self about one moment—now—and about one place—here."[67] Humans who experience transient global amnesia, for example, have no sense of the past or the future but do have a sense of self with respect to present events and objects. Damasio maintains that many animal species possess core consciousness. He distinguishes core consciousness from what he calls "extended consciousness," which requires reasoning and memory, but not language, and involves enriching one's sense of self with autobiographical details and what we might consider a representational sense of consciousness. Extended consciousness, of which there are "many levels and grades," involves a self with memories of the past, anticipations of the future, and awareness of the present.[68] Although Damasio argues that extended consciousness reaches its most complex level in humans, who have language and sophisticated reasoning abilities, he maintains that chimpanzees, bonobos, baboons, and even dogs may have an autobiographical sense of self.[69] Even if most animals do not have extended consciousness, most of the animals we routinely exploit undoubtedly have at least core consciousness, which means that they are self-conscious.

In the past twenty years, cognitive ethologists and others have confirmed that animals, including mammals, birds, and even fish, have many of the cognitive characteristics once thought to be uniquely human.[70] Animals, including mammals, birds, and even fish, possess considerable intelligence and are able to process information in sophisticated and complex ways. They are able to communicate with other members of their own species as well as with humans; indeed, there is considerable evidence that nonhuman great apes can use symbolic language to communicate with humans. The similarities between humans and animals are not limited to cognitive or emotional attributes alone. Many argue that animals exhibit what is clearly moral behavior as well. For example, Frans de Waal states that "honesty, guilt, and the weighing of ethical dilemmas are traceable to specific areas of the brain. It should not surprise us, therefore, to find animal parallels. The human brain is a product of evolution. Despite its larger volume and greater complexity, it is fundamentally similar to the central nervous system of other mammals."[71] There are numerous instances in which animals act in altruistic ways toward unrelated members of their own species and toward other species, including humans.

Although it is clear that animals other than humans possess characteristics purported to be unique to humans, it is also clear that there are differences between humans and other animals. For example, even if animals are self-aware on some level, that does not mean that animals will recognize themselves in mirrors (although some nonhuman primates do) or keep diaries or anticipate the future by looking at clocks and calendars; even if animals have the ability to reason or think abstractly, that does not mean that they can do calculus or compose symphonies. Yet for at least two related reasons, the humanlike varieties of these characteristics cannot serve to provide a morally sound, non-arbitrary basis for denying the right not to be treated as property to animals who may lack these characteristics.[72]

First, any attempt to justify treating animals as resources based on their lack of supposed uniquely human characteristics begs the question from the outset by assuming that certain human characteristics are special and justify differential treatment. Even if, for instance, no animals other than humans can recognize themselves in mirrors or can use symbolic language to communicate, no animals other than nonhumans are able to fly, or breathe underwater, without assistance. What makes the ability to recognize oneself in a mirror or use symbolic language better in a moral sense than the ability to fly or breathe underwater? The answer, of course, is that *we* say so. But apart from our proclamation, there is simply no reason to conclude that characteristics thought to be uniquely human have any value that allows us to use them as a non-arbitrary justification for treating animals as property. These characteristics can serve this role only after we have assumed their moral relevance.

Second, even if all animals other than humans lack a particular characteristic beyond sentience, or possess it to a different degree than do humans, there is no logically defensible relationship between the lack or lesser degree of that characteristic and our treatment of animals as resources. Differences between humans and other animals may be relevant for other purposes—no sensible person argues that we ought to enable nonhuman animals to drive cars or vote or attend universities—but the differences have no bearing on whether animals should have the status of property. We recognize this inescapable conclusion where humans are involved. Whatever characteristic we identify as uniquely human will be seen to a lesser degree in some humans and not at all in others.[73] Some humans will have the exact same deficiency that we attribute to animals, and although the deficiency may be relevant for some purposes, most of us would reject enslaving such humans or otherwise treating them exclusively as means to our ends.[74] For example, even if animals are not self-aware in the same sense that normal humans are, the same is true of some humans. Many humans, such as those who have a severe mental disability, do not have an autobiographical sense of self-consciousness; but we do not enslave such people or regard it as permissible to use them as we do laboratory animals. Nor should we. We recognize that a mentally disabled human has an interest in her life and in not being treated exclusively as a means to the ends of others even if she does not have the same level of self-consciousness that is possessed by normal adults; in this sense, she is similarly situated to all other sentient humans, who have an interest in being treated as ends in themselves irrespective of their particular characteristics. The fact that she may not have a particular sort of self-consciousness may serve as a non-arbitrary reason for treating her differently in some respects—it maybe relevant to whether we make her the host of a talk show, or give her a job teaching in a university or allow her to drive a car—but it has no relevance to whether we treat her exclusively as a resource and disregard her fundamental interests, including her interest in not suffering and in her continued existence, if it benefits us to do so.

The same analysis applies to every human characteristic beyond sentience that is offered to justify treating animals as resources. There will be some humans who also lack the characteristic, or possess it to a different degree than do normal humans. This "defect" may be relevant for some purposes, but not for whether we treat humans exclusively as resources. We do not treat as things those humans who lack characteristics beyond sentience merely out of some sense of charity: we realize that to do so would violate the principle of equal consideration by using an arbitrary reason to deny similar treatment to similar interests in not being treated exclusively as a means to the ends of others.[75]

In sum, there is no characteristic that serves to distinguish humans from all other animals for purposes of denying to animals the one right that we extend to all humans. Whatever attribute we may think makes all humans special and thereby deserving of the right not to be the property of others is shared by nonhumans. More importantly, even if there are uniquely human characteristics, some humans will not possess those characteristics, but we would never think of using such humans as resources. In the end, the only difference between humans and animals is species, and species is not a justification for treating animals as property any more than was race a justification for human slavery.

If we extend to animals the one right that we extend to all humans irrespective of their particular characteristics, then animals will become moral persons. To say that a being is a person is merely to say that the being has morally significant interests, that the principle of equal consideration applies to that being, that the being is not a thing. In a sense, we already accept that animals are persons; we claim to reject the view that animals are things and to recognize that, at the very least, animals have a morally significant interest in not suffering. The status of animals as property, however, prevented their personhood from being realized.

The same was true of human slavery. Slaves were regarded as chattel property. Laws that provided for the "humane" treatment of slaves did not make slaves persons because, as we have seen, the principle of equal consideration could not apply to slaves. We tried, through slave welfare laws, to have a three-tiered system: things, or inanimate property; persons, who were free; and in the middle, depending on your choice of locution, "quasi-persons" or "things plus"—the slaves. That system could not work. We eventually recognized that if slaves were going to have morally significant interests, they could not be slaves anymore, for the moral universe is limited to only two kinds of beings: persons and things. "Quasi-persons" or "things plus" will necessarily risk being treated as things because the principle of equal consideration cannot apply to them.

Nor can we use animal welfare laws to render animals "quasi-persons" or "things plus." They are either persons, beings to whom the principle of equal consideration applies and who possess morally significant interests, or things, beings to whom the principle of equal consideration does not apply and whose interests may be ignored if it benefits us. There is no third choice. We could, of course, treat animals better than we do; there are, however, powerful economic forces that militate against better treatment in light of the status of animals as property. But simply according better treatment to animals would not mean that they were no longer things. It may have been better to beat slaves three rather than five times a week, but this better treatment would not have removed slaves from the category of things. The similar interests of slave owners and slaves were not accorded similar treatment because the former had a right not to suffer at all from being used exclusively as a resource, and the latter did not possess such a right. Animals like humans, have an interest in not suffering at all from the ways in which we use them, however "humane" that use may be. To the extent that we protect humans from suffering from use as resources and we do not extend the same protection to animals, we fail to accord equal consideration to animal interests in not suffering.

If animals are persons, that does not mean that they are human persons; it does not mean that we must treat animals in the same way that we treat humans or that we must extend to animals any of the legal rights that we reserve to competent humans. Nor does this mean that animals have any sort of guarantee of a life free from suffering, or that we must protect animals from harm from other animals in the wild or from accidental injury by humans. As I argue below, it does not necessarily preclude our choosing human interests over animal interests in situations of genuine conflict. But it does require that we accept that we have a moral obligation to stop using animals for food, biomedical experiments, entertainment, or clothing, or any other uses that assume that animals are merely resources, and that we prohibit the ownership of animals. The abolition of animal slavery is required by any moral theory that purports to treat animal interests as morally significant, even if the particular theory otherwise rejects rights, just as the abolition of human slavery is required by any theory that purports to treat human interests as morally significant.[76]

III. Conclusion: False Conflicts

The question of the moral status of animals addresses the matter of how we ought to treat animals in situations of conflict between human and animal interests. For the most part, our conflicts with animals are those that we create. We bring billions of sentient animals into existence for the sole purpose of killing them. We then seek to understand the nature of our moral obligations to these animals. Yet by bringing animals into existence for uses that we would never consider appropriate for any humans, we have placed nonhuman animals outside the scope of our moral community altogether. Despite what we say about taking animals seriously, we have already decided that the principle of equal consideration does not apply to animals, and that animals are merely things that have no morally significant interests.

Because animals are property, we treat every issue concerning their use or treatment as though it presented a genuine conflict of interests, and invariably we choose the human interest over the animal interest. In the overwhelming number of instances in which we evaluate our moral obligations to animals, however, there is no true conflict. When we contemplate whether to eat a hamburger, or buy a fur coat, or attend a rodeo, we do not confront any sort of conflict worthy of serious moral consideration. If we take animal interests seriously, we must desist from manufacturing such conflicts, which can only be constructed in the first place by ignoring the principle of equal consideration and by making an arbitrary decision to use animals in ways in which we rightly decline to use any human.

Does the use of animals in experiments involve a genuine conflict between human and animal interests? Even if such need for animals in research exists, the conflict between humans and animals in this context is no more genuine than a conflict between humans suffering from a disease and other humans we might use in experiments to find a cure for that disease. Data gained from experiments with animals require extrapolation to humans in order to be useful at all, and extrapolation is an inexact science under the best of circumstances. If we want data that will be useful in finding cures for human diseases, we would be better advised to use humans. We do not allow humans to be used in the way that we do laboratory animals, and we do not think that there is any sort of conflict between those who are afflicted or who may become afflicted with a disease and those humans whose use might help find a cure for that disease. We regard all humans as part of the moral community, and although we may not treat all humans in the same way, we recognize that membership in the moral community precludes such use of humans. Animals have no characteristic that justifies our use of them in experiments that is not shared by some group of humans; because we regard some animals as laboratory tools yet think it inappropriate to treat any humans in this way, we manufacture a conflict, ignoring the principle of equal consideration and treating similar cases in a dissimilar way.

There may, of course, be situations in which we are confronted with a genuine conflict, such as the burning house that contains a human and an animal, where we have time to save only one. Such emergency situations require what are, in the end, decisions that are arbitrary and not amenable to satisfying general principles of conduct. Yet even if we would always choose to save the human over the animal in such situations, it does not follow that animals are merely resources that we may use for our purposes.[77] We would draw no such conclusion when making a choice between two humans. Imagine that two humans are in the burning house. One is a young child; the other is an old adult, who, barring the present conflagration, will soon die of natural causes anyway. If we decide to save the young person for the simple reason that she has not yet lived her life, we would not conclude that it is morally acceptable to enslave old people or to use them for target practice. Similarly, assume that a wild animal is just about to attack a friend. Our choice to kill the animal in order to save the friend's life does not mean that it is morally acceptable to kill animals for food, any more than our moral justification in killing a deranged human about to kill our friend would serve to justify our using deranged humans as forced organ donors.

In sum, if we take animal interests seriously, we are not obliged to regard animals as the same as humans for all purposes any more than we regard all humans as being the same for all purposes; nor do we have to accord to animals all or most of the rights that we accord to humans. We may still choose the human over the animal in cases of genuine conflict—when it is truly necessary to do so—but that does not mean that we are justified in treating animals as mere resources for our use.[78] And if the treatment of animals as resources cannot be justified, then the institutionalized exploitation of animals should be abolished. We should care for domestic animals presently alive, but should bring no more into existence. The abolition of animal exploitation could not, as a realistic matter, be imposed legally unless and until a significant portion of us took animal interests seriously. Our moral compass will not find animals while they are lying on our plates. In other words, we have to put our vegetables where our mouths are and start acting on the moral principles we profess to accept.

If we stopped using animals as resources, the only remaining human/animal conflicts would involve animals in the wild. Deer may nibble our ornamental shrubs; rabbits may eat the vegetables we grow. The occasional wild animal may attack us. In such situations, we should, despite the difficulty inherent in making interspecies comparisons, try our best to apply the principle of equal consideration and to treat similar interests in a similar way. That will generally require at the very least a good-faith effort to avoid the intentional killing of animals to resolve these conflicts, where lethal means would be prohibited if the conflicts involved only humans. I am, however, not suggesting that the recognition that animal interests have moral significance requires that a motorist who unintentionally strikes an animal be prosecuted for an animal equivalent of manslaughter. Nor do I suggest that we should recognize a cause of action allowing a cow to sue the farmer. The interesting question is why we have the cow here in the first instance.

Notes

©2003 by Gary L. Francione. Many thanks to Anna Charlton, Cora Diamond, Marc Hauser, and Alan Watson for their helpful comments, and to the Dean's Research Fund of Rutgers University Law School—Newark for research support. The ideas and arguments discussed here were developed and are expanded in GARY L. FRANCIONE, ANIMALS, PROPERTY, AND THE LAW (1995), GARY L. FRANCIONE, INTRODUCTION TO ANIMAL RIGHTS: YOUR CHILD OR THE DOG? (2000), and GARY L. FRANCIONE, RAIN WITHOUT THUNDER: THE IDEOLOGY OF THE ANIMAL RIGHTS MOVEMENT (1996). Footnote references will direct the reader to further discussion in these books. An extended version of this essay appears in ANIMAL RIGHTS (C. Sunstein & M. Nussbaum eds., 2004). This essay is dedicated to Emma and Simon, two blind dogs who help me to see things clearly.

1. *See* GARY L. FRANCIONE, INTRODUCTION TO ANIMAL RIGHTS: YOUR CHILD OR THE DOG? 1–9 (2000).
2. The humane treatment principle reflects our recognition that animals are sentient: they can suffer pain or distress. Not all animals may be sentient, and it may be difficult to draw the line separating those who are from those who are not. Yet most of the animals we routinely exploit are clearly sentient. Scientists generally accept that animals are sentient. For example, the U.S. Public Health Service states that "[u]nless the contrary is established, investigators should consider that procedures that cause

pain or distress in human beings may cause pain or distress in other animals." U.S Department of Health and Human Services, National Institutes of Health, *Public Health Service Policy and Government Principles Regarding the Care and Use of Animals*, *in* INSTITUTE OF LABORATORY ANIMAL RESOURCES, GUIDE FOR THE CARE AND USE OF LABORATORY ANIMALS 117 (1996).

3. N.Y. AGRIC. & MKTS. LAW § 353 (Consol. 2002).
4. DEL. CODE. ANN. tit. 11, §§ 1325(a)(1) & (4) (2002).
5. Protection of Animals Act, 1911, c. 27 § 1(1)(a) (Eng.).
6. 7 U.S.C. §§ 2131–2159 (2003).
7. Cruelty to Animals Act, 1876 (Eng.).
8. Animals (Scientific Procedures) Act, 1986 (Eng.).
9. 7 U.S.C. §§ 1901–1907 (2003).
10. *See* GARY L. FRANCIONE, ANIMALS, PROPERTY, AND THE LAW 20–26 (1995).
11. Animals (Scientific Procedures) Act, 1986, c. 14, § 5(4) (Eng.).
12. For a discussion about the necessity of animal use for food, sport hunting, entertainment, and clothing, see FRANCIONE, *supra* note 1, at 9–30.
13. It may be argued that we like the taste of meat because our ancestors ate meat and we inherited the disposition to do so. But that is no different from saying that we continue to be sexist because our ancestors were and we inherited a disposition in favor of patriarchy. Moreover, the cause of our liking meat (or patriarchy) is irrelevant as far as moral justification is concerned. *See id.* at 171–72.
14. *See id.* at 31–49.
15. The status of animals as property has existed for thousands of years. Indeed, historical evidence indicates that the domestication of animals is closely related to the development of the concepts of property and money. The property status of animals is particularly important in Western culture for two reasons. First, property rights are accorded a special status and are considered to be among the most important rights we have. Second, the modern Western concept of private property, whereby resources are regarded as separate objects that are assigned and belong to particular individuals who are allowed to use the property to the exclusion of everyone else, has its origin in God's grant to humans of dominion over animals. *See id* at 50–54; FRANCIONE, *supra* note 10, at 24–49. *See generally id.* (discussing the status of animals as property as a general matter, and in the context of anticruelty statutes and the federal Animal welfare Act). The effect of the property status of animals on our treatment of them is discuused in David Hambrick's essay in this volume.
16. GODFREY SANDYS-WINSCH, ANIMAL LAW 1 (1978).
17. T. G. FIELD-FISHER, ANIMALS AND THE LAW 19 (1964).
18. To the extent that animal uses, such as certain types of animal fighting, have been prohibited, this may be understood more in terms of class hierarchy and cultural prejudice than in terms of moral concern about animals. *See* FRANCIONE, *supra* note 10, at 18.
19. *See id.* at 139–42.

20. *See id.* at 224. For a discussion of the Animal Welfare Act, see *id.* at 185–249.
21. *See id.* at 142–56; FRANCIONE, *supra* note 1, at 58–63.
22. Murphy v. Manning, 2 Ex. D. 307, 313–14 (1877) (Cleasby, B.).
23. *See* FRANCIONE, *supra* note 10, at 127–28; FRANCIONE, *supra* note 1, at 66–67. This presumption not only insulates customary practices from being found to violate anti-cruelty laws, but also militates against finding the necessary criminal intent in cases involving non-customary uses. *See, e.g.,* Commonwealth v. Barr, 44 Pa. C. 284 (Lancaster County Ct. 1916). *See infra* notes 25–28 and accompanying text.
24. 16 I.L.R. 325, 335 (C.P.D. 1885) (Murphy, J.). In Britain, the dehorning of older cattle was found to violate the anticruelty statute but only because dehorning had been discontinued and was no longer an accepted agriculture practice. *See* Ford v. Wiley, 23 Q.B. 203 (1889). In his opinion, Hawkins, J., noted that the fact that the practice had been abandoned by farmers who were acting in their economic self-interest was proof that the practice was unnecessary. *See id.* at 221–22.
25. *See* FRANCIONE, *supra* note 10, at 135–39; FRANCIONE, *supra* note 1, at 63–66.
26. 572 A.2d 416 (D.C. 1990).
27. *Id.* at 420.
28. *Id.* at 421.
29. *See* FRANCIONE, *supra* note 10, at 156; FRANCIONE, *supra* note 1, at 67–68. In recent years, many states have amended their anticruelty laws and have increased penalties for at least certain violations. It remains to be seen whether this will make any real difference because most animal uses will remain exempt and there will still be problems with proof of criminal intent.
30. *See* FRANCIONE, supra note 10, at 65–90, 156–58; FRANCIONE, *supra* note 1, at 69–70.
31. *See* FRANCIONE, *supra* note 10, at 27–32.
32. Commonwealth v. Lufkin, 89 Mass. (7 Allen) 579, 581 (1863). *See* FRANCIONE, *supra* note 10, at 137–38, 153–56; FRANCIONE, *supra* note 1, at 70–73.
33. 444 A.2d 855 (R.I. 1982).
34. 447 A.2d 493 (Md. Ct. Spec. App. 1982).
35. 375 S.E.2d 893 (Ga. Ct. App. 1988).
36. 477 A.2d 1115 (D.C. 1984).
37. 172 Misc.2d 564 (N.Y. Crim. Ct. 1997).
38. 478 S.2d 13 (Ala. Crim. App. 1985).
39. 384 N.W.2d 620 (Neb. 1986).
40. ROBERT GARNER, ANIMALS, POLITICS AND MORALITY 234 (1993).
41. *See* FRANCIONE, *supra* note 1, at 13, 73–76, 181–82. *See generally* GARY L. FRANCIONE, RAIN WITHOUT THUNDER: THE IDEOLOGY OF THE ANIMAL RIGHTS MOVEMENT (1996) [hereinafter FRANCIONE, RAIN WITHOUT THUNDER] (discussing unsuccessful efforts by the animal protection movement to obtain animal welfare laws that exceed the minimal standards required to exploit animals).

42. For example, McDonald's, the fast-food-chain, announced that it would require its suppliers to observe standards of animal welfare that went beyond current standards: "Animal welfare is also an important part of quality assurance. For high-quality food products at the counter, you need high quality coming from the farm. Animals that are well cared for are less prone to illness, injury, and stress, which all have the same negative impact on the condition of livestock as they do on people. Proper animal welfare practices also benefit producers. Complying with our animal welfare guidelines helps ensure efficient production and reduces waste and loss. This enables our suppliers to be highly competitive." Bruce Feinberg & Terry Williams, *McDonald's Corporate Social Responsibility, Animal Welfare Update: North America, at* http://www.mcdonalds.com/corporate/social/marketplace/welfare/update/northamerica/index.html (Mar. 3, 2003). The principle expert advisor to McDonald's states: "Healthy animals, properly handled, keep the meat industry running safely, efficiently and profitably." TEMPLE GRANDIN, RECOMMENDED ANIMAL HANDLING GUIDELINES FOR MEAT PACKERS 1 (1991).

43. *See* FRANCIONE, *supra* note 1, at 81–102. A reason not to treat similar cases in a similar way must not be arbitrary and thereby itself violate the principle of equal consideration.

44. Animals—human and nonhuman—might occasionally choose to experience pain or suffering in order to obtain benefits. This does not mean that they lack an interest in avoiding pain and suffering.

45. The principle of equal consideration also failed in other systems of slavery, but because of differences among these systems, I confine my description to North American slavery. For a discussion of various systems of slave law, see ALAN WATSON, SLAVE LAW IN THE AMERICAS (1989); ALAN WATSON, ROMAN SLAVE LAW (1989); Alan Watson, *Roman Slave Law and Romanist Ideology*, 37 PHOENIX 53 (1983).

46. Chancellor Harper, *Slavery in the Light of Social Ethics, in* COTTON IS KING, AND PRO-SLAVERY ARGUMENTS 549, 559 (E.N. Elliott ed., 1860).

47. Stanley Elkins and Eric McKitrick, *Institutions and the Law of Slavery: Slavery in Capitalist and Non-Capitalist Cultures, in* THE LAW OF AMERICAN SLAVERY 111, 115 (Kermit L. Hall ed., 1987) (quoting WILLIAM GOODELL, THE AMERICAN SLAVE CODE IN THEORY AND PRACTICE 180 (1853)). For a discussion of slave law in the context of animal welfare law, see FRANCIONE, *supra* note 1, at 86–90; FRANCIONE, *supra* note 10, at 100–12.

48. 13 N.C. (2 Dev.) 263, 267 (1829).

49. 26 Va. (5 Rand.) 678, 678 (1827).

50. *Id.* at 680.

51. WATSON, SLAVE LAW IN THE AMERICAS, *supra* note 45, at xiv.

52. *Id.* at 31 (quoting Justinian).

53. Even after the abolition of slavery, race continued to serve as a reason to justify differential treatment, often on the ground that whites and people of color did not have similar interests and, therefore, did not have to be treated equally in certain respects, and often on the ground that race was a reason to deny similar treatment to similar

interests. But abolition recognized that, irrespective of race, all humans had a similar interest in not being treated as the property of others.

54. Bernard E. Rollin, *The Legal and Moral Bases of Animal Rights, in* ETHICS AND ANIMALS 103, 06 (Harlan B. Miller & William H. Williams eds., 1983). *See* FRANCIONE, *supra* note 1, at xxvi–xxx. For a general discussion of the concept of rights and rights theory in the context of laws concerning animals, see FRANCIONE, *supra* note 10, at 91–114. This notion of rights is adopted in Alex Pollen's essay.

55. Similar concepts have been recognized by philosophers and political theorists. Kant, for example, maintained that there is one "innate" right—the right of "innate *equality*," or the "independence from being bound by others to more than one can in turn bind them; hence a human being's quality of being *his own master*." IMMANUEL KANT, THE METAPHYSICS OF MORALS, §§ 6:237–38, at 30 (Mary Gregor trans. & ed., Cambridge Univ. Press 1996). This innate right "grounds our right to *have* rights." ROGER J. SULLIVAN, IMMANUEL KANT'S MORAL THEORY 248 (1989).The basic right not to be treated as property is different from what are referred to as natural rights insofar as these are understood to be rights that exist apart from their recognition by any particular legal system because they are granted by God. For example, John Locke regarded property rights as natural rights that were grounded in God's grant to humans of dominion over the earth and animals. The basic right not to be treated as property expresses a proposition of logic: if human interests are to have moral significance (*i.e.*,if human interests are to be treated in accordance with the principle of equal consideration), then humans cannot be resources. For a further discussion of this basic right and the related concept of inherent value, see FRANCIONE, *supra* note 1, at 92–100. *See also* HENRY SHUE, BASIC RIGHTS, (2d ed. 1996).

56. Human experimentation is prohibited by the Nuremberg Code and the Helsinki Declaration. Torture is prohibited by the International Convention against Torture and Other Cruel, Inhuman or Degrading Treatment or Punishment. The notable exception to the protection provided by the basic right is compulsory military service, which is controversial precisely because it does treat humans exclusively as means to ends in ways that other acts required by the government, such as the payment of taxes, do not.

57. *See* FRANCIONE, *supra* note 1, at 94, 131–33.

58. Some claim that the relevant difference between humans and nonhumans is that the former possess souls and the latter do not. For a discussion of this and other purported differences, see *id.* at 103–129. Ian Tomb discusses some of these characteristics in his essay.

59. CHARLES DARWIN, THE DESCENT OF MAN 105 (Princeton Univ. Press 1981). *See* JAMES RACHELS, CREATED FROM ANIMALS: THE MORAL IMPLICATIONS OF DARWINISM (1990).

60. DARWIN, *supra* note 59, at 105.

61. *Id.* at 76, 77.

62. Self-awareness is considered important because if animals do not have any sort of continuous mental existence, then death is supposedly not a harm to them and we

may, therefore, use and kill them for our purposes if we treat them "humanely." *See* FRANCIONE, *supra* note 1, at 133–42.

63. DONALD R. GRIFFIN, ANIMAL MINDS: BEYOND COGNITION TO CONSCIOUSNESS 274 (2001).

64. *Id.*

65. *Id.*

66. *Id.*

67. ANTONIO R. DAMASIO, THE FEELING OF WHAT HAPPENS: BODY AND EMOTION IN THE MAKING OF CONSCIOUSNESS 16 (1999).

68. *Id.*

69. *See id.* at 198, 201.

70. *See, e.g.,* GRIFFIN, *supra* note 63; MARC D. HAUSER, THE EVOLUTION OF COMMUNICATION (1996); MARC D. HAUSER, WILD MINDS: WHAT ANIMALS REALLY THINK (2000); READINGS IN ANIMAL COGNITION (Marc Bekoff & Dale Jamieson eds., 1996); SUE SAVAGE-RUMBAUGH & ROGER LEWIN, KANZI: THE APE AT THE BRINK OF THE HUMAN MIND (1994).

71. FRANS DE WAAL, GOOD NATURED: THE ORIGINS OF RIGHT AND WRONG IN HUMANS AND OTHER ANIMALS 218 (1996).

72. There are problems in relying on similarities between humans and animals beyond sentience to justify the moral significance of animals. *See* FRANCIONE, *supra* note 1, at 116–19. For example, a focus on similarities beyond sentience threatens to create new hierarchies in which we move some animals, such as the great apes or dolphins, into a preferred group, and continue to treat other animals as our resources. There has for some years been an international effort to secure certain rights for the nonhuman great apes. This project was started by the publication of a book entitled THE GREAT APE PROJECT (P. Cavalieri & P. Singer eds., 1993), which seeks "the extension of the community of equals to include all great apes: human beings, chimpanzees, gorillas, and orang-utans." *Id.* at 4. I was a contributor to *The Great Ape Project. See* Gary L. Francione, "Personhood, Property, and Legal Competence," *in id.* at 248–57. The danger of *The Great Ape Project* is that it reinforces the notion that characteristics beyond sentience are necessary and not merely sufficient for equal treatment. Hélène Landemore recognizes a similar point in her essay. In my essay in *The Great Ape Project,* I tried to avoid this problem by arguing that although the considerable cognitive and other similarities between the human and nonhuman great apes are sufficient to accord the latter equal protection under the law, these similarities are not necessary for animals to have a right not to be treated as resources. *See id.* at 253. For an approach that argues that characteristics beyond sentience are necessary and not merely sufficient for preferred animals to have a right not to be treated as resources in at least in some respects, see STEVEN M. WISE, DRAWING THE LINE: SCIENCE AND THE CASE FOR ANIMAL RIGHTS (2002) and STEVEN M. WISE, RATTLING THE CAGE: TOWARD LEGAL RIGHTS FOR ANIMALS (2000).

73. Some argue that although certain humans may lack a particular characteristic, the fact that all humans have the potential to possess the characteristic means that a hu-

man who actually lacks it is for purposes of equal consideration distinguishable from an animal who may also lack it. *See, e.g.,*Carl Cohen, *The Case for the Use of Animals in Biomedical Research*, 315 NEW ENG. J. MED. 865 (1986). This argument begs the question because it assumes that some humans have a characteristic that they lack and thereby ignores the factual similarity between animals and humans who lack the characteristic. Moreover, in some instances, animals may possess the characteristic to a greater degree than do some humans.

74. A notable exception to this view is Peter Singer, who argues that in certain circumstances, we may use some humans as resources for the benefit of other humans. *See, e.g.,* PETER SINGER, PRACTICAL ETHICS 186 (2d ed. 1993).

75. In this sense, the equality of all humans is predicated on a factual similarity shared by all humans irrespective of their particular characteristics beyond sentience: all humans have an interest in not being treated exclusively as means to the ends of others. All humans value themselves even if no one else values them. *See* FRANCIONE, *supra* note 1, at 128, 135 n.18. Moreover, justice (not charity) may require that we be especially conscientious about protecting humans who lack certain characteristics precisely because of their vulnerability.

76. *See* FRANCIONE, *supra* note 1, at 148. The theory presented here differs in fundamental respects from that proposed by Peter Singer. *See* PETER SINGER, ANIMAL LIBERATION (2d ed. 1990). Singer, who is a utilitarian, claims to apply the principle of equal consideration to animal interests but he rejects the notion that animals have the right not to be treated as resources. Therefore, he does not advocate the abolition of animal exploitation; rather, he argues that we ought to regulate animal use in a way that gives equal consideration to animal interests. For a number of reasons, Singer's attempts to accord equal consideration to the interests of animals that are property are unsuccessful. *See* FRANCIONE, *supra* note 1, at xxxii, 135–48; FRANCIONE, RAIN WITHOUT THUNDER, *supra* note 41, at 156–60, 173–76. I maintain that any theory that regards animals as having morally significant interests must recognize that animals have a right not to be treated as resources even if the theory otherwise rejects rights. *See* FRANCIONE, *supra* note 1, at 148.

The theory presented here is also different in significant respects from that of Tom Regan. *See* TOM REGAN, THE CASE FOR ANIMAL RIGHTS (1983). Regan argues that animals have rights and that animal exploitation ought to be abolished and not merely regulated, but he limits protection to those animals who have preference autonomy and he thereby omits from the class of rightholders those animals who are sentient but who do not have preference autonomy. The theory presented in this essay applies to any sentient being. Regan uses the concept of basic rights and although he does not discuss the property status of animals or the right not to be property, he maintains some animals should have a right not to be treated exclusively as means to human ends. Moreover, Regan does not acknowledge that this basic right can be derived solely from applying the principle of equal consideration to animal interests in not suffering, or that it must be part of any theory that purports to accord moral significance to animal interests even if the theory otherwise rejects rights. For a further discussion of the differences between my theory and that of Regan, see FRANCIONE, *supra* note 1, at xxxii–xxxiv, 94 n.25, 127–28 n.61, 148 n.36, 174 n.1.

77. A common argument made against the animal rights position is that it is acceptable to treat animals as things because we are justified in choosing humans over animals in situations of conflict. *See, e.g.* Richard A. Posner, *Animal Rights*, Slate Dialogues, *at* http://slate.msn.com/id/110101/entry/110129/ (June 12, 2001).

78. The choice of humans over animals in situations of genuine conflict does not necessarily represent speciesism because there are many reasons other than species bias that can account for the choice. *See* FRANCIONE, *supra* note 1, at 159–62.

Section 3—Cognitive Science

NEARLY EVERY ARGUMENT ABOUT ANIMAL WELFARE relies on certain assumptions about animal cognition. Cognitive science promises to provide two key pieces of information: the constraints on non-human mental experiences, and the constraints on non-human behaviors. These, in turn, are thought by many to dictate the constraints on our own duties towards animals. The more animals can think and behave like us, the more seriously we must consider their rights.

The essays in this section focus primarily on the mental experiences of animals. To begin with, do they experience pain? Is their experience confined to the moment, or can they abstract from specific instances? Are they conscious beings at all? Do they experience morally relevant emotions like guilt, indigence, and duty? These questions are considered critical because animals that cannot experience certain types of thoughts or emotions, it is argued, are not owed full moral consideration. Similarly, critics wish to know what behaviors can be reasonably expected of animals. Can they inhibit selfish temptations? Are they motivated by moral considerations? To what extent, if any, can they participate in a human moral community?

The answers to these questions depend, at least to some extent, on whether animals possess a core set of cognitive capacities. Abstract reasoning, self-reflection, theory of mind, conscious desires, and linguistic communication have all been proposed as acid-tests for moral desert. Whether some animals can meet these strict cognitive standards remains a contentious point, and this section grapples head-on with the evidence for both sides of the debate.

Lewis Petrinovich, an animal learning psychologist, adds a final twist to the cognitive science perspective in his commentary, claiming that the evolution of the human mind plays a critical role in shaping the nature of our moral judgments. Cognition, in Petrinovich's view, is not merely a tool to be used by our ethical sense, it is the tool that crafts our ethical sense and that serves to justify our attitudes toward animals. Excluding animals from the realm of moral consideration is not speciesism, but a natural consequence of our evolved psychology to favor kin.

Aping Ethics

Behavioral Homologies and Nonhuman Rights

Fiery Cushman

Introduction

"He who understands the baboon," penned Charles Darwin, "will do more towards metaphysics than Locke" (Darwin and Barrett 1987). Darwin's wry assessment appears in a private journal from 1838, and it reveals much more than the young biologist's distaste for philosophical speculation. His success as a theoretician derived from decades of painstaking observation and empirical study, and it was these methods in which he invested full faith. Among Darwin's greatest insights was that scientific study applies as much to human affairs as to the natural world—in short, that philosophers might benefit from a little biology.

Today, the behavioral sciences provide perspective to philosophers that is just as important and infinitely more nuanced. At one of the more salient junctions of their disciplines, philosophers and biologists are taking more seriously the question of our obligations to nonhuman beings. It is rapidly becoming an unavoidable conclusion that animals share with humans not only common ancestors, but a common suite of behaviors and mental experiences. This is especially true of humans' closest relatives, primates such as the chimpanzee and bonobo. Indeed, behavioral research has unmasked beneath simian faces perhaps the most human quality of all: a moral faculty.

It goes without saying that there is no clear consensus on whether animals meet the criteria for moral worth—quite to the contrary, there is substantial disagreement over what the criteria ought to be. This conflict has deep historical roots. Jeremy Bentham, the father of utilitarian philosophy, argues that the key issue concerning animal welfare is not "Can the *reason?* nor, Can they *talk*? but Can they *suf-*

fer?" (Bentham, Burns, et al. 1996). Bentham's mantel is worn today by Peter Singer, who advocates for the rights of animals on precisely these grounds, but his approach is by no means universally accepted. Immanuel Kant, a representative of the deontological tradition in philosophy, disposes of the matter by declaring that "Animals are not self-conscious and are there merely as a means to an end" (Kant 1999). Kant's position is apparently that a being must have the cognitive capacity to experience a moral wrong in order to enjoy the protection of moral rights. This view is well represented today, although authors on both sides of the fence disagree over which cognitive abilities ought to count.

Especially since the 1975 publication of Singer's *Animal Liberation*, there has been a vibrant and complex debate over the philosophy of animal rights. During the same period, jump-started by works such as Don Griffin's *Animal Consciousness*, Frans de Waal's *Chimpanzee Politics*, and Premack and Woodruff's classic paper on primate "theory of mind," the cognitive sciences have witnessed an explosion of research on the nature of nonhuman minds and social behavior. This essay will not attempt to provide definitive answers for either the philosophical or biological debates, but rather to facilitate communication between them. Given certain philosophical questions, what biological or psychological facts can be brought to bear on the question of animal rights?

First, in answer to Bentham's challenge, I consider the question of animal suffering. Do animals experience pain? In what ways is it similar to human pain? Do they merely experience pain, or are they reflectively aware of it? Next, I consider whether animals experience moral sentiments. Do they self-reflect as moral beings? Do they hold their peers morally accountable? Do they categorize actions as right and wrong? At each nexus between philosophy and science a common theme emerges: humans ought to be taking far more seriously the moral standing of other animals, and nonhuman primates in particular.

Pain and Suffering

Peter Singer, the preeminent philosopher of animal rights, takes Bentham's lead, declaring that "the limit of sentience (using the term as a convenient, if not strictly accurate, shorthand for the capacity to suffer or experience enjoyment or happiness) is the only defensible boundary of concern for the interests of others." If Singer and Bentham are correct that the critical issue at stake is whether animals suffer, and if physical pain is one form of suffering, then the matter is solved, for there are certainly animals besides humans that experience pain.

The case for pain in nonhumans is so strong because of the concordance of two lines of evidence: physiological and behavioral. If humans shared only the neurological mechanisms of pain with other vertebrates, it might be written off as a homologous structure (an adaptation of an identical structure to different tasks), and there would still be substantial uncertainty whether the similar neurological mechanisms caused identical perceptual experiences. Likewise, if only certain behaviors were shared, it might be argued that they are analogous behaviors of independent origin and, once again, potentially linked to different perceptual experiences. Yet among nearly all vertebrates, shared physiological structures are associated with strikingly similar perceptual inputs and behavioral responses. Nociception, the process by which noxious stimuli are detected by peripheral neurons, is present among all vertebrates and some invertebrates (Wise 2000). The parts of the brain responsible for processing pain are present in nearly all vertebrates and are highly conserved among the closest relatives of humans. While the human brain has undergone rapid and significant evolution since human and chimpanzee lineages diverged, most of this development has occurred in other parts of the brain devoted to higher-level reasoning, not perceptual experience (Singer 1975). Furthermore, most vertebrates exhibit similar responses to stimuli, exhibit the same anxieties, and employ the same avoidance mechanisms as humans.[1] Simply put, there is little reason for us to doubt the existence of pain in many nonhuman animals besides the sort of brute epistemic skepticism that doubts if even fellow humans experience pain. Such skepticism has an appropriate place in philosophy, but strongly violates the principle of parsimony, which guides experimental science.

At least in higher-order vertebrates, the conclusions reached above generalize to mental states with more emotional content than physical pain, such as fear and depression. Studies of the neurochemical and environmental interactions leading to mental distress and disorder in humans often depend on the use of laboratory animal models precisely because the relationship between experience, brain, and behavior observed in humans holds true, at some reasonable level, for other vertebrates as well.[2] When deprived of a social environment, even the laboratory mouse—by no means a Goliath of the mental world—exhibits marked physiological and behavioral changes including defects in learning ability, hormone levels and brain neurochemistry (Valzelli 1973). The concordance of physiological and behavioral evidence suggests that it is not only appropriate to attribute emotional content to the mental states of many animals, but justified and relevant to the debate over animal welfare.

Some philosophers insist, however, that the experience of pain is not enough—that a higher order processing of experience is requisite for moral consideration. Awareness, consciousness and self-reflection are frequent candidates for this higher order mental state. Definitions of these terms are often contradictory, or absent altogether, but this may not reflect intellectual sloppiness so much as the blurred lines of the natural world. For the sake of rigor, I will set the bar as high as possible: for the experience of pain to count, the animal must be able to reflect on its own position as an individual experiencing pain. This is the position adopted by the philosopher Peter Carruthers, for instance.

The litmus test of an animal's sense of self is an elegant experiment devised in the 1970s by Gordon Gallup, in which subjects are surreptitiously marked with a red dot on one eyebrow and one ear and then exposed to a mirror. Human infants under the age of two and most monkeys will not spontaneously touch the marked area while looking in the mirror, suggesting that they do not recognize the image as a representation of the self.[3] Older children and most adult great apes pass the mirror test, however, first touching the marked areas while looking in the mirror and subsequently using the mirror to investigate normally unobservable parts of the body. Among a few great apes who have learned sign language, individuals such as Washoe and Nim have signed "me" in response to their own reflections (Wise 2000). The ability of many great apes to recognize their own reflection is our best evidence yet that they can form an abstract representation of themselves as physical and causal agents. Not only can they perceive their own body, they appear to conceive of it (Povinelli and Cant 1995).

Whether animals are aware of themselves as mental beings is a far trickier question. Current experimental methods are unable to explore the precise content of an animal's beliefs about itself. Rather, research over the last 25 years has centered around the question of whether animals have knowledge of *other* animals' mental states. In 1978 Premack and Woodruff claimed to have answered this question affirmatively, based on research with their chimp Sarah. The issue continues to be hotly debated, and experts within the field have not reached consensus (Heyes 1998). I will directly address the evidence for a theory of mind in some nonhuman primates in the following section; suffice it to say for now that the question is open. Nor it is obvious that a theory of *others'* minds presupposes a theory of one's *own* mind. Protocols that more directly measure primate self-awareness are necessary.

These shortcomings notwithstanding, it is likely that Bentham's acid test of suffering is easily met by many nonhuman animals. The experiential phenomenon of physical pain is almost certainly shared between diverse taxa of vertebrates. In higher vertebrates, it appears to determine behaviors in a manner very similar to human pain. Moreover, despite lingering uncertainties, it is at least a defensible position that our closest relatives can reflect on their own experience of pain. Yet, while these empirical facts have proven more than sufficient to convince a number of philosophers that animals deserve moral consideration, plenty of critics remain. A common assertion is that moral rights should only be granted to those organisms who can experience violations as morally wrong. The remainder of this essay undertakes to demonstrate that some primates meet even this stringent criterion.

II. The Moral Faculty

Recent reviews of morality among nonhuman animals have focused on the distinction between moral agents and moral patients. A normal human adult is a moral agent: somebody not only worthy of moral consideration, but capable of moral reasoning and beholden to moral behavior. A human infant, on the other hand, is a moral patient: somebody still deserving of moral treatment, but incapable of reasoning morally and therefore not morally culpable. It is often argued that animals are moral patients, but not moral agents.[4]

Unfortunately, the agent/patient distinction is often conflated with a different question: whether animals possess any moral faculty. The distinction is subtle, but important. Some critics have falsely reasoned from the appropriate claim that animals are not moral agents equivalent to humans to the dubious assertion that animals are incapable of moral reasoning at any level. To be sure, no nonhuman animal can engage in the sort of abstract moral reasoning typical of even the least educated human, and thus it is unlikely that any nonhuman animal would qualify as a moral agent in human society. Ultimately, however, I consider the agent/patient distinction to be the domain of philosophers—an interesting question, but one unanswerable by scientific methods. On the other hand, the question of whether animals have any moral faculty falls squarely to empirical scientists. Rather than letting the philosophical question of moral agency in animals define the empirical question of a moral faculty in animals, I advocate the opposite approach. As with all domains of cognition, the moral faculty need not be an all-or-nothing proposition. It is not enough to claim that animals do not experience morality in a sufficiently human way for agency; the question is how, if at all, they experience morality at all.

To date, attempts to provide an answer have too often ignored the evolutionary perspective that, as Darwin recognized, is fundamentally important to all biological research. To find moral sentiments in animals, researchers must look at behaviors that have evolved in the environment of typical social interactions, not those induced in contrived laboratory settings.

The debate over theory of mind in nonhuman primates, arguably a prerequisite for the experience of moral sentiment, is illustrative of the importance of an ethological perspective.[5] Dozens of experimental and observational procedures have been used to assess theory of mind in nonhuman primates. Many of the most credible ones involve deception or imitation. If animals are capable of deliberately lying to each other, this might suggest they can abstractly represent others' mental states. Likewise, if animals have the ability to teach and to learn from such instruction, this might suggest the ability to recognize another's intentions and states of knowledge.

Anecdotal evidence from field ethologists has indicated for decades that chimpanzees have many of the hallmarks of a theory of mind: behaviors like deception and teaching, which indicate that chimpanzees attribute mental states such as perception, knowledge and belief to members of their own species.[6] A striking example is the chimpanzees of West Africa, where juveniles learn from their parents how to use stone anvils and hammers to crack nuts. The evidence is strongly against this behavior being innate; rather, it appears to be culturally transmitted. Most striking of all, in a few rare cases proficient chimpanzees have been observed actively teaching their offspring—correcting inappropriate behavior, demonstrating the proper technique and even repositioning the tools in the hands their "pupils." Although decades of observation have only yielded a handful of these breakthrough observations, there is evidence of similar behavior in other taxa. Researches have observed killer whales teaching their young how to stalk and capture prey, and vervet monkeys appear to teach juveniles how to sound situation-specific alarm calls by rewarding correct calls and punishing incorrect ones (Caro and Hauser 1992, Rendell and Whitehead 2001). Significantly, these behaviors are manifested only towards naïve individuals. Field observations of deception are much more numerous, spanning a variety of situations in a diversity of species (Byrne and Whiten 1988). Observations of learning and deception indicate that chimpanzees and other species are able to form judgments about what their peers know and do not know, and modify their behavior in order to supply or withhold key information (de Waal 2001). Yet behavioral research in the lab has largely failed to duplicate field observations of teaching, deception, and other behaviors indicative of a theory of mind, leading to a widespread doubt that nonhuman primates possess the cognitive capacity for such behavior.

The disparity between ethologists and experimentalists is rooted in the failure of laboratory settings to replicate the natural conditions of the animal test subjects.[7] For instance, Daniel Povinelli has run numerous experimental procedures to discern whether chimpanzees have the concept "to see" (Povinelli et al. 2000). The chimps have failed, but always at unnatural tasks that require atypical behaviors (pointing, for instance) and demand the chimps to apply a theory of mind to human experimenters. In sharp contrast, Brian Hare recently published a breakthrough study involving food competition—a natural setting—in which the subjects had to apply the "to see" concept to members of their own species (Hare et al. 2000). Hare's chimpanzees passed the theory of mind test with flying colors. Not only did the subjects use knowledge about each other's mental states, they were able to apply this information in order to subvert the desires of dominants. As Hare's work demonstrates, the evidence for a theory of mind in many nonhuman primates is very strong, when looked for in the appropriate places (Wise 2000). Cognitive scientists must remind themselves that theory of mind is not an emergent property of mega-minds, but a mental tool evolved for social behavior in the natural environment.

The same errors that plague research into theory of mind among primates also permeate the literature on animal morality. As a consequence, researchers attempting to locate moral agency in animals have uniformly come up short—the best candidates for moral behavior, they claim, are nothing more than specific, domain-specific solutions to adaptive problems in social life. True moral agency, they assert, requires the ability to abstract ethical principles to novel situations. This approach fails to recognize two key points, however. First, animals may experience moral sentiments without being capable of moral agency. Second, nearly all behaviors are best explained as adaptive responses to specific problems, and just as with theory of mind, social interactions are precisely where researchers ought to be looking for moral sentiment.

A case in point comes from Marc Hauser's recent review of animal cognition, *Wild Minds*. Hauser maintains that, among other shortcomings, animals do not have the inhibitory control necessary for moral agency (Hauser 2000 and personal communication). Hauser is probably correct that animals do not have the inhibitory control necessary for moral agency in a human context, but this does not mean that they cannot experience moral sentiments. In any event, his claim is an instructive example of how previous attempts to locate animal ethics have looked for the wrong behaviors in the wrong places. Hauser bases his argument on experiments in which chimps cannot inhibit innately programmed actions, such as reaching for the larger of two piles of food, even when consistently punished for the behavior by being given the smaller pile. But is this truly the kind of inhibition necessary for moral behavior? It seems rather like criticizing humans for not being able to inhibit the kicking response when tapped on the knee.

As a foil, consider an experiment by the ethologist Eduard Stammbach. The lowest ranking members of several macaque groups were rewarded with large quantities of food for correctly pressing a sequence of levers on a machine. Once the low ranking animals learned the sequence, they were released into their social group with the machine and with other animals that were naïve with respect to the appropriate sequence. Initially the dominant members tried to gain exclusive access to the levers, but upon discovering that the levers would not work for them, the dominant members relinquished access. Their next strategy was to allow the low-ranking members to access food, but then to immediately chase them away and claim the full reward. In response, the low-ranking members went on strike, refusing to provide any food. Finally, the high-ranking members began to groom and coddle the low-ranking members, "inhibiting all aggression," in Hauser's words, and sharing the rewards with the low-ranking members (Hauser 2000).

If nothing else, these results demonstrate that some primates can inhibit reaching for large piles of food. The result also indicates that this capacity may not be domain-general, but rather specific, revealing good control in some contexts and poor control in others. But there is a broader methodological point. As with the theory of mind experiments (to which this research is also very applicable), to elicit a typical behavior it is necessary to employ protocols that put subjects in a natural, social setting with conspecifics.

Hauser objects that cases of inhibition such as these simply represent animals' "innately specified expectations about . . . the general psychology of members of their social group," which "evolve as the result of statistical regularities." From an evolutionary perspective, however, this isn't an objection, but rather the main point! Of course morality—the innate expectations of permissible and impermissible behavior—evolved as the result of statistical regularities of behavior. Hauser concludes from his discussion of inhibition that the innate rigidity of animal minds "won't work with the general goals of a moral society" that might, for instance, have to "facilitate the greatest good for the greatest number" (Hauser 2000). While he is certainly correct that animals cannot perform on this intellectual plane, this only goes to show why the category of moral agency creates confusion and evades the more fundamental issue of whether animals have a moral faculty.

Animals are not fully capable moral agents in human society, but this does not mean that they lead amoral lives. Rather, social interactions between animals demonstrate a rich variety of social rules, norms and expectations that strongly indicate a sense of right and wrong. Rhesus macaques expect members of their social group to call out when they discover food, and silent members are punished without regard to rank on the social hierarchy. By contrast, individuals exterior to the social group never call, and are never punished when the group learns of their discovery (Hauser 2000). A fascinating experiment with a chimpanzee named Sheba involved two groups of humans bringing her juice. One group accidentally spilled the juice, while the other deliberately threw it on the ground. In apparent anger Sheba would threaten the intentional spillers, but she did not react angrily to the accidental spillers. Given a choice in future trials, Sheba would request juice from accidental spillers over intentional spillers (Povinelli and Godfrey 1993). David Premack's chimp Sarah would, given the ability to choose outcomes to videotaped dilemmas, choose pleasant outcomes for her favorite keepers and unpleasant outcomes for her least favorite (Povinelli and Godfrey 1993). Nor is punishment the only outcome of moral conflict; reviewing the research on peacemaking among primates, Hauser writes, "many primate societies have evolved systems to reduce the day-to-day tensions of living a life in the company of others. This system is certainly an important part of getting along in a society with rules" (Hauser 2000).

Are these cases of animals responding with moral indignation? Since it is impossible to solicit a first-hand account, we cannot know for sure whether Sheeba's threats against deliberate spillers, for instance, are accompanied by a sense of having been wronged, or simply represent an innate reflex, devoid of any moral content. But when the cases of consciousness, pain, and suffering seem obvious, why not bridge the identical epistemic gap in the case of morality? Animals are morally wronged (that is, expected norms are violated), and consequently behave as if they *felt* morally wronged. Why deny the moral experience?

Perhaps the most important shortcoming of the excuse that animal emotions are "merely" adaptive responses to social life is simply that human moral sentiments are best explained adaptively as well. Moral agency may depend on rational thought that transcends innate emotive responses, but moral intuitions about fairness and basic social rules are apparently hard-wired in the human mind.[8] Psychologists and behavioral economists have synthesized data from more than a dozen primitive cultures on fairness in economic interactions. Strikingly, individuals seem to have a concept of fairness that, from an economic perspective, is irrational. Although cultural determinants predict much of the variation between individuals, it appears that variation hovers around a mean innately determined, rather than rationally derived (Henrich, Boyd, et al. 2001). As such, the cross-cultural concepts of economic fairness underlying these observations might best be explained as domain-specific adaptations for social behavior. These moral intuitions are precisely the ones which cognitive and ethological research increasingly find evidence for in our closest primate cousins.

There are at least two replies to this argument worth careful consideration. Hauser frequently makes use of the distinction between domain-specific and domain-general abilities (Hauser 2000). Whereas humans can apply cognitive skills to a variety of unfamiliar tasks, comparable skills in animals have typically evolved only in the narrow domains that applied to their daily lives during the relevant adaptive history. I suspect Hauser's complaint that apparently moralistic attitudes in animals are merely evolved social expectations to be rooted in his conviction that human morality depends on its generality across novel social interactions.[9] In my view, however, moral feelings are moral feelings whether they apply generally or specifically. We should not expect chimpanzees to have the capacity for human moral behavior any more than humans can be expected to behave according to "chimpanzee politics," as Frans de Waal termed them. But we should recognize chimpanzee politics for what tit is: a moral system, albeit one more primitive. Nor should we forget that our own moral emotions, however generally applied, probably first evolved as domain-specific adaptations for social life.

A second objection is that the "argument by analogy" is simply insufficient.[10] What distinguishes the observation of apparently "moral" behavior in primates from the foolhardy anthropomorphism of dog lovers who claim that "virgin bitches 'save' themselves for future 'husbands,'" assuming "Victorian values in an animal not particularly known for its sexual fidelity"?[11] The best response to this criticism is to point to the rapidly mounting evidence that great apes (but, by and large, *not* monkeys) possess a theory of mind and have the capacity to deceive, punish, inhibit, and reward. They have complex social interactions governed by rules but also characterized by flexibility. They recognize the boundaries of their social groups, form friendships and enmities, make peace and make war. The argument by analogy is inescapable, at least so long as animal communication remains inadequate for first-hand accounts, but it is an argument gaining in strength year by year and study by study.

It bears repeating that no animal displays even a pale image of the colorful range of moral sentiments in humans. Determining whether animals have the right kinds of moral faculty for true agency is a matter of philosophy, not biology. Nevertheless, biology can contribute an important insight to the debate: as both experimental and evolutionary psychology dig closer at the roots of the moral faculty, the experiences of humans and animals appear more and more similar in kind, if separated by a chasm of degree.

Conclusion

In the 1960s, Stanley Wechkin and a group of colleagues investigated empathy and altruism among rhesus macaques (Wechkin et al. 1964). One monkey, the actor, was trained to pull on either of two chains to receive food. Then another monkey, the receiver, was introduced in an adjacent cage, while the actor's chains were rewired. One chain would still deliver food to the actor, but the other administered a shock to the receiver. Most monkeys substantially reduced the number of pulls to the shocking chain. Several monkeys stopped using either chain; one starved itself for 12 days before it would pull either chain. Monkeys who had been shocked before were significantly less likely to shock their neighbors, as were monkeys with prior social contact (Hauser 2000). In short, these macaques seem to have behaved according to the golden rule.

Before presenting this data, Marc Hauser writes, "The fact that I discuss this work should not, however, be read as an endorsement. It is most definitely not." He later comments, "For many, the experiments described above are unethical because we should not harm animals for our own intellectual benefit" (Hauser 2000). Some philosophers take this reasoning to be sufficient: if animals experience pain, we ought to avoid causing it. Others demand that the animals in question not only experience pain, but experience the "rightness" and "wrongness" of actions. Their question is this: does the actor macaque who avoids shocking the receiver want the receiver not to experience pain in the same way that Marc Hauser does not want the receiver to experience pain?

There are many reasons for the actor to avoid shocking the receiver that make no appeal to right and wrong. Perhaps actor monkeys are frightened by the abnormal contortions of their shocked neighbors. Perhaps they are afraid they will be shocked, or fear long-term retribution, or simply act reflexively to avoid pain in conspecifics. But I believe that these explanations do not best account for the data. They ignore the adaptive roots of moral behavior and the evolutionary ties which bind us to our primate cousins. When we look closely at human morality, we see sociality; when we look closely at primate sociality, we see morality. Indeed, the best explanation for these data is provided in *The Descent of Man* by Darwin, whose clairvoyant musings on evolutionary biology continue to astound modern researchers. Darwin recognized the fundamental unity between animal social instincts and human moral instincts as well as the inherent limits of the comparison, and so to him I give the final word:

> The moral sense perhaps affords the best and highest distinction between man and the lower animals; but I need say nothing on this head, as I have

> so lately endeavored to show that the social instincts—the prime principle of man's moral constitution—with the aid of active intellectual powers and the effects of habit, naturally lead to the golden rule, "As ye would that men should do to you, do ye to them likewise"; and this lies at the foundation of morality. (Darwin 1974)

Notes

1. *Animal Experimentation: Report by the Senate Select Committee on Animal Welfare.* (The Australian Government Publishing Service, Canberra, 1989), pp. 44–48.
2. "Emotional events in young mammals can have major, long-lasting effects on the neurochemistry of the developing brain—and therefore on mood and behavior."
3. But see Hauser, (1995) , which suggests that cotton top tamerins pass the mirror test, and that monkeys may fail for methodological reasons. Hauser's observation that subjects may simply be uninterested in minor markings on their own body may explain why even some chimps do not pass the mirror test.
4. See, for instance, Hauser 2000 and Petrinovich 1999.
5. The argument is commonly made that animals cannot experience moral indignation at each other without a concept of the "other" as a mental being.
6. For a brief, general defense of the ethological approach, see Green (1998). For a review of animal deception see Whitten and Byrne (1988). For reviews of chimp teaching and learning see Whitten, Goodall, et al. (1999).
7. I focus on the ethology/laboratory division, but Premack and Premack make important points about methodological errors in current theory of mind empirical protocols. See Premack (2003).
8. This comment will inevitably strike some as obvious and others as absurd; hopefully both camps will accept, however, that it is fruitless to argue the point anew in this essay. For a comprehensive defense of the statement, see Darwin (1974).
9. Eliot Sober has advocated a related position, well worth consideration. See Sober (1993).
10. See Povinelle, D. J., et al. (2000). While his argument is directed specifically at theory of mind, the methodological points apply generally.
11. See de Waal (2001), paraphrasing Elizabeth Marshall Thomas's *The Hidden Life of Dogs.* In my own view, the rampant anthropomorphization of dog behavior owes to extraordinary selective pressures operating on domesticated pet breeds to behave according to human social expectations. In short, we selectively breed dogs adept at making us believe they think like humans.

References

Bentham, J., J. H. Burns, et al. (1996). *An introduction to the principles of morals and legislation.* Oxford, Clarendon Press.

Byrne, R. W., and A. Whiten (1988). *Machiavellian intelligence: Social expertise and the evolution of intellect in monkeys, apes, and humans.* Oxford, Clarendon Press.

Caro, T. M., and Hauser, M.D (1992). "Is there teaching in nonhuman animals?" *Quarterly Review of Biology* 61: 151.

Darwin, C. (1974). *The descent of man and selection in relation to sex.* Detroit, Gale Research Co.

Darwin, C., and P. H. Barrett (1987). *Charles Darwin's notebooks, 1836–1844: Geology, transmutation of species, metaphysical enquiries.* Ithaca, Cornell University Press.

de Waal, F. B. M. (2001). *The ape and the sushi master: Cultural reflections by a primatologist.* New York, Basic Books.

Green, S. M. (1998). "Anecdotes, omniscience and associative learning in examining the theory of mind." *Behavioral and Brain Sciences* 21: 122.

Hare, B., et al. (2000). "Chimpanzees know what conspecifics do and do not see." *Animal Behavior* 59: 771–785.

Hauser, M. D. (2000). *Wild minds: What animals really think.* New York, Henry Holt.

Hauser, M. D., J. Kralik, C. Botto, M. Garrett, and J. Oser (1995). "Self-recognition in primates: Phylogeny and the salience of species-typical traits." *Proceedings of the National Academy of Sciences* 92: 10811.

Henrich, J., R. Boyd, et al. (2001). "Cooperation, reciprocity and punishment in fifteen small-scale societies." *American Economic Review,* May.

Heyes, C. M. (1998). "Theory of mind in nonhuman primates." *Behavioral and Brain Sciences* 21(1): 101–14; discussion 115–48.

Kant, I. (1999). "Lectures on ethics." In H. Kuhse and P. Singer (Eds.), *Bioethics: An anthology.* Malden, Blackwell Publishers: 459.

Mlot, C. (1998). "Probing the biology of emotion." *Science* 280(5366): 1005–7.

Petrinovich, L. (1999). *Darwinian dominion.* Cambridge, MIT Press.

Povinelli, D. J., and J. G. Cant (1995). "Arboreal clambering and the evolution of self-conception." *Quarterly Review of Biology* 70(4): 393–421.

Povinelli, D. J., et al. (2000). "Toward a science of other minds: Escaping the argument by analogy." *Cognitive Science* 24(3).

Povinelli, D. J., and L. R. Godfrey (1993). "The chimpanzee's mind: How noble in reason? How absent in ethics?" In M. H. Nitecki and D. V. Nitecki (Eds.), *Evolutionary Ethics.* Albany, State University of New York Press.

Premack, D., and A. J. Premack (2003). *Original intelligence: Unlocking the mystery of who we are.* New York, McGraw-Hill.

Rendell, L., and H. Whitehead (2001). "Culture in whales and dolphins." *Behavioral and Brain Sciences* 24(2): 309–24; discussion 324–82.

Singer, P. (1975). *Animal liberation: A new ethics for our treatment of animals.* New York, New York Review of Books: Distributed by Random House.

Sober, E. (1993). Altruism, egoism, and morality. In M. H. Nitecki and D. V. Nitecki (Eds.), *Evolutionary ethics.* Albany, State University of New York Press.

Valzelli, L. (1973). "The 'isolation syndrome' in mice." *Psychopharmacologia* 31(4): 305–20.

Wechkin, S., Masserman, J. H., and Terris, W. (1964). "Shock to a conspecific as an aversive stimulus." *Psychonomic Science* 1: 47–48.

Whitten, A., and R. W. Byrne (1988). "Tactical deception in primates." *Behavioral and Brain Sciences* 11: 223–273.

Wise, S. M. (2000). *Rattling the cage: Toward legal rights for animals.* Cambridge, Mass., Perseus Books.

Wright, R. (1994). *The moral animal.* New York, Vintage Books.

Cognitive Beasts

The Thoughts and Feelings of Animals

Robbie Silverman

IN MOST SCIENTIFIC AND POPULAR CIRCLES the instrumental use of animals is considered morally legitimate. We raise and kill them for food, perform experiments on them to cure our diseases, keep them in captivity, and hunt them for sport. We treat animals this way because we view them as fundamentally different from human beings. Whereas humans are conscious beings, able to perceive the world around them, express desires, and employ language to communicate with others, animals are widely considered to lack these cognitive abilities. As a result, we often assume that we are free to employ them for our own ends, just as we use a car, a plow, a toy, or a tomato.

This view, however widespread, is wrong; there is no clear dividing line between the cognitive abilities of humans and of animals. Animals think, feel, communicate, and anticipate. They are aware of themselves and others around them. They have desires and they have goals. Some mammals, including dolphins and primates, are able to follow complicated commands, employ language, and express emotions. Primates demonstrate an awareness of number theory and physical laws on par with very young children. Chimpanzees can recognize themselves in a mirror, and appear to manifest reflective consciousness, the ability to reflect on their own state of being. Nor is consciousness limited to these animals; even insects seem to possess perceptual consciousness, the ability to be aware of things that are around them.

Animals demonstrate consciousness in three ways: first, through their versatile responses to changing conditions, including tool use, structure building, food foraging, and the predator-prey relationship; second, through neurobiological activity, which is strikingly similar to humans'; and third, through their communicative ability, which in recent years has been found to far exceed previous understanding. Animals certainly do not think, feel, or communicate in the same way that humans do, but we cannot dismiss them as mindless automatons. They do possess consciousness, and we must change our laws and our societal institutions to serve their needs and respect their rights.

It is extremely difficult to characterize animal consciousness. We understand and define human consciousness by communicating with other humans, using language to share subjective experiences. Although this option is not available with animals, we can observe them in the field and in the laboratory, and this information points unequivocally to some form of animal consciousness.

Our closest animal cousins, such as monkeys and great apes, demonstrate cognitive abilities on par with young human children. They seem to possess self-awareness, a form of reflective consciousness that is often cited as a uniquely human trait. For example, many chimpanzees recognize themselves in a mirror, rather than mistaking their reflection for another chimpanzee. Chimps that have been marked by paint on the forehead while asleep will spontaneously touch the paint mark after observing it in a mirror (Griffin 2001). Even more remarkably, a recent study has shown that chimps can recognize themselves even in mirrors that distort their images. This implies a degree of abstractional ability, as they can abstract from a distorted image to perceive themselves (Kitchen, Denton et al. 1996).

Primates also manifest an understanding of simple number theory and physical laws. Rhesus monkeys appear to possess a rudimentary understanding of arithmetic akin to that of very young human children. Human infants are able to recognize that one plus one is exactly two, and that two minus one is exactly one. Rhesus monkeys also appear to possess the same mathematical expectations, staring longer at and expressing more interest in physical arrangements where, by an experimenter's sleight of hand, these expectations are not satisfied (Hauser 1996). Similarly, both monkeys and infants seem to share an innate understanding of fundamental physical laws. Both will stare longer at violations, such as when an object appears to fall through a solid shelf (Griffin 2001).

There is also evidence for a lower order of consciousness, perceptual awareness, outside of the primate family. One indicator of perceptual awareness is the versatility that animals show in responding to changing circumstances. Animals choose between competing courses of action, exercise foresight in planning for future occurrences, remember past events and past actions, and exhibit wants and desires. Animals seem to exhibit goal-oriented behavior both in the wild and in the lab. In a lab, for instance, animals come to expect food at a specific place at a specific time every day. If they fail to receive this food, they express annoyance, frustration, or disappointment.

Animals have desires and preferences, and they can make choices. Several experiments have shown the complex choices that bees make when gathering food.

They select certain sources of food based on color and distance, and they adjust their preferences when circumstances change. Experiments conducted by Marian Dawkins have demonstrated a strong preference among chickens for chipped wood in their cages. Given two compartments, one with chipped wood and one without, chickens will always choose the one with the chips. They will continue to choose this compartment even if they have to push through a weighted door to enter it, to the point of injuring themselves (Hauser 1999).

Many of the complex choices that animals make are not innately "programmed"; rather, they represent a process of complex decision-making. Oystercatchers, a type of large bird that lives along beaches, catch mussels for food. These birds employ two distinct methods to do this. If the mussels are completely exposed by the surf, and hence tightly shut, oystercatchers will pick them up and then crack their shells against a hard patch of sand. If the mussels are still in shallow water, however, and thus slightly open, oystercatchers will pry their shells open with their bills and eat the flesh. This decision-making process is not innate; oystercatchers learn how to appropriately match the technique to the situation from their parents, indicating that they possess the ability to make a situational decision based on previous experience (Griffin 2001).

Some animals exhibit an incredible memory store. Clark's nutcrackers, for instance, collect as many as 33,000 pine seeds in an autumn, which they then hide in shallow holes, about four seeds per hole. To survive in the spring and winter, they must remember and visit 3,000 of these caches, recognizing them even when the ground is covered with snow (Pearce 1997). To accomplish this mental feat the birds employ mental landmarks (Griffin 2001).

Competitive selection over evolutionary time between predators and prey has also produced quite complex cognitive abilities. Both predators and prey demonstrate a clear perceptual awareness of the other. Often, this awareness can register the most minute distinctions. Hyenas, for example, search out the old, weak, and sick among possible prey, and they act based on this preference (Griffin 2001). Group hunting, which occurs among such diverse creatures as lions, hawks, and otters, requires coordination, a division of labor, and signaling communication. These animals are aware of each other, communicate with one another, and make choices to produce a desired outcome.

Animals also exhibit goal-driven behavior when constructing various artifacts, such as nests, huts, egg compartments, or food traps. Common goals include attracting mates, providing for offspring, or procuring food. Animals seem to recognize that engaging in certain behavior will produce a desired result. Furthermore, animals are able to adapt their structures based on the physical landscape or availability of resources. Perhaps the most extravagant example of nest-building occurs among bowerbirds. Male bowerbirds construct extraordinarily elaborate bowers to attract mates. They seek out snail shells, feathers, and colored dyes as decoration, and males will steal desirable material from one another. This is not entirely a programmed behavior; finding decorations seems to involve a conscious choice, and young males will learn from older males the best way to construct a successful bower (Griffin 2001).

The construction and use of tools also illustrates animals' cognitive abilities. Once defined as a trait restricted only to humans, tool use is now recognized throughout the animal kingdom. Chimpanzees find a branch, strip it of its leaves, carry it to a termite nest, insert it, pull it out, and feast off of the clinging termites. Ants fashion sponges out of leaves and use them to transport liquids to the colony. Gulls drop shellfish against asphalt, stones, or other hard surfaces to get at the meat inside. The use of tools is a goal-driven, conscious behavior. Don Griffin writes, "Even in relatively simple cases the tool is a separate object from the food it helps the animal to obtain or the process for which it is used. Therefore, selecting or preparing a tool indicates awareness of whatever it serves to accomplish" (Griffin 2001).

Complex behaviors are not the only manifestation of animal cognition; the growing study of neurobiological factors also provides evidence. To begin with, there is no single physical instantiation of consciousness. The brain does not include a localized point that serves as the root of conscious thought, nor is there a set configuration of brain waves that demonstrates consciousness. Science has yet to uncover a clear dividing line between a conscious brain and an unconscious brain. Furthermore, while human brains are much more complex than the brains of animals, the basic building blocks of the nervous system remain largely the same—they are regulated by the same genes, composed of the same molecules, and arranged in the same cellular and macroscopic structures. Some comparative studies of animal and human brain waves do exist, and similar brain lesions in humans and chimps seem to result in correlate patterns of behavior. Furthermore, REM sleep and dreaming appears to be widespread among both mammals and birds (Griffin 2001). Human and nonhuman brains are similar enough in structure and function that there is no reason to deny the possibility of conscious life in nonhumans.

Perhaps the most compelling arguments for animal consciousness come from the study of animal communication, which seems to offer a window into their consciousness. Language was once considered a unique characteristic of humankind. While it still appears true that no system of communication in the animal kingdom approaches the richness or complexity of human language, animals of all kinds have developed methods to convey information to their fellows. Chickens produce alarm calls to warn others about approaching danger, and these calls differ depending on the location of the threat. Even more significantly, the audience that the chicken has affects the frequency of the alarm. Chickens are aware of other chickens around them and modify their behavior accordingly. The number of alarm calls that a young rooster gives upon seeing a hawk depends on his audience. He gives fewer when alone, more when females or young chicks are present than for other adult males, and more when familiar females are present than for unfamiliar females. Young roosters are also much less likely to call when in the presence of a female of another species. Similarly, young roosters are more likely to signal the presence of food when in the presence of females than when alone or with other males (Marler, Karakashian, et al. 1991). Vervet monkeys have also developed a system of conveying information. They produce three different types of grunts for different predators, and their vocalization changes when addressing dominant or subordinate fellows (Griffin 2001). The changing patterns of calls suggests that animals have the option to withhold signaling based on their desire with respect to others, and indicate a conscious decision-making processes.

Higher-level animals communicate in very complex ways. Dolphins have a signature whistle and can imitate the signature whistle of others, possibly as a type of name-calling. Dolphins are also very communicative and very social. In the wild, dolphins aid other dolphins that are sick or injured by pushing them to the surface to enable them to breathe. In captivity, they can learn to interpret and follow very complex commands. Chimpanzees, meanwhile, can learn more than 100 words in American Sign Language. They appear to fully conceptualize the meaning of these words, and can apply them to new objects and use them in new situations. Apes taught to communicate will often spontaneously ask for things they want (Griffin 2001). One male bonobo named Kanzi learned to use a keyboard simply by watching his mother being taught, without undergoing formal training on his one. Once trained, he learned a vocabulary of more 140 words that he was able to use spontaneously. Kanzi's comprehension of spoken English approached that of a human two-and-a-half-year-old child, and his word production was similar to that of a one-and-a-half-year-old child (Rumbaugh and Savage-Rumbaugh 1994).

Irene M. Pepperberg has been able to train African grey parrots to communicate in remarkable ways. She was able to teach one parrot, Alex, to use a vocabulary of several names, colors, and shapes, by establishing a rival game with another human trainer acting as competition for the parrot. Using this method, the parrot learned to identify more than 100 different objects. The parrot could answer questions regarding the color and shape of objects with 80 percent accuracy. Four-fifths of the time, the parrot could also accurately identify the characteristic—color, shape, or matter—shared by two objects (Pepperberg 1991). In addition, Alex had command of the numbers two through six, and could answer how many objects were present (Griffin 2001). Alex's talents are significant not only from a linguistic perspective. In addition, such data indicates a high degree of conceptualization about numbers, shapes, sameness, and other abstract concepts.

One of the most astounding systems of animal communication is manifested by the honeybee. Honeybees engage in a complex "dance language," first described by Karl von Frisch, in which a member of the nest will produce a series of movements, including loops, walks, and waggles, to convey information to fellow bees. These dances reveal a very complex set of information regarding the nature, distance, and desirability of food sources. The cognitive ability of bees, at least in relation to locating food, may indeed approach that of mammals (Griffin 2001).

Animals, therefore, are far from mindless robots. They perceive other animals and objects around them, and change their own actions based on that information. Some possess the ability of self-recognition. They use tools, build elaborate structures, and possess remarkable memories and conceptions of spatial relations. They have needs, wants, and desires. They communicate with one another, often in astounding ways, and some have learned to communicate with humans.

Our current treatment of animals utterly fails to take into account their cognitive abilities. Cognitive science cannot justify a system that so readily distinguishes between animals and humans for there is truly no dividing line for consciousness. The black-and-white distinction that we have created is entirely unscientific. People cannot continue to treat animals as property and use them solely to satiate their own appetites for meat, money, or pleasure, without considering the interests of the animals themselves.

References

Griffin, D. R. (2001). *Animal minds: Beyond cognition to consciousness.* Chicago, University of Chicago Press.

Hauser, M. (1999). "Final club fowls." *The Harvard Crimson*, December 10. Online at http://www.thecrimson.com/article.aspx?ref=98893.

Hauser, M. D., P. MacNeilage, and Ware, M. (1996). "Numerical representations in primates." *Proceedings of the National Academy of Sciences* 93(4): 1515–1516.

Kitchen, A., D. Denton, et al. (1996). "Self-recognition and abstraction abilities in the common chimpanzee studied with distorting mirrors." *Proceedings of the National Academy of Sciences* 93(14): 7405–7408.

Marler, P., S. Karakashian, et al. (1991). "Do animals have the option of withholding signals when communication is inappropriate? The Audience effect." In C. A. Ristau (Ed.), *Cognitive ethology: The minds of other animals: Essays in honor of Donald R. Griffin.* Hillsdale, Lawrence Erlbaum Associates.

Pearce, J. M. (1997). *Animal learning and cognition.* East Sussex, Psychology Press.

Pepperberg, I. M. (1991). "A communicative approach to animal cognition: A study of conceptual abilities of an African grey parrot." In C. A. Ristau (Ed.), *Cogni-*

tive ethology: The minds of other animals: Essays in honor of Donald R. Griffin. Hillsdale, Lawrence Erlbaum Associates.

Rumbaugh, D. M., and E. S. Savage-Rumbaugh (1994). "Language in comparative perspectives." In N. J. Mackintosh (Ed.), *Animal learning and cognition.* San Diego, Academic Press.

An Argument from Cognitive Science against Increasing Legal Rights for Animals

Justin Jungé

THE ANIMAL RIGHTS MOVEMENT IS COMPOSED of many varied organizations with unique purposes and goals, yet most animal rights activists are motivated by one particular concern: to cause animals to experience pain is a moral violation. This essay argues that no such moral issue is at stake in our treatment of animals because animals lack the cognitive capacity to experience pain in a significant sense—the psychological dimension where moral and ethical considerations are relevant. This view rests on three claims: 1) There is a distinction between pain and suffering that relates to cognitive capacity. 2) Human laws and moral responsibilities are applicable to suffering only, and pain is only given consideration when it can be the direct cause of suffering. 3) Animals lack the cognitive capacity to suffer, and consequently do not qualify for human legal and moral rights.

If those in favor of increasing animals rights are motivated by an empathetic concern for animals, rather than a perceived moral obligation to minimize the causes of animal pain, then the degree to which animals are cognitively capable of pain is of critical importance. Consider the following rationale: "I have conscious experiences that deserve the protection of a legal system. I'm pretty sure that my lovable dog has some sort of conscious experiences too. So my dog (and probably some other intelligent animals) should be protected by our legal system." Following this logic there are two important questions: Can animals consciously experience pain? And, How does experience of pain factor into consideration of our moral obligations and legal rights?

The answers to both of these questions hinge on a distinction between pain and suffering. Pain will be defined as the physical perceptual experience, and suffering as the reflective psychological dimension of an experience. At first glance, it might not seem intuitive to draw a line between pain and suffering because it often appears that, if not identical, they are at least causally inseparable: pain causes suffering. But closer examination reveals that this is not always the case and that there can be a clean dissociation of the two. Consider the case of childbirth versus stillbirth. The pain of childbirth is excruciating, but it is often distinctly lacking any degree of suffering. Stillbirth, on the other hand, is accompanied by a huge amount of suffering, which can last long after the physical pain is over and forgotten. It need not, however, entail any more physical pain than childbirth. Indeed, humans have the capacity to suffer as the result of verbal abuse, which is clearly independent of any physical pain.

To place the distinction between pain and suffering within the larger framework of cognitive science requires an operational definition of consciousness. Defining consciousness is a difficult yet crucial undertaking, and a strict definition has the potential to preclude the serious consideration of any animals as conscious. To avoid introducing such a bias, I will give up home field advantage and use an illustrative dichotomy put forward by a scientist who would likely disagree with the overall conclusions of this paper, Don Griffin. Griffin remains an advocate for animal consciousness, defining it loosely and distributing it widely throughout the animal kingdom. Drawing a line between perceptual and reflective consciousness, a distinction critical to the following argument, Griffin writes, "The former . . . [perceptual consciousness] includes all sorts of awareness, whereas the latter [reflective consciousness] is a subset of conscious experiences in which the content is conscious experience itself." To apply these terms to the categories of pain and suffering, pain is defined as occurring in the realm of perceptual consciousness, and suffering as exclusively residing at the higher level of reflective consciousness. To define what it means to suffer—as well as to experience suffering itself—can only be accomplished within a cognitive framework capable of reflective consciousness.

Some good examples of suffering are profound hopelessness, the understanding that one is the victim of injustice, and the fear of death as an eternal state. Clearly it is not just the emotional or perceptual component that constitutes suffering, but rather the deep understanding of the significance of our experiences within a larger framework. Examining suffering in this light, it is apparent that reflective consciousness is a prerequisite to suffering. For example, one must be capable of abstracting about the significance of a current perceptual state of physical pain or emotional discomfort in relation to a set of abstract ideals and standards in order to suffer a genuine feeling of injustice. Likewise, it requires a well-developed concept of extended time frames in order to grasp the significance of one's own death and see the ways in which physically painful experiences may bring this death closer. These are just a few illustrative examples, but they demonstrate the degree to which high-level cognition can extend perceptual pain into the reflective realm of psychological suffering.

Legal and moral restrictions are designed to protect us not from pain, but from suffering. The reason that human laws and moral concerns focus on protecting individual humans from experiencing pain is because almost anytime that a normal human adult is unwillingly subjected to a perceptually painful experience, there is a corollary potential for suffering. Exceptions to this rule are accounted for in our laws; whereas there are laws aimed at the prevention of domestic abuse and battery, rape and assault, we have no enforced laws that prevent childbirth or self-inflicted pain such as masochism.[1] It might be objected that this line of reasoning leaves it permissible to cause types of pain that are not typically associated with suffering. By definition, however, if the human does not desire the pain, then it would entail suffering. Furthermore, it would be acceptable to inflict pain on a willing masochistic recipient because they would, also by definition, not suffer.

Another objection involves so-called "marginal cases." Young human children and some mentally handicapped adults do not posses the cognitive capacity discussed here. Does the previous logic exclude them from moral consideration? Certainly not. A perfectly consistent line of reasoning extends legal rights to all members of a species, who, on average, demonstrate reflective consciousness, and may require protection from suffering caused by pain. Finding a nonhuman candidate for this has so far proved an impossible task.

If animals are incapable of suffering because they lack the cognitive tools, then human law should not concern itself with protecting animals from pain—their unreflective minds already protect them completely from the possibility of suffering. As such, the burden of proof is on the advocates in favor of improving animal rights to demonstrate that animals do indeed posses abilities that can only be adequately explained by reflective consciousness and could consequently allow the potential for suffering. A careful review of the relevant empirical literature will leave most animal rights activists disappointed; the evidence for reflective consciousness is simply not there. Nevertheless, most of the remainder of this paper will be aimed at addressing this issue and refuting several exemplary anecdotes that some might consider as candidates for the task of demonstrating reflective consciousness in the animal kingdom.

Since it is difficult to directly prove or disprove reflective consciousness in the animal kingdom, a useful place to begin is with the notion of abstraction, one of the cognitive prerequisites of reflective consciousness. The neuroscientist John Dowling has given an illustrative example of perceptual abstraction, a likely predecessor of mental abstraction. A frog will use the perceptual information of a moving fly to actively respond and catch the fly for a meal. However, the frog will completely ignore a dead fly lying on the ground beside it, despite the fact that this could make an equally good meal (Dowling 2001). The frog lacks an abstract representation of the fly that would allow it to generalize from the flying object in the air to the dead object next to it. Animals with better cognitive equipment could easily make such a move. For example, a wolf will kill prey for food or eat a carcass that is already dead.

In this sense, the notion of abstraction is exemplified by a particular category applying to multiple physical things.

Higher levels of abstraction apply not to specific objects, but to categories themselves. For example, color is the abstraction that applies to the categories of purple, blue and yellow. Minds endowed with this second-degree of abstraction can begin to make the move toward reflective consciousness. Although it is theoretically possible (though almost certainly not the case) that animals represent low level abstractions at the level of reflective consciousness, it would be difficult, or perhaps even impossible, to prove that an animal's mind worked this way, because there are more simple explanations available. Nevertheless, there are tools for the task, and behavioral observation and experimentation can address the question with carefully considered qualifications.

Reflective consciousness requires abstraction because it requires the content of a thought to be consciousness itself, an abstract category. As such, it must either combine abstract categories from independent domains of knowledge,[2] or be removed at least two degrees from perceptual input. Any behaviors absent of these qualifications could be explained more parsimoniously by appealing to lower-level abstraction paired with some type of conditioned learning. For instance, the concept of color is an example of an abstraction that does not qualify as reflective. Color is a perceptual attribute, so the abstract concept of color is only one abstraction away from a perceptual input. If an animal were capable of categorizing objects by color, this could be accomplished by linking color perception to a simple abstraction—and this feat would not require reflection. However, the category of prime numbers appears to meet the criterion also necessary for reflective consciousness. To form this category relies on the abstract attribute of a specific quantifier (for example labeling the item as 2, 11, 17, etc.) that cannot be perceptually perceived, and also an abstract qualifier of divisibility. To return to the realm of morality, the ability to suffer injustice requires an abstract notion of fairness combined with an abstracted concept of right and wrong, and the ability to understand the significance of death requires an abstract representation of an extended time frame along with an abstract distinction between living and non-living.

At this point it may seem that I have set up an impossible test for animals to pass. After all, how can we possibly know whether or not animals posses a notion of right and wrong, or grasp the significance of death? Although it may seem unlikely that any nonhuman animal could do this, it is equally unlikely that we could learn such information without a revolution in interspecies communication. What has actually been argued, however, is that if any animal were to definitively demonstrate that it possessed reflective consciousness, it would be prudent to treat it as possessing the potential to suffer. This is an empirically verifiable criterion; what is needed is an abstract quality that relates directly to physical qualities, and can be utilized to produce observable results. Functionality, the concept that links physical object properties to their potential for useful manipulation, serves this role. Marc Hauser (2000) has used laboratory experiments to demonstrate that certain primates can learn to identify the functional attributes of tools and manipulate these tools to obtain a reward. This research provides valuable insight into the potential for at least one type of abstraction in nonhuman primates, and shows that certain primates may be one (large) step away from demonstrating reflective consciousness. Hauser's primates learned functional attributes only when applied in concert with their innate object knowledge. If they or any other animals could learn functional attributes that applied to a substance outside this domain of innate object knowledge (for example, the functionality of elasticity or magnetism), this would be a strong suggestion of the kind of cognition required for reflective consciousness. To accomplish this task would require an animal to form an abstract notion about a learned object property, and the most probable way to accomplish this is through reflective awareness. This is just one example of the kind of advanced abstraction-related behavior that would indicate reflection. Now that the bar has been set, it is easy to see how the behavior that some cognitive scientists have claimed is indicative of high-level abstraction and reflection simply falls short. The often impressive animal feats sometimes considered as evidence for high-level cognition can be explained with a lower-level form of abstraction.[3]

Early in the twentieth century Wolfgang Köhler demonstrated that chimpanzees were capable of applying some object knowledge to spontaneously solve a mechanical problem to obtain a food reward (for instance, stacking boxes to reach a bunch of bananas). This is evidence of functional abstraction in a controlled context. However, he also found that the chimpanzees could not extend this problem solving ability when the reward was not readily visible. Even when repeatedly given the opportunity, they would not take a box from one room and bring it with them into the room where they could use it functionally, because this involved a short delay between the opportunity to obtain the tool and use it. Kohler found this example, along with many other observations, as ample evidence against chimpanzees' ability to hold an abstract concept in mind for a significant time frame. A functional property is not high-level abstraction. Chimpanzees are the closest genetic relatives of human beings, and if they are such a large step away from reflective consciousness it may be a good indication of how far away the rest of the animal kingdom is.

Animal communication is a field well suited to the search for a behavior indicative of reflective consciousness. If an animal could consciously represent an abstract concept well enough to communicate this concept to other animals, then this would be the kind of reflective consciousness required for suffering. In fact, there are claims that vervet monkeys do something quite like this. Vervets have three distinctive alarm calls: one for hawks, one for leopards, and one for snakes. The first observations of these monkeys assumed that these alarm calls were representing the predators in an abstract manner of arbitrary sounds.[4] However, other observations reveal that these vervet monkeys have made leopard calls in response to the sight of a snake eating one of their fellow monkeys. This type of evidence indicates that the vervet calls may in fact be related to degree of danger rather than serving as specific abstract references to particular predators. And this explanation suggests an internal mediator utilizing emotional response—possibly degree of fear—rather than symbolic abstraction.

The examples of primate tool use and communication are widely considered some of the best candidates for high level thought among nonhumans. These are quite impressive abilities and, taken along with other data from the field, demonstrate that in some ways we have not departed too far from our animal relatives. Viewed beside the human capacity for reflective thought and abstraction, however, these abilities are dwarfed. Human cognition is responsible for the existence of moral codes, and moral codes are responsible for the protection of humans against pain that our cognitive capacity can magnify into suffering. The fact that many people would like to protect our animal relatives from pain demonstrates that these people have healthy levels of empathy, but their concern is also misguided. Efforts to improve the lives of animals should not consider it a moral issue or pursue legal action to achieve their goals. Nature has already protected animals against the cruelty of suffering by keeping them blissfully ignorant of the abstract world of reflective thought where suffering can exist.

Notes

1. The exception to this is suicide, which, somewhat ironically, U.S. law prohibits.
2. A knowledge domain can be loosely defined as a set of knowledge that is categorically similar in a cognitively significant way. For example, things relating to number and quantification could be a knowledge domain, or things related to the distinction between alive and dead.
3. Sometimes this class of explanation needs to be paired with evidence of conditioning or other learning.
4. By arbitrary, it is meant that the actual acoustics of the calls do not bear any significant relationship to the predators—for example, they do not mimic noises made by the predators.

References

Dowling, J. (2001). *Neurons and networks: An introduction to behavioral neuroscience.* Cambridge, Harvard University Press.

Griffin, D. R. (2001). *Animal minds: Beyond cognition to consciousness.* Chicago, University of Chicago Press.

Hauser, M. D. (2000). *Wild minds: What animals really think.* New York, Henry Holt.

Köhler, W., and E. Winter (1925). *The mentality of apes.* New York, Harcourt, Brace & Company.

Evolved Aspects of Morality Determine Legal Rights of Animals

Lewis Petrinovich

THESE THREE EXCELLENT ESSAYS are representative of the range of arguments regarding the reasons to extend rights to animals. The pro argument by Robbie Silverman is that there is no clear dividing line between the cognitive abilities of humans and other animals. This position leads to the conclusion that "People cannot continue to treat animals as property, to use them solely to satiate their own appetites for meat, money, or pleasure, without considering the interests of the animals themselves." This essay sets the rights bar quite low: rights should be extended to all animals that have consciousness. Consciousness is indicated by any animal that "seems to possess perceptual consciousness, the ability to be aware of things that are around them." Consciousness is extended to insects (ants and honeybees are mentioned), and it is stated that "we must change our laws and our societal institutions to serve their needs and respect their rights." Accepting this criterion to justify rights is so broad that all animals that have biological systems to warn them of harmful conditions (and all do), would qualify. It is intuitively difficult to accept the proposition that construing rights so broadly will enable us to formulate adequate guidelines regarding the permissible treatment of animals. It is difficult to accept the proposition that insects should be accorded the same rights as humans.

The con argument by Justin Jungé rejects using the criterion of the ability to experience pain and suffering as sufficient to extend rights to an organism. The sufficient criterion is argued to be the possession of reflective consciousness, which makes it possible to magnify the possibility of pain into suffering. If animals lack the cognitive tools to reflect on the possibility of pain, "human law should not concern itself with protecting animals from pain—their unreflective minds already protect them completely from the possibility of suffering." This view excludes most animals from the realm of rights because "Nature has already protected animals against the cruelty of suffering by keeping them blissfully ignorant of the abstract world of reflective thought where suffering can exist." Possessing a high level of cognition is argued to make moral codes possible and necessary in order to protect humans against such suffering. It is concluded that, although some primates demonstrate high levels of cognitive abilities, they do not meet the stringent criterion required for reflective consciousness.

Fiery Cushman argues that some nonhuman primates qualify for rights. Although all animals can suffer pain, the position is taken that only our "closest relatives" (nonhuman primates) can reflect on their own experience of pain, and that this level of mental ability is relevant to the debate on animal welfare. Cushman argues that moral rights should only be granted to those organisms who can experience violations as morally wrong, and that some primates meet this stringent criterion.

An Evolutionary Perspective

The concept of rights is central to the arguments presented in these three essays. I suggest that the concept of rights should be dispensed with, and the issues more profitably viewed from an evolutionary perspective. As I discussed in my book, *Darwinian Dominion* (1999), there is an intuitive appeal to the idea that individuals of many species have moral rights that should be respected. An important consideration is how such moral rights should be grounded, and I argue that there can be an evolutionarily mandated biological grounding that will make the whole idea of rights superfluous.

When considering the human condition, a large number of positive rights have been suggested, ranging from those involving basic aspects of existence (needs) to ones that reflect more particular desires and interests. Among the positive rights that can be grounded on needs are those to life, to reproduce, to die with dignity, to privacy, to freedom, to respect, to control one's own body, to housing, and to freedom of expression. Several negative rights have also been suggested, including freedom from hunger, harm, torture, imprisonment, execution, and suffering. If these rights are considered to be natural rights, they should be grounded in terms of basic biological existence in order to raise the claims above the level of platitudes that lack substance, mainly being aimed to excite a sympathetic emotional response.

Most will agree that the basic needs necessary to sustain the existence of organisms should be met, and that this basic level should be extended to animals. These needs can be specified objectively, can be applied to most objects, and can exist without any cognitive component. In this sense, *need* refers to objective states of being, and its existence can be determined through analysis of an organism (or machine) as a machine, looking at the way the system is built, how it operates, and how it is powered. This means that all animals should be allowed to eat, drink, have opportunities to breed, and afforded freedom of movement. Social animals should be allowed to interact with conspecifics and have environmental supports for social interaction. Although in an ideal world there might be no pain, suffering, or deprivations, within the natural ecology such conditions do exist: animals (conspecific and allospecific) harm one another, and animals are prevented from gaining access to food, water, and shelter due to inter- and intra-specific competition. Therefore, the situation is much more complicated than it might appear from a cursory reliance to let natural conditions prevail.

A step beyond merely respecting an animal's needs should be taken to ground moral rights in a manner that respects another level of biological reality. This step involves evolved patterns of interaction that initiate a social bond that admits a neonate as an individuated member of its species. This social bond provides the organism with the status of *personhood* as a member of its species community. It does not depend on the level of neonatal rationality (for neonates of most species undoubtedly have little) but on the emotionally based social bond that develops between the neonate and its community. With many species, and particularly humans, there is an extended period during which the neonate requires intensive care following birth. This period of care sets into motion evolved emotional actions and reactions based on a set of evolved behavioral processes that enhance the likelihood the neonate will survive. Such survival is necessary if the neonate is ultimately to contribute to the reproductive success of the parents—the payoff in the evolutionary lottery.

The moral standing conferred by personhood entitles the neonate to have its welfare protected, and, for social species, confers duties and responsibilities on parents and other members of the social community. The primary caregiver is the mother, with the father and immediate kin having a biological as well as social investment, as does the community at large. The environment of evolutionary adaptation would have been composed of small, biologically organized communities, and the members of each would have had a genetic relationship that would produce an investment to enhance the likelihood the neonate would survive.

These social bonds have an emotional base, leading both neonate and caregivers to emit appropriate signals and engage in behaviors that will lead conspecifics to respond in ways that might be conducive to survival. They do not depend on the rational state of the infant, and impose duties on all within the community. These community members are moral agents, and should accept caretaking responsibilities. These social bonds reflect an evolved nature that develops in the normal course of existence, certainly for many bird species, probably for all mammalian species, and certainly for the human species.

Concentrating on humans, this view emphasizes the family as a universal human institution. Through the process of natural selection, individuals are produced who are not simply tuned to be skilled at reproduction, but also to be skilled at parenting—although some turn out not to be skilled at either. Kinship ties are the essence of a family, and they establish child-care obligations. This schema emphasizes the importance of strong evolved sensory, perceptual, and motor systems that extend moral standing to impaired human neonates as well as to those who turn out to be normal, and confers the status of personhood that is unique to the species—the neonate is one of us.

At this stage, an infant has the standing of a moral patient, a standing that also can be enjoyed by animals; but the human infant displays uniquely human emotional responses to members of the human community and these displays evoke the attribution of emotional capacities to the neonate, setting it apart from beings of other species that are entitled to welfare respect. This special human standing is due, not to the infant's potential, but is based on the evolved social dynamics among humans.

The conception of an emotional bond that establishes the initial social contract does not depend on mere sentimentality, but represents a biologically evolved social contract that enhances the ultimate evolutionary payoff—the increase in inclusive fitness that represents the currency of reproductive success in evolutionary systems. These evolved dispositions can be considered to be spontaneous pre-moral tendencies, and they exist within many nonhuman species as well. They are fostered genetically, serve to resolve problems of survival, mimic the appearance of calculation and purposiveness, and if internalized, will become adapted normative conventions in behavior.

The unfolding of the social program enhances cooperation, reciprocation, and supports legal norms that secure biological needs. This evolutionary argument is based on well-understood and generally accepted biological principles involved in the evolution of all sexually reproducing organisms.

Although it is relatively easy to identify needs, it is more difficult when the levels of desires and interests are involved because these imply the existence of mental components that cannot be observed directly, but must be inferred from behavior and its outcomes. Differences of opinion regarding the relative importance of different rights based on desires and interests cause major conflicts between people who champion different sets of rights to be primary. In many cases it is not possible for opposing parties to reach agreement because so many different rights based on desires and interests have been offered as stipulated primitives. Although it is difficult to specify the nature of basic desires and interests, behavioral scientists (Dawkins 1990) have contributed greatly to our understanding of many factors that influence the physical and psychological well-being of laboratory and zoo animals. They have characterized aspects that are essential to the welfare of animals, both in natural and confined circumstances. The intent of these investigators is to use knowledge regarding species-specific behaviors to design living spaces and guide experimental designs that will provide understanding of the particular species, as well as to support broad generalizations across species. It is doubtful that the concept of rights can provide a useful foundation for the moral realm, and I believe it should be restricted to legal structures that are mapped onto the evolved moral foundation.

Speciesism, Racism, and Sexism

My argument is avowedly speciesist and anthropocentric, in the sense that human agents have characteristics that contribute a unique moral standing, with attendant duties and responsibilities toward all moral agents and patients. Speciesism is based on a reasonable biological imperative that enhances the survival of individual young, which enhances the likelihood of the community's continuation. The species unit is basic to evolutionary change. Species come and go, they breed with other members of their species, they only rarely breed with members of other species, and if they do, seldom are viable and fecund hybrid offspring produced. The concept of a species is basic to biology because it focuses on actions of interbreeding individuals sharing characteristics that permit them to adapt to demands of the environment in which they find themselves. These demands direct the development of species characteristics that can be quite different from those possessed by other breeding populations, and the geographic separation of two breeding populations of a species is one important path leading those separated populations to become species. Behavioral tendencies evolve that enhance the likelihood offspring will survive, and themselves be able to reproduce and continue the parents' lineage. The biologically crucial unit of the reproducing species embodies qualities that carry considerable moral relevance as well—these involve tendencies to favor members of one's own species, family members, kin, neighbors, and community members.

Animal-activist philosophers, such as Peter Singer (1975) and Tom Regan (1983), argue that speciesism is based on the same prejudices as sexism and racism, a point I have disputed at length (Petrinovich 1999). Racism is impermissible, and most agree that human slavery is based on an inadmissible use of the race of humans to justify the institution. If speciesism is considered to be the same as racism, then enslaving animals as pets, guides, or companions cannot be justified unless it is admitted that there *is* a critical difference which is based on the fact that they are not of the human species—in short, speciesism. I cannot accept the proposition that the permissibility of keeping a pet dog or cat belongs on the same dimension as human slavery. There is a moral discontinuity between pet owning and human slavery. I suggest the analogy between racism and speciesism is not valid because biologically ordained moral considerations are being introduced—and they *do* make a difference. The tired charge of speciesism should be dropped, with attention devoted to exploring why there is a stronger moral imperative against enslaving humans than nonhumans—against eating humans than nonhumans (Petrinovich 2000).

Humans have kept other humans as slaves, and also keep pets. However, human slaves generally were treated in a different manner from animals, and laws reflected that difference. In general, it is permissible to eat animal moral patients (at least those that are not common house pets), but not human patients. As I noted in *Darwinian Dominion* (Petrinovich 1999), if a cult defended the practice of cannibalism on the grounds that they restricted their practice to neonate humans, even the most dedicated carnivores among us would be unimpressed with that justification, and no doubt the strongest legal action would be taken against those individuals.

When considering pets the situation is different than for other animals; when an animal is accepted as a pet, the owner (or companion, if you wish) assumes a special set of social contractual duties and responsibilities to maintain a pet's welfare, which accords the pet a special moral status. Although pets are accorded a special status, no one would argue that they should be allowed to engage in many of their natural behaviors, such as a dog urinating on handy upright objects and rolling in excrement. Dogs are subjected to housebreaking, a procedure that could well be considered to be cruel to the dog, forcing it to behave in an unnatural fashion for the rest of its life. On the other hand, most well-fed, well-cared-for, and housebroken dogs give no indication of wanting to escape the family home. When some presumably well-treated human slaves were given the opportunity to leave their masters after the Civil War, they did not accept the opportunity. I don't believe many would argue that pet owners should be required to give a similar opportunity to their pets to leave if they so desired.

Another question concerns whether sexism and speciesism rest on the same prejudicial base. There are many differences between male and female humans; the distribution of physiological and mental characteristics for the two sexes reveals high overlap (except for matters most intimately related to reproduction). The proper test is to allow all individuals an equal opportunity to compete, and it is likely that many females would be able to achieve at a higher level than most males in a large number of endeavors in which they are not permitted to compete, and that some would perform as well as most successful males.

Not to be judged on the basis of ability is clearly an instance of sexism, but this is not analogous to the comparisons made across species. Each species has a unique emotional attachment to those of its own kind, and there is little overlap in those critical aspects of emotional bonding that establish the personhood that determines moral standing in the human community. It can be argued that in terms of language and cognitive abilities, no species overlaps any normal human distribution (with the possible exception of some of the Great Apes—although I consider the case not to be strong).

It should be determined whether there is *any* overlap between humans and other animals in those characteristics that are accepted to justify full moral standing. In short, it is necessary to agree on criteria, to agree on methods of evaluation and classification, and to make the required observations.

Singer (1979) argued that if humans have special relations with marginal beings—human and nonhuman moral patients—favored relations must be justified on grounds other than affectionate regard; morality should not be tied too closely to our affections. To the contrary, I suggest these affections represent an evolved tendency that supports emotional bonding in the service of differential reproductive success, that they are an essential part of those biological predispositions promoting a cohesive community, and that this affectionate basis is highly relevant to morality—conferring the status of human moral patient on neonates and the cognitively disabled. When matters are cast in terms of evolutionary biology, we can meet the test that those humans influenced by our actions have a moral claim that is not grounded on sentimentality, but on a respect for basic aspects of the human social contract.

With human personhood there is a moral standing that does not entail the duties of moral agency, but which confers a higher moral standing than enjoyed by moral patients of other species. This greater standing is a function of reproductive interactions that produced the offspring, and of the reproductive investment the offspring represents.

I argue for two distinct classes of moral patients: human and nonhuman. The former class includes such individuals as the human mental defective, the senile, and the very young child; the latter, all nonhuman animals. Both classes are entitled to have their welfare protected, but neither can be expected to understand right and wrong. (On this point I differ from the conclusions of Cushman in his contribution to this volume).

It is evolutionarily sound to expect that, in many instances, animals (including humans) would be more sensitive to covenants respecting members of their own species than they would those involving members of other species. It usually is considered natural and reasonable for humans to favor members of the human species, kin, and community when moral decisions are to be made. The same is true for many social, sexually reproducing species, such as squirrels and many birds.

This schema emphasizes the importance of strong biological tendencies, extends moral standing to impaired neonates as well as to those who will become normal adults, and confers a status of personhood that is unique to the human animal—the human neonate is recognizably one of us. While we should show respect for a newborn puppy or kitten, and be concerned with its welfare, that concern has a different emotional base and tone from that enjoyed by the human neonate as a result of the processes of emotional bonding that occur immediately between the mother and neonate.

A member of any species may legitimately give members of its own species more weight than it gives members of other species. If lions were moral agents, they could not be criticized for putting other lions first. In fact, we do not condemn animals for killing animals of their own or other species—ascribing this to their animal nature. However, when an animal kills a human, it is usually considered justifiable to kill the animal, presumably to deter further killing of humans by that animal, but most likely in retribution. It is evolutionarily sound to expect that in many instances, animals (including humans) would be more sensitive to covenants respecting members of their own species than they would to those that involve members of other species.

Many animals can be assumed to have awareness and interests, and for this reason are due respect and are able to suffer, and some may be subjects-of-a-biographical-life. Silverman presents a host of relevant evidence for these cognitive capacities in his essay. There is no doubt these animals have a moral standing as patients, and this standing requires moral agents to at least respect their welfare.

The final stage in moral development takes place when the individual moves from the status of a moral patient to that of a moral agent with full moral standing that confers freedoms and duties: freedom from harm and freedom of welfare and respect, and duties and responsibilities to extend those freedoms to others. This stage of agency is based on rational and cognitive criteria that make it possible to have the sense of a continuing autobiographical self, an ability to understand rules, causation, and intentionality, and to reason. Nonhuman animal species should be evaluated by the same criteria as those used to establish moral agency for humans. All members of a given species should be considered individually in order to determine whether there are crucial differences—and I argue that the biologically mandated human social contract is one such difference. This social contract is based on a universal set of features shared by neonate and caregivers, and on the dance of actions and reactions.

One could ask whether an individual animal, say a chimpanzee raised with humans and coached to communicate at a level that cognitively qualifies it as a moral agent, should have the same moral agency as a human. I believe that this chimp should be accorded the status of a chimp moral agent, allowing it the rights and privileges of a human moral agent. It should be emphasized, however, that aspects crucial to human social bonding would be lacking, and that the entire scenario requires a unique (human) environmental structure that normal chimps would lack. Therefore, the status of moral agent would apply to this one chimp only, and not to the entire species, and I wonder if the chimp would be liable to all the legal sanctions applied to humans.

A central problem is how to assess the relative utilitarian value of certain practices and outcomes. Moral theories must deal with the problem of determining the relative strength and importance of different, often incommensurable values—especially when a decision must be made regarding the relative strength of the same value for different individuals, or different values for the same or different individuals. The status of moral agency involves high levels of cognition, and I believe that the notion of rights should remain at the legal level, and if construed properly would be adequate to protect the interests of animals.

Legal Status of Animals

At the legal level, animals are considered to be the personal property of their owners. This view denies animals any rights that stand against human owners, and legal regulations regarding animals generally facilitate the most efficient exploitation by the owner. Laws regulating the use of animals prevent the waste of animal property by actions that kill them or cause suffering when it is against a legitimate economic purpose (Francione 1995). Viewed in this way, the legal test for cruelty to animals is not based on the actions themselves, but on whether they result in some human benefit, and are actions that use commonly accepted treatments.

Francione argued that our legal treatment of animals is goal-based on two levels: one is to provide maximum benefits to people from animal exploitation, and the second is to seek humane treatment of animals and protect them from unnecessary suffering. There are serious problems involved in reaching agreement regarding the meaning and limits of the terms "humane" and "unnecessary."

Tannenbaum (1995) believes that American law dealing with animals is sensible and serviceable. He considers animals not to be just another kind of personal property, but to be a "seminal kind of personal property." He noted that they represent the first items of personal property common people possessed throughout history, and they were among the earliest subjects of litigation. The early legal status of animals was as property without interests; one could harm one's own animals, but not those belonging to someone else; the harm was considered to be done to the owner rather than the animal.

A second construal of property invokes the concept of cruelty. Cruelty statutes forbid the affliction of unnecessary or unjustifiable pain, distress, or discomfort upon an animal. It is illegal to fail to provide one's dog or cat with sufficient food or water, or leave it outside in the cold or in a hot automobile on a summer day. However, it is permissible to not play with a pet or to not make it happy. In Tannenbaum's view this interpretation protects animals, and creates legal duties regarding them—affording adequate legal rights for animals and protecting their interests. Tannenbaum argues that this possession of legal rights by animals does not confer legal standing, and recommends that cruelty laws be amended so that the most serious kinds of animal abuse and neglect would be felonies. This second view still considers animals to be property, but insists they should be treated fairly as moral patients. I believe the notion of rights should remain at this second legal level, and that such a conception is adequate to protect the interests of animals.

Conclusions

Kinship obligations are strong because they are part of evolved human nature. We favor the interests of our species over the welfare of animals of other species for the same reasons we favor those of our own kin and members of our community. The norm of reciprocity is universal and reasonable, especially among humans who can reason and communicate with such facility.

The evolutionary perspective involves what I have dubbed a liberal utilitarianism. The interests and welfare of innocent human moral agents override those of innocent human or nonhuman moral patients, other things being equal. Empirical studies of moral dilemmas (Petrinovich, O'Neill, et al. 1993) support the reasonableness of the evolutionary argument, with species and fitness always emerging as the major factors influencing people's resolution of moral dilemmas. To sustain the privileges that moral agency confers, it is necessary to accept the duties and responsibilities owed moral patients in order to avoid compromising the patients' status of innocence.

Adopting a scheme of morality based on principles of evolutionary development makes it possible to avoid quarrels regarding at what place in the phylogenetic scale a dividing line should be drawn to separate those with rights from those without. All living things deserve respect for their welfare, but the welfare of some will override that of others whenever welfare choices must be made. In the moral realm there are justified biological realities that make it understandable why humans extend more consideration to other humans; the legal realm should reflect and respect those realities. All of the above supports the argument that animal welfare should receive strong consideration and be protected in our pursuit of human interests.

References

Dawkins, M. (1990). "From an animal's point of view: Motivation, fitness and animal welfare." *Behavioral and Brain Sciences* 12: 1–9.

Francione, G. L. (1995). *Animals, property, and the law.* Philadelphia, Temple University Press.

Petrinovich, L. (1999). *Darwinian dominion*. Cambridge, MIT Press.

Petrinovich, L., P. O'Neill, et al. (1993). "An empirical study of moral intuitions: Toward an evolutionary ethics." *Journal of Personality and Social Psychology* 64: 467–478.

Petrinovich, L. F. (2000). *The cannibal within.* New York, Aldine de Gruyter.

Regan, T. (1983). *The case for animal rights.* Berkeley, University of California Press.

Singer, P. (1975). *Animal liberation: A new ethics for our treatment of animals.* New York, New York Review of Books: Distributed by Random House.

Singer, P. (1979). *Practical ethics.* Cambridge, Cambridge University Press.

Tannenbaum, J. (1995). "Animals and the law: Cruelty, property, right . . . Or how the law makes up in common sense what it may lack in metaphysics." *Social Research* 62(3).

Section 4—Biomedical Research

THIS SECTION ADDRESSES a particularly real consequence of the proposal at hand. The prospect of increasing the legal status of animals out of the realm of property threatens to upset, if not entirely eliminate, the use of animals in biomedical research. The essays in this chapter outline the existing controversy in the biomedical industry over the use of animal subjects.

As the essays in this section explain, this debate typically has three major fronts. Perhaps the most common dispute over the use of animals in biomedical research involves a tricky cost/benefit analysis between the cost of animal life and the benefit to humans of medical advances. Another aspect of this controversy maintains that, independent of costs and benefits, animals possess certain rights that should unconditionally protect them from use in laboratory experiments. Yet another position holds that that there can be no cost/benefit analysis because biomedical research involving animals is purely useless.

Despite the ultimate conclusions of each author, the fundamental principles to which they appeal are largely the same. Andrew Rowan, a professor of veterinary medicine and animal rights and a vice president of the Humane Society of the United States, proposes that the important question is not whether we should or should not use animals in biomedical research, but the extent to which we should work to eliminate the harm caused animals in biomedical research. Most of the student essays concede that in its ideal form, where the benefit to human life is tremendous, the use of animals in laboratory research is warranted. Similarly, none of the authors deny that there is ample room for improvement in current biomedical research practices. Finally, most authors acknowledge that the debate over biomedical research is further complicated by the possibilities for the future. With new and improved biomedical technology on the horizon, the issues over animal testing are sure to change drastically, if not become entirely moot. On the other hand, with advances in fields like genetics, the issues of animal testing may become even more relevant.

A Critical Review of Animal Experimentation

Moral and Practical Problems, Alternatives and Necessary Changes

Frances Chen

EXACT TOTALS HAVE NEVER BEEN TALLIED, but the best estimates indicate that 20–35 million vertebrate animals are used each year in the United States for research, testing, and teaching purposes.[1] Figures so staggeringly large are difficult to grasp, but the estimate is comparable to something between the entire human population of the state of New York (19 million), and of California (34.5 million). Animal experimentation gained a foothold in Western medicine centuries ago, when medical knowledge was relatively shallow and religious tenets prohibited research on human cadavers (Greek and Greek 2000). Although the large majority of advances in medical knowledge have since been made through human studies, animal experimentation continues, propelled by the inertia of a medical establishment unwilling to uproot conventional yet clearly flawed practices in favor of better but unfamiliar ones, by dependable funding from poorly informed government programs and agencies, and by the pressures of an even less well-informed public opinion (Greek and Greek 2000).

Inertia, however, is a sadly inadequate justification for the dismal fates of so many millions of animals. When the moral and practical aspects of animal experimentation are carefully examined, it becomes clear that the exploitation of other species for the purposes of our own species is unethical, and that animal research is superfluous even when properly employed and dangerous when not. Furthermore, our society's dependence on interventional, rather than preventative, medical practices is misguided. Our efforts and funds must be redirected from the abuse of other species to the development of alternative research techniques and a more holistic approach to medicine in general. The removal of animals from the status of property will be a crucial step in this process, jump-starting a paradigmatic shift and, ultimately, increasing the health and welfare of all species, including our own.

Moral issues

Despite important advances in the treatment of laboratory animals, shockingly cruel practices in biomedical research and product testing still endure. Physiologist and animal researcher Barbara Orlans (1993) describes a few infamous examples, including the Draize test, in which possibly irritant or toxic substances are dripped into the eyes of conscious rabbits. The rabbits are restrained, often with only their head protruding from a holding device, to prevent them from touching or scratching their inflamed eyes. The eyes are then observed over a period of many days for signs of tissue damage; the damage is then given a rating to indicate the irritancy potential of the substance.

Orlans's description of the LD50 (median lethal dose) test is particularly horrifying:

> To conduct this test, various doses of a drug or other substance are administered to groups of animals to determine the lethal dose at which half the number of animals die. . . . Reports from the past show that LD50s were determined for substances like paper, lipstick, and distilled water. The animals were virtually blown up with excessive volumes forced down tubes into the stomach. . . . The deaths are often protracted, taking days, weeks, or even months. During this time, the animals may exhibit typical symptoms of poisoning such as vomiting, diarrhea, paralysis, convulsions, and internal bleeding. Since death is the required endpoint, dying animals are not put out of their misery by euthanasia. (Orlans 1993)

Even the less unfortunate animals that escape experiments involving physical pain and death frequently suffer extreme psychological or emotional stress, even beyond the context of the experiment. Naturally social animals are kept isolated in bare metal cages, ostensibly for the purposes of sterility and uniformity of living conditions. Deprived of social contact and mental enrichment, these animals often become depressed or insane (Goodall 1989).

How can we determine whether this is a morally acceptable way to treat animals? Some argue that the ascent of our species to the top of the food chain gives us the right to use animals as we see fit, but this is a frighteningly amoral foundation upon which to base our treatment of those less powerful than we. How we *should* act constitutes a limited subset of how we *can* act, and the purpose of a moral system is to delineate the "should," not to default to the "can."

One traditional consideration is pain, a universal and primary concern in our species. Although we are often insensitive to animal pain because animals are unable to communicate it as unambiguously as humans can through language, animals respond to stimuli we would find painful with some of the same physiological hallmarks of pain: increased heart rate, sweating, and release of stress hormones. The most explicit response, however, is also the most persuasive—the overwhelming behavioral urge to avoid the source of pain.

Pain, so universally experienced, is a paramount consideration in the moral calculations of many philosophers. The eighteenth-century philosopher and jurist Jeremy Bentham, for instance, argued that all behavior is based on seeking pleasure and avoiding pain, and thus the only objective way to measure the morality of an action—its "goodness" or "evil"—is by the resultant amount of pleasure or pain. "Pleasure," he wrote, "is in itself a good: nay, . . . the only good: pain is in itself an evil; and, indeed, without exception, the only evil; or else the words good and evil have no meaning" (Bentham, Burns, et al. 1996). If pleasure and pain are the currency of morality, then animals, with their clear ability to experience pain, must be included within our moral calculations.

Others suggest, however, that the intelligence, consciousness, or other cognitive characteristics of our species increase our capacity to suffer relative to other animals, thus justifying the infliction of pain on animals if it will result in the reduced suffering of humans. Under closer examination, this view is morally untenable, for it is founded on categorical assumptions about individual members of a species based solely on their species membership. Such "speciesism," as this type of discrimination has been called (Ryder 1991), is driven by a powerful human propensity to group individuals by superficial or even arbitrary characteristics—the same propensity which causes racism. No logical argument, however, can support the emotional biases which cause either racism or speciesism. Generalizations about the group or species to which an individual belongs may or may not be true for that particular individual; discrimination based merely upon the group membership of that individual is illogically and ethically indefensible.

The assumption that every member of the human species has some cognitive capacity which distinguishes it from any other species is an absolute fiction. Undoubtedly, certain individual members of our own species—often referred to as "marginal cases"—do not meet any of the criteria that have been suggested to separate our species from others in a morally relevant way. To cite an extreme example, imagine a severely mentally-retarded or brain-dead human with no potential for recovery. If we maintain the position that intelligence or consciousness is the metric by which we justify testing or the infliction of suffering, we must logically consider these humans more morally appropriate subjects for experimentation than some chimpanzees and gorillas (Frey 2002).

Persistent debaters might resist such a disturbing conclusion, arguing that the suffering of these human individuals' relatives and loved ones would still make it unethical to experiment upon them. But can this argument be supported consistently? Are we willing to subject an unwanted orphan to torture simply if he or she has a reduced capacity to suffer and no friends and family who will suffer either? If we hesitate to experiment on humans with limited cognitive capacities, we must also rethink our willingness to experiment upon individual animals who can be distinguished from these humans only by the label of their species membership and not by any cognitive characteristic.

Even if every individual human were more intelligent or conscious than every nonhuman animal, that fact alone still would not automatically grant us rights over other species. We imbue our prized intellect and consciousness with special relevance in our moral calculations, but is this an objectively valid assessment of morally relevant criteria, or just a manner of justifying our actions to ourselves? As Benjamin Franklin mused ironically in his *Autobiography*, "so convenient a thing it is to be a reasonable creature, since it enables one to find or make a reason for everything one has a mind to do." If one wanted to argue for the superiority of dolphins over humans, supporting evidence might easily be found in their highly-developed ability to form abstract mental representations through echolocation—a sensory-cognitive ability endowed by biology which humans simply lack. Each species has characteristics that make it "special" or "superior," and it is extremely difficult to dissociate oneself from the biases of one's own species membership to determine *a priori* which characteristics should be considered relevant to the morality of testing or inflicting suffering on any species.

To underscore the unwarranted arrogance of the human position, psychologist Richard Ryder (1991) provides a thought experiment in which the tables are turned upon humans:

> If some creatures from outer space invaded Earth and proved to be stronger or vastly more intelligent than ourselves, would they be justified in ordering us to be vivisected? They might explain to us that, after all . . . they would keep us in perfectly clean and hygienic cages and that they naturally regretted having to perform severe experiments upon us but that it was, unfortunately, necessary for the benefit of their own species. (Ryder 1991)

If we would protest such treatment by another species, only moral hypocrisy can account for our own such use—justified in terms of abstract criteria like "intelligence" and "consciousness"—of other species with the capacity to suffer.

Practical Arguments

More pragmatic individuals have claimed that the issue of experimentation is really not a question of morals at all, but rather one of necessity. All moral argumentation, they say, becomes irrelevant in consideration of the "need" for animal experimentation for the further advancement of science and health. Yet, the claim that animal experimentation is a necessity is hardly a foregone conclusion. While scientists and researchers who work with animals are quick to list advancements supposedly developed with the aid of animal research, they do not report the far more numerous cases in which animal research has failed to produce beneficial results. In fact, a careful review of the medical advancements commonly attributed to animal testing reveals that nearly all of the critical initial discoveries and observations occurred with human subjects. Animal testing is more often used as a means of confirming hypotheses based on human studies and observations; animal testing itself has provided few substantive discoveries (Greek and Greek 2000).

In a speech a few years ago, Christine Stevens, president of the Animal Welfare Institute, informed the House Subcommittee on Labor, Health, and Human Services that 400,000 chemicals had been screened on mice in the past thirty years. Although some drugs were found which were effective against leukemia and lung tumors in mice, these successes had never carried over to humans. Stevens concluded that "chemical trials with human lung cancer victims have been disappointing . . . the 'war against cancer' has been . . . an expensive failure based on the excessive reliance which has been placed on animal experiments and tests" (quoted in Kaufman 1989).

Furthermore, as Ryder (1991) has pointed out, "to attempt to justify the *certain* suffering of animals against some future, as yet *uncertain* benefit, seems to be an unwarranted gamble." We will also never know if these same advances could have been made with other techniques—techniques that we have failed to develop due to our single-minded dependence on animal research.

It is no mystery why animal experimentation has been so ineffectual; animal physiology differs from human physiology in fundamental yet often unpredictable ways, and hence animals respond differently than humans to many drugs and treatments tested on them. Consequently, effective treatments for humans may be overlooked because of their ineffectiveness in animal tests, and seemingly effective drugs may be completely ineffective or even harmful to humans. Significant side effects, such as headache and nausea, are often not readily observable in animals (Kaufman 1989). As if these differences were not enough, the gap between humans and animals is widened by the highly unnatural conditions of isolation, stress, and lack of exercise under which animals are kept. These conditions alter animals' behavior and physiology to such a degree that extrapolation to healthy humans becomes even more inappropriate (Fox 1990).

The case of thalidomide serves as a cautionary tale against relying on animal models to test drugs for human use. Thalidomide, a drug which had been tested on rodents, was prescribed in the early 1960s to pregnant women to relieve morning sickness. In 1960, many of these women gave birth to children with digestive tract abnormalities and incomplete or missing limbs (Monamy 2000). Thalidomide immediately underwent intensive testing on pregnant animals of many species, but it was not until 1962 that birth defects comparable to those noted in humans were found in laboratory animals (Monamy 2000). Then-unknown differences between species in gestation timing masked the results of many experiments—even those experiments specifically designed to produce malformed young. There will always be unknown differences between species; thus, it will always be impossible to certify the effectiveness and safety of drugs and treatments tested solely on animals. Michael Fox, senior scholar of bioethics at the Humane Society of the United States, has even asserted that "animal safety tests amount to little more than a public relations campaign to dispel public concern and, at best, give a false sense of security" (Fox 1990).

The Draize and the LD50 tests, apart from being morally repugnant, are also scientifically and practically flawed. Results even within a single species vary depending upon the weights, ages, and sexes of the subjects; extrapolation between species is even less reliable (Kaufman 1989). The LD50 test has been condemned for repeated examples of its lack of reproducibility: among different labs which used their own standard procedures, numerical values for LD50 tests of PCP ranged from 44 to 523 mg/kg, and for sodium salicylate from 4.150 to 800 mg/kg (Orlans 1993). Kaufman goes on to criticize the practical inapplicability of the LD50: "LD50 data cannot be applied to most human poisoning victims, because the quantity and even the type of substance(s) ingested are often unknown. Finally, in an emergency, one needs to know how much of a substance is dangerous and which organs are at risk, but the LD50 indicates only the meaningless statistic of how much is lethal to 50% of individuals" (Kaufman 1989).

Similar criticisms have been leveled against the Draize test. In addition to moral objections against the frivolous infliction of pain in order to test primarily nonessential cosmetic products such as eye makeup, the Draize test has been attacked as unreliable. When the Draize data for 14 household and cosmetic products were compared to accidental human eye exposures, the toxicity predicted by the Draize test differed from the actual toxicity to humans by factors of between 18 to 250 times (Kaufman 1989).

Alternatives and Changes

The continuation of these inhumane and ineffective techniques cannot be justified. Still, some have argued that animal research must continue because alternative methods have not been found for many procedures currently in use. Recent history has proven, however, that the finding of alternative methods depends on the *commitment* of researchers to the quest for alternative methods. Unfortunately, there is currently little incentive for animal researchers to devote themselves to finding alternative methods. On the contrary, the medical establishments that receive funding for animal research, and particularly those individuals who make their living through animal research, often have the greatest incentive to defend animal testing and maintain the popular perception that it is necessary. Until stricter laws protecting animals are implemented, we can hardly expect the established research traditions, and the myth that animal experimentation is necessary, to change.

A change in the legal status of animals would result in both the elimination of certain research techniques, and a push to find better alternatives in biomedical research and safety testing. Public pressure on firms to find and use alternatives to the Draize and LD50 tests, for instance, has resulted in the development of many alternative techniques which involve less suffering and are at least as effective as the original tests. Orlans (1993) describes several of these techniques. The CAM assay removes a small piece of shell from a chick egg without damaging the underlying membrane. No pain is perceived by this membrane because it lacks nerve cells, but it reacts to toxins with easily recognizable signs of inflammation. Testskin, which consists of skin cells grown on sheets and attached to a synthetic skeleton and circulatory system, has been used successfully by several major companies in safety tests of various chemicals. Moreover, physical tests are not always necessary, because toxicity can often be predicted from analyses of a substance's chemical structure and properties. Scientists have been able to save time and money by rejecting—before ever subjecting animals to painful tests—a number of novel chemicals, based on toxicity predictions generated by intricate computer models used in tandem with other tests (Orlans 1993).

On a more fundamental level, however, our society should rethink its overall outlook on medicine and health. Interventional techniques, as Fox (1990) has argued, are only superficial, temporary patches to a damaged system. Our society's misguided focus on short-term solutions is creating a dangerous dependence on "symptom-oriented medical treatments for human patients who would benefit more from preventive medical procedures" (Fox 1990). Most diseases are at least partially caused by environmental and lifestyle factors, and as Fox suggests, "if the environment and our food, air, and water were cleaned up, along with our dietary habits, food-processing procedures, and agricultural practices, there would be little need for dramatic organ transplants or life-saving open heart operations." The primary task of the medical establishment should be to take a more holistic approach to human health. If efforts were focused on finding more ways to prevent the occurrence of disease, the need for research to find cures and new interventional techniques for disease would decrease dramatically.

Conclusion

Not only is animal experimentation morally indefensible, it is also unnecessary for the advancement of science and medicine. Mistaken assumptions about it have been perpetuated by scientific tradition and the misconceptions of the public. By removing animals from the status of property and compelling the scientific community to develop new foundations for research and testing, we will finally be able to see the flaws in the current moral and practical arguments in favor of animal research.

Slavery was once considered to be a necessity, and thus moral arguments against it were given minimal consideration, completely disregarded, or even twisted in order to support the status quo. The speciesist arguments which attempt to justify the exploitation and suffering of animals are no more logical than the racist arguments which once justified the exploitation and suffering of slaves; furthermore, animal experimentation is no more a medical necessity than slavery was an economic one. Two centuries from now, our descendents may judge us for our stance on animal experimentation. Whether history remembers our age as passive followers of outdated traditions, or as progressive challengers of one of the primary moral issues of our time, is up to us.

Note

1. There is no national data on this, and estimates range from 17–70 million, but most sources, including Hendee, Fox, and Orlans, place the estimate somewhere between 20–35 million.

References

Bentham, J., J. H. Burns, et al. (1996). *An introduction to the principles of morals and legislation*. Oxford, Clarendon Press.

Fox, M. W. (1990). *Inhumane society: The American way of exploiting animals.* New York, St. Martin's Press.

Frey, R. G. (2002). "Ethics, animals, and scientific inquiry." In J. P. Gluck, T. DiPasquale, and F. B. Orlans (Eds.), *Applied ethics in animal research: Philosophy, regulation, and laboratory applications.* West Lafayette, Purdue University Press: 13–24.

Goodall, J. (1989). "Primate research is inhumane." In J. Rohr. (Ed.), *Animal rights: Opposing viewpoints*. San Diego, Greenhaven Press.

Greek, C. R., and J. S. Greek (2000). *Sacred cows and golden geese: The human cost of experiments on animals.* New York, Continuum.

Hendee, W., J. Loeb, et al. (1988). *Use of animals in biomedical research: The challenge and response.* Chicago, American Medical Association.

Kaufman, S. (1989). "Most animal experimentation does not benefit human health." In J. Rohr (Ed.), *Animal rights: Opposing viewpoints.* San Diego, Greenhaven Press.

Monamy, V. (2000). *Animal experimentation: A guide to the issues*. Cambridge, Cambridge University Press.

Orlans, F. B. (1993). *In the name of science: Issues in responsible animal experimentation.* New York, Oxford University Press.

Ryder, R. (1991). "Speciesism." In S. E. Rosenbaum (Ed.), *Animal experimentation: The moral issues.* Buffalo, Prometheus Books.

Why Animals Should Own Their Genes, and, Therefore, Own Themselves

Jonathan Flombaum

THIS ESSAY EXAMINES THE PRACTICE of knockout patenting as a case study in genetic ownership. Its goal is to demonstrate that a serious consideration of what owning genes or genetic information might mean in the future, both philosophically and practically, forces us to reconsider the practice of knockout patenting, in particular, as well as our regard for animals as property, in general. I conclude that animals are entities that should not be subject to ownership by humans in any form.

Before I begin this argument, however, I must make two important disclaimers. First, I will make a few claims about the broader implications of moving animals into the status of personhood. Despite the fact that ownership and property are inherently legal concepts, the arguments herein are fundamentally philosophical. I try to make the general case that animals should not be property, motivated by the specific implications of this status to "knockout" patenting. Can we eat animals? Can we experiment on them? Can we keep them in captivity? These questions, and many others, are related to how we categorize animals with respect to property, but it is not obvious, I think, exactly how. One example should make this point clear. If animals were no longer property, we might be inclined to think of them in a position similar to children. At the same time, I think, we may be inclined to believe that they could not be used for experiments of any sort. However, respectable labs, government funding, and loving parents readily submit infants to experiments with behavioral methods identical to those employed by some animal researchers. Perhaps, then, even were animals not considered property they could still be tested in behavioral experiments? Because I think that this issue and others do not have a clear resolution, I shall remain agnostic about them in this essay.

Disclaimer number two is that I am not making a moral argument in the traditional philosophical sense. The case I make in this paper is one that I personally believe to be true, though not exclusively for the reasons that I present. My own moral intuitions tell me that animals are not property, but I do not think that these intuitions should be convincing to others (just as I would hope that others not try to convince me on the basis of their moral convictions alone). In fact, I would like to say up front that the arguments in this paper are not really moral at all. The arguments that I make for what *ought* to be are not based upon a discovery that I claim to make of some determination of what *is*. Instead, they are based upon intuitions that I hope you and I will share about how we *want* things to be. In other words, to borrow a dichotomy characterized by Alan Dershowitz (2002) I aim not to discover that animals should not be considered property, but I invent this notion because I think it is of practical importance for me and like-minded people. I argue that declassifying animals as property is consistent with a general picture of the type of world that many people want.

It seems, then, that the place to start is by characterizing what it is that I think people want. I think that people want ownership of their genes, and with good reason. That is, I think that Americans would be uncomfortable if a piece of paper listing their genetic sequence rested in a government office somewhere. I think that they would be uncomfortable with these sequences being used to restrict their freedoms, for example, by imposing curfews upon people whose genetic sequence allegedly implies a tendency towards violent crimes. Moreover, I think that even the most capitalistic and free-market-oriented of Americans would hate the idea of a company being able to buy access to their sequence, or even a fraction of it, in order to better market products to them. Certainly, Americans would not tolerate the government or a company's right to keep a sample of somebody's DNA against his or her will, but I think that this discomfort extends even to pieces of paper that list nucleotide sequences. In short, DNA as a chemical structure is interesting because of the information that it represents. I believe that in the future people will want to secure the right to own and protect the actual DNA that they are built of, and the information, however abstractly represented, that it conveys.

Why do I think that these rights are and ought to be important to anyone who understands genetics? The first reason is somewhat more philosophical than practical, and it is one that evolutionary biologists have articulated for over 20 years, but has yet to fully enter into our modern theories of "personhood," "identity," and related notions. This is, simply put, that we *are* our genes. Richard Dawkins (1986) argues from the perspective of evolutionary biology that natural selection does not always act on the individual organism. Instead, he favors a "gene's eye perspective" of evolution. In these terms it is not clear to what extent we pass genes into the next generation, and to what extent we are just vehicles that our genes create for passing themselves along into the next generation. In other words, there is a real biological sense in which who we are is really who *our genes* are.

I am not claiming that this perspective on the level of evolutionary selection has legal implications, or that any particular evolutionary perspective may have other implications. I am merely arguing that considering the point that Dawkins (1986) makes with respect to evolution and genes, the lines between a full-grown organism and a genetic code are blurred. My phenomenal experience in this world tells me that who I am right now has a whole lot to do with who I am in my memories—a matter independent of genes. But, on the other hand, this conventional sense of self and identity is complicated by modern genetics and evolutionary theory. (Exactly how is a topic for extensive discussion by philosophers and biologists.) For the moment, however, perceiving the fact that there is a relationship between my sense of "self" and my genes makes me feel protective of those genes. Consider a simple thought experiment: A mad scientist has built a program that can make any robot behave exactly like you. Extensive tests confirm that the robot answers questions exactly how you do before the question is even asked of you. Your best friends cannot tell a difference between you and the robot on the phone, not only because it sounds like you, but also because it says what you would say. Do you feel comfortable with the scientist selling this program to a toy company planning on marketing "you" robots?

The second, more practical reason why we should like to retain ownership of our genes is that to allow state or corporate ownership of our "genes" could easily lead to violations of other rights that we value and have previously affirmed. It seems obvious that this type of genetic information is readily prone to abuse; for example, a company could know exactly what products I may not be able to resist,. If this sounds a bit like science fiction and not a bit like science, just consider the possibility of health insurance companies using an analysis of your actual genes to deny you health coverage. Consider, further, a company requiring "gene tests" that screen for markers associated with violence or laziness, and denying someone a job on such a basis. It seems obvious, at least to me, that avoiding these frightening scenarios requires securing legal control and ownership of this information about ourselves, whether it is represented on paper, in bits, or in a double helix.

That we will always have this control, however, is an assumption that I think we should realize will be challenged in the near future. Here is why: Long-dormant provisions of patent laws permitting the ownership of specific genotypes have been increasingly exploited as research into genetic modification has gather steam. Usually this occurs when a scientist develops what is known as a knockout mouse. This is a mouse that has been slightly altered genetically for two reasons: (1) to demonstrate the causal relationship between a genotype and a phenotype and (2) to be able to breed mice with phenotypes that one would like to study. It is important to be very clear about what one owns when one owns such a patent. The patents represent ownership of intellectual property. In the case of genetic engineering, they arise from the demonstration of a relationship between a genotype and a phenotype. Nobody wants a patent because they want to own this idea or discovery in an abstract sense; rather, they want such a patent because it means that no one can profit from this idea without paying them royalties. Thus, people cannot use or breed mice with a patented knockout because they are not allowed to benefit from someone else's discovery of how genotype leads to phenotype. One last point needs to be made about what can and cannot be patented. In most cases of patented genetic modifications, patents have been issued for gene-phenotype relationships that have been experimentally created and do not naturally occur. However, the potential exists to patent a naturally occurring phenotype. If I can demonstrate through knockout experiments a definite relationship between a genotype and a phenotype, even if the phenotype is rather common, I can patent that discovery. I would then have ownership over a naturally occurring phenotype (and genotype).

I think that it is important to declassify animals as property; otherwise, the day is not far away when human knockouts and gene sequences will be patentable as well. Imagine that you are walking in a public place, and some hair falls from your head to the ground. What if someone picks this up, and then extracts your DNA, finally patenting it. This is surely a case that would make you very uncomfortable. Our intuition—or at least mine—is that we have a priori ownership of our genes. But this intuition is not legally protected under the current status quo because we do not extend these rights of self-ownership, at the genetic and organism levels, to other animals. Biotechnology companies will argue in court that precedents set in decisions with mice that allow for genetic patents allow for human patents as well. The argument might go something like this: "I have a cell in my lab that I admittedly got from Jonathan Flombaum's skin that was left in a public place. I have demonstrated a causal link between a genotype and phenotype in this cell by manufacturing knockout versions of this cell; therefore, I now own the perturbed version of Mr. Flombaum's genotype. Indeed, this is no different from the court's decision to allow for the ownership of experimentally modified mouse genes." If we want to prevent this circumstance we must assert that genotypes are owned by organisms, who, in turn, own themselves. We must assert that animals are not property, but independent, and therefore that they have the right to own their own genes. This guarantees humans the right to own their own genes as well, preventing a nightmare age of people running to patent as many genotypes as they can and, similarly, preventing the type of genetic abuses of power that anyone who has seen a small number of science fiction movies can easily imagine.

Once companies and government agencies can secure the right to own, study, and analyze a person's genes, it seems impossible to stop them from using this information in the abusive ways that I discussed above, such as limiting health care coverage or threatening job security. Our laws do not protect us from these abuses in any obvious way. That a company, for example, cannot discriminate against me on the basis of race, religion, or creed, does not mean that they cannot discriminate against me because they think I am unqualified. The concern here is that arguments about one's qualification will be generated from genetic information. One might contend: "But genes do not exclusively determine how one will behave." I agree entirely, but this is not what is at stake. Consider the fact that insurance companies can already limit coverage based on one's family history. The argument, "just because my father had heart disease does not *necessarily* mean that I will have heart disease" does not hold water. How hard would it be, then, for an insurance company with access to my genotype to further constrain my coverage based on what I perceive to be an inaccurate and genetically deterministic perspective? Could I ever force them to care about the fact that I eat right if they are convinced that I will develop heart disease anyway?

Perhaps, however, there is a simpler solution to the problems that I outlined above. Why not just say that humans and other animals are different, and therefore, that humans may own their own genotypes though animals may not? Animals are property, after all, and humans are not. Unfortunately, in this case, the slippery slope between animals and humans is far more slippery than usual, especially with respect to the nature of the legal forums in which the debates over human patenting will take place. This is because there is no clear line at which to distinguish human genes and animal genes; they are both very similar sequences of nucleotides. Being sentient, feeling pain, being conscious, and many other mental categories that we use to distinguish between animals and humans have no obvious connection to why or why not an individual should own its own genes. To protect our rights legally from the self-interested corporations who will make just this argument, we must assert the strong case that any gene sequence, and therefore, any organism, regardless of how sentient it is, cannot be owned.

There are also independent reasons for asserting the right to self-ownership of animals, which do not depend on the analogy between animals and humans. We can easily imagine abuses of genetic power emerging only from ownership of animal genotypes. For example, companies owning gene patents might not allow poor countries, who cannot afford to pay royalties, to benefit from different medical research programs and therapies. We have already seen that this is the case for drug patents. Extending self-ownership to animals will prevent this abuse as well. What the argument really boils down to then is that we must give ownership of genes to the organisms that they belong to, in order to ensure that the new age of genetic discovery does not just lead to new methods for abusing power through technology.

I would like to admit that the proposal and logic that I have laid out above open the door to some very difficult and serious questions. If genes and organisms are entities that cannot be owned, then what about plants? The views in this paper commit me to the view that plants own themselves and their genes, and that they cannot really be considered property. Indeed, I am wholly supportive of this view insofar as it would outlaw patenting plant knockouts and genetically altering them,. I add as well, as I did in the introduction, that further implications of this view—i.e., can we eat plants, sell plants, grow them, etc.—do not follow exclusively from the views of genetic ownership I have presented. With respect to eating plants, why should the fact that the we cannot patent their genes mean that we cannot eat them? Perhaps we will decide that not being property gives an organism a right not to have pain inflicted upon it, a concern that certainly does not apply to flora.

To conclude, this view of genetic ownership—one in which no organism can be owned by another organism—will afford humans the most protection of their own rights in the future. I think that a genetic perspective forces us to look beyond cognitive categories and to recognize that living things, genetically speaking, are really amazingly similar, and therefore, that they may deserve some common rights. I think that this view guarantees our own rights with respect to each other, and that it keeps things like genes and the information that they contain outside of the reach of corporate greed and political abuse.

References

Dawkins, R. (1986). *The blind watchmaker*. New York, Norton.

Dershowitz, A. M. (2002). *Shouting fire: Civil liberties in a turbulent age*. New York, Little, Brown, and Company.

Nonhuman "Pain" and Animal Rights

Lisa Guttentag

HAD ANIMALS BEEN GRANTED legal personhood decades ago, few people reading this would be alive. Yet the goal of this paper is not to scare legal authorities into relinquishing rights of nonhuman animals. I will not rattle off the immeasurable benefits brought by animal research, which include the rabies vaccine, insulin for type-1 diabetics, and the procedure for liver transplants. Any well-read person is already familiar with these. Though debaters on both sides often beg the question, the deeper issue surrounding the ethics of animal research lies with the query: At what cost?

Every moral dilemma requires a weighing of two alternatives that cannot, but must, be exchanged for identical moral currency. To set most moral boundaries, such as the legal driving age, the courts must weigh human life against human freedom, two human commodities which we humans can appraise based on our own experience in the world. To set the boundary for legal personhood, however, human pain must be weighed against a commodity whose weight we can only estimate indirectly, the apparent pain of nonhuman animals. In this paper, I explain the irrationality of the two arguments, utilitarian and rights-based, that are brandished against animal research.

First, if we are to grant legal personhood to nonhuman animals, we should realize exactly what such an action would entail. Animals as legal "persons" could not participate in even the pleasantest of scientific procedures. The Declaration of Helsinki adopted by the World Medical Assembly in 1996 stipulates that "in any research on human beings, each potential subject must be adequately informed of the aims, methods, anticipated benefits and potential hazards of the study and the discomfort it may entail," but that "in the case of legal incompetence, informed consent should be obtained from the legal guardian in accordance with national legislation" (Brody 1998). Appointing an appropriate legal guardian for every animal on earth, as Francione himself admits in his manifesto for animal personhood, *Animals, Property, and the Law,* would be an impossible task. Though Francione suggests righting the messy problem by appointing organizations already advocating for animal rights, such as PETA, as guardians to act in the best interest of whole groups of animals, it is unlikely that such organizations, after fervently campaigning against animal research, would allow their wards to participate in the most innocuous experiments. Barred from taking part in any type of research, animals could contribute absolutely nothing to scientific pursuits. The resulting decrease in research would negatively impact both humans who could benefit from medical or psychological advances and nonhuman animals themselves whose behavior and physiology could have been investigated in the laboratory.

Most arguments against animal research have invoked a Benthamite reduction of costs and benefits into pain and pleasure. The common motto of animal research opponents that "a rat's pain is a dog's pain is a monkey's pain is a human's pain" implies that the moral weight of any physical sensation depends only on the vehemence with which an animal avoids it. By this reasoning, nonhuman "pain" should be factored into utilitarian calculations alongside, and equivalent to, that of humans. However, contrary to anti-animal-research assertions, even this overly simple conception of morality, due to progress made in recent years in preventing the pain of nonhuman subjects, only leads one to support animal research more fervently. Unlike most defenders of animal research, who highlight the immensity of the human pain which it has prevented, I will focus on the other side of the equation: the meagerness of the nonhuman "pain" it apparently causes.

The term "animal research," for some, conjures up images of cute, furry creatures with their hair matted and covered in bandages, staring pathetically from between the bars of a cramped cage. However, concern over animal welfare has ensured that for any creature, whether cute and furry or not, research inflicts as little "pain," or as little of the nonhuman experience of pain, as possible. Numerous legal statutes and institutional practices which guard against nonhuman pain have been established to appease those who use Benthamite calculations as the basis of their moral arguments.

The legislative regulation of animal research began in 1876 with the Animals Act of Britain. The Animals Act required that any research potentially inflicting animal pain be approved by the Home Office, that anesthetics minimize animal pain, that the suffering of animals following the experiment be immediately terminated by killing the animal, and that any experiment involving animals somehow "advance knowledge" (Brody 1998). Though few advances in animal welfare were made for most of the twentieth century, since the 1980s many nations, including nearly all European countries, the United States, Canada, and Australia, have legally refined and extended the principles that the Animals Act first articulated.

During the past few decades, legal and institutional policies around the world have increasingly incorporated the "3 R's" principle, first proposed by Russell and Burch in 1956 in *The Principles of Humane Experimental Technique*. According to the seminal book, researchers should seek to replace live research animals with biotechnical materials such as in vitro cultures and phylogenetically higher animals with lower ones, reduce the number of animals used in research, and refine the techniques employed to minimize nonhuman "pain." Data from the early 1990s illustrates the international success of policies that aim to promote these three R's, still listed explicitly among the aims of many animal research laboratories. The overall number of nonhuman animals, especially "higher" ones, employed for research purposes has been greatly reduced; while Canadian institutes used 2,699,012 animals for scientific purposes in 1975, only 2,115,006 were used in 1992, with national authorities citing an increase of 600% in the number of fish used and a concurrent decrease in all other animals. In Britain, similarly, the 5.45 million research procedures carried out in 1976 had decreased to 2.8 million by 1993 (Brody 1998). When the replacement of animals is impossible, refinement of experimental technique has nevertheless mitigated the "pain" inflicted by experiments and lowered the number of apparently painful experiments themselves. In the United States, in 1991, 61 percent of nonhuman animal medical procedures involved no pain or distress, 33 percent involved pain alleviated by an anaesthetic, analgesic, or tranquilizer, and a mere 6 percent involved pain which, for scientific reasons, could not be alleviated by drugs. While photographs of bandaged animals may be heart-wrenching, statistics reveal that the human pain prevented by animal research, even if it is illogically equated with the "pain" of nonhuman animals, far outweighs it.

Moreover, the quest to discover new experimental techniques that reduce, refine, or replace animal uses is still gathering steam. The European Center for the Validation of Alternative Methods (EVCAM) funds research aimed at finding methods to replace animal experimentation (Brody 1998) as does the Johns Hopkins Center for Alternatives to Animal Testing in the United States, which has distributed over $4.5 million for research during the past twenty years (see http://altweb.jhsph.edu). Alternatives developed that have spared huge quantities of nonhuman "pain" include a procedure that replaces the LD50 test of acute toxicity, which reduced the number of animals required to determine the lethal dose of a substance from 50–100 to only 3–8. Thanks to many organizations and researchers, animal "pain" endured during animal research continues steadily to decrease.

Utilitarianism justifies animal research. However, the very mention of "utilitarianism" leads many to crinkle their noses in disgust. A more complex principle of morality which goes beyond a simple calculation of pain and pleasure to forbid, for example, harvesting the organs of a living human, also demands a more complex evaluation of animal research. Even "rule utilitarianism," which preserves pain and pleasure calculations while avoiding their intuitive moral contradictions, sums the consequences of animal research in a way that finishes by supporting it; while rule utilitarians assert that the mere knowledge of an innocent person being slaughtered will incite sufficient psychological pain in humans to outweigh any pain it might immediately prevent, no Dr. Doolittle–type animal language enables the transmission of such morbid knowledge between nonhumans, and so knowledge of physical pain adds no psychological pain to nonhuman totals.

Rights-based arguments for and against animal research, because they are based on different premises, often fly uselessly by each other. While proponents usually assume that humans take priority in moral matters, opponents refuse to grant priority to a single species, decrying the arguments of the other side as "species-chauvinist." So that the following argument lines up on the same logical plane as animal rightists' claims, I have formulated it not to be species-chauvinist, but "self-awareness-chauvinist." I will not launch into a philosophical explanation of why such chauvinism is appropriate to moral reasoning. However, in order to combat the arguments that threaten their pursuits, animal researchers must argue within the same framework as their opponents.

No brand of utilitarianism, even rule utilitarianism, can be a legitimate basis for the moral repugnance of animal research. Yet many animal rightists base their arguments instead on the conviction that animals possess an inherent *right* to be free of physical or psychological pain. The source of this mysteriously inherent right is rarely explained. Such a natural right is rarely conferred by moral philosophers upon lower life forms, such as insects; even more rarely upon inanimate life, such as trees; and never upon inanimate objects, such as furniture. Presumably, therefore, the rights which Americans deem "self-evident" are not bestowed by humans on anything merely possessing life, but rather on any being possessing the complex neural connections that bring it closer to the human experience of "consciousness." According to most animal rightists, the rights conferred on a being depend on its degree of "consciousness," "autonomy," or "self-awareness," qualities that are aspects of the human experience of the world.

Nonhuman animals, however, do not possess anything akin to the consciousness which humans anthropomorphically grant their animal cousins. When comparing human pain with nonhuman animal pain, most humans necessarily imagine nonhuman pain simply as a reduced version of their own suffering. However, because it lacks the human experience of consciousness to lend it moral weight, nonhuman animal "pain," independently of its impact on humans, does not merit the creation of a right under the implied consciousness-based criterion.

Nonhuman animals, though they do not use language or construct societies, perform complex behaviors that seem to stem from consciousness. In *Animal Rights: A Beginner's Guide*, a few of the factoids presented as evidence that nonhumans "deserve our respect" are: bats have five times the hearing range of humans; English sheep dogs can read hand signals from a mile away; birds and marine animals such as horseshoe crabs use celestial navigation; and many fish emit electrical impulses and are highly sensitive to changes in electric fields (Achor 1996). In his book *Rattling the Cage*, Stephen Wise formalizes the allocation of desert by behavioral ability, implicit in animal rightists' arguments, by creating four levels of "autonomy" into which he places animals based on behavior. For example, honeybees, because they can communicate the distance and direction to a food source with a finely tuned "dance language," have surpassed level I to be placed in Wise's level II, "non-humans which might someday be found to have a near-human degree of self-awareness."

The early emergence in the phylogenetic tree of animals who nevertheless earn a high "autonomy ranking" hints at the inadequacy of Wise's classification system. A single complex behavior is not, in fact, a proxy for autonomy. In every animal's constant flow of environmental input and behavioral output, a certain output may be selected for, regardless of whether the input takes a detour through consciousness on the way. A honeybee's dash at the same angle to the sun as that of a distant food source does not indicate that the bee consciously recognized and formulated a description of the food's location. Rather, bees that ran in the appropriate direction before taking off to feed, perhaps millions of years ago in preparation for a long flight, enjoyed a higher mating success than nest mates, and so the honeybee dance language evolved. The unconscious algorithm that paired a journey to food with the corresponding dance earned a seat over evolutionary time in the honeybee brain.

Like the honeybee, many animals display remarkable navigation or communication skill but lack flexible behaviors that reveal autonomy and self-awareness. Such nonhuman animals cannot experience "pain" as humans understand it. The awareness that an event is painful is an essential ingredient in our experience of pain; people who have undergone a painful ordeal during a subjectively important event, such as a sporting competition, often report that they "did not feel pain." Without the direction of subjective attention toward a painful stimulus through the constant self-monitoring of sensation, "pain" as humans conceptualize it, pain which includes an understanding of its consequences, does not exist.

If a behavior can be so simply selected for in nature, one wonders what distinguishes conscious human behaviors from unconscious nonhuman ones. The central difference between these two distinct types of behavior lies in their degree of flexibility. Psychologists have pointed out that only human language is characterized by *productivity*, the inclusion of components which can form an infinite number of messages. The novel combinations of words in human utterances indicate that these components must have been deliberately arranged before jaw and lip muscles formed them. While instances of behavior that are both complex and flexible, like the communication of new ideas, suggest self-awareness, those that adhere to an inflexible pattern, like the honeybee dance language, do not. Calculators, indeed, can solve numerical problems far faster than can human beings; however, calculator-rightists, unlike animal-rightists, do not exist.

If pain as humans conceptualize it only exists when available for conscious appraisal, according to a Benthamite calculation nonhumans can morally be slaughtered indiscriminately. Even injuring a person in a vegetative state, it seems, would not be morally objectionable. Indeed, to a comatose person, the actions of an assailant would cause no pain at all.

However, one notable result of humans' self-awareness and sociality is the existence of "networks of empathy" in human, and not nonhuman, society. Any breach of a human's rights, even if that human has lost all potential of self-awareness, evokes sufficient psychological pain in any member of his "empathy network," which includes family members, friends, neighbors, and almost anyone who learns of the breach of rights, to make the action, even by utilitarian standards, morally repugnant.

These same networks of empathy extend to the nonhuman world, a world to which humans fallaciously, but unavoidably, attribute human sensation. The suffering of animals brings humans, whether it ought to or not, psychological pain; it is by virtue of this human psychological pain that nonhuman "pain" carries moral weight. Present efforts to develop alternatives to animal testing are commendable. However, the meager moral pull of nonhuman "pain" should not budge the tremendous weight of the millions of human lives saved by animal research.

References

Achor, A. B. (1996). *Animal rights: A beginner's guide.* Yellow Springs, WriteWare.

Brody, B. A. (1998). *Ethics of biomedical research: An international perspective.* New York, Oxford University Press.

Francione, G. L. (1995). *Animals, property, and the law.* Philadelphia, Temple University Press.

The Importance of Animal Testing in Biomedical Research

Virginia Vance

Introduction

BIOMEDICAL RESEARCH HAS UNDOUBTEDLY CONTRIBUTED immeasurably towards the reduction of human and animal suffering. Yet, this progress notwithstanding, some animal rights activists advocate raising animals from the status of property to that of children, a proposal that would prohibit the use of animal subjects in biomedical research. I argue that should the status of animals be changed in this way, it would prove deleterious to human society. Contrary to the claims of these activists, such a change would not cause a decrease in suffering, but rather, a pronounced increase. This essay will first review some of the key achievements of biomedical research on animals, such as the development of numerous vaccinations, surgical procedures and heart disease treatments, and the identification of key carcinogenic agents. Of course, animal testing is not justified in every situation, and the second half of this essay broadly sketches the sort of calculations necessary to weigh the costs of research to animal subjects against the benefits of such research to human and animal patients. Applying a consistent, pragmatic standard to all cases of animal experimentation will allay the fear that animals are being needlessly harmed while allowing important and otherwise unattainable medical advances to carry forward.

Vaccines

All vaccines available today have undergone trials on laboratory animals, and with good reason. Only a complete organism can be used to determine the effectiveness of a vaccine in stimulating protective immunity to a disease. Though some preliminary assessments of vaccine reactivity can be made using *in vitro* tests, no vaccine can be considered safe to use on humans until it is tested *in vivo*.

Furthermore, the necessity of such vaccination research can hardly be underplayed. Vaccines have controlled or eradicated some of our most deadly infectious diseases, including smallpox, rabies, yellow fever, poliomyelitis, and measles. With a mortality rate of 90 percent, smallpox was the deadliest infectious disease in America during the seventeenth and eighteenth centuries. Jenner discovered the vaccine for smallpox in 1796 while studying how milkmaids that contracted cowpox were subsequently immune to smallpox (Leader and Stark 1987). In 1967, the World Health Organization (WHO) launched a global campaign to eradicate smallpox. The last recorded case of smallpox occurred in Somalia in 1977, and in 1980 the WHO declared the disease officially eradicated.

The poliovirus, *poliomyelitis*, was another epidemic that spread across America beginning in the early 1900s. No effective treatment was available until the 1950s when Salk and Sabin developed a vaccine from tissue cultures of monkey kidney cells. Primates are the only animals besides humans that are susceptible to the poliovirus, so without them as test subjects the vaccine could never have been developed and safely tested. The incidence of *poliomyelitis* has fallen from 58,000 cases in 1952 to less than ten a year since 1984 (Hendee, Loeb, et al. 1988).

Despite this progress, there are still many infectious diseases for which no effective vaccines exist. Two of the most prevalent human infectious diseases, malaria and HIV, have no vaccines. Work on the development of a malaria vaccine has been facilitated by continuous tissue culture growth in animals. The two stages in the cycle of the malaria parasite that vaccine research is currently targeting are the sporozoite, the form injected by the mosquito into the patient's bloodstream, and the merozoite, the blood form of the parasite. Researchers are working on synthesizing the key proteins embedded in the sporozoite and merozoite surface, which produce immunity when injected into animal tissues (Leader and Stark 1987). The animal model systems of birds, rodents and monkeys are essential for testing each stage of new vaccines.

Much of the progress in the development of treatments for AIDS, the first infectious disease with a mortality rate of nearly 100 percent, is based on the interaction between research into the human disease and research into similar conditions afflicting animals. The feline leukemia virus, for instance, causes a depression of functions of the lymphoid cells that leads to immunologic deficiencies, much as HIV does in humans. These observations from cats have contributed to understanding the nature of human AIDS. Other useful models include the tropic virus HTLV-III, which in macaque monkeys produces a disease very similar to AIDS, and a virus in African green monkeys that is reportedly a relative of HIV (Leader and Stark 1987). Such observations have led researchers to believe that AIDS evolved in Africa from the simian form, eventually becoming adapted to humans. Chimpanzees are critical to AIDS research because until recently they have been the only animals that can be infected with HIV without showing the symptomology of humans. New strains of transgenic rabbits have been developed that are susceptible to HIV (Fan, Challah et al., 1999). Nevertheless, because primates are humans' closest genetic relatives, they will continue to be vital to finding and testing AIDS therapies.

Surgery

Experiments on laboratory animals have been vital in the development of modern surgical practices. Common procedures in blood transfusions, setting bone fractures, cardiac surgery, microsurgery and organ transplants, all depend on preliminary animal trials. A veterinarian in the 1930s developed the Stader splint for treating dog fractures. The splint, which used pins held by a frame, represents the first use of external fracture fixation, a technique now frequently used to repair human fractures (Leader and Stark 1987. The first cardiopulmonary bypass performed on a human heart utilized a heart-lung machine that was developed and tested on animals (Ludbrook 1987). The techniques of microsurgery, which involve repairing nerves, blood vessels, tendons, and the replacement of limbs, were all perfected on animals before being used on humans; they are also of vital importance to animal health, almost independently of their value to humans.

Perhaps the surgical field most dependent on animal subjects is organ transplantation. The rate of organ acceptance has been greatly improved by advances in our understanding of the genetics of the major histocompatibility complex (MHC) and of MHC-linked genes affecting growth and development. MHC molecules control the immune system's recognition of organs. If a patient's immune system recognizes a transplanted organ as belonging to an outside cell type, the body will reject the organ and the transplant will fail. Immunogenetic work with transgenic rats has enabled researchers to identify the key MHC genes responsible for organ recognition (Gill, Smith, et al. 1989). Donors and patients are now screened for these genes, as an appropriate match greatly increases the chance of organ acceptance.

The surgical procedures involved in organ transplantation have also been developed and improved due to work on animals. The first successful kidney transplants were performed in dogs in the late 1950s. This early breakthrough laid the foundations for transplantation of the liver, heart, lungs, and various other organs (Leader and Stark 1987). Animals still have an important role to play in transplantation research. The rat has been an important model for transplants of brain and other neural tissues. Transplantation of tissue into the brain is one of the most promising therapies for a variety of disorders involving damage to the central nervous system. The potential clinical value of neural grafts lies in the replacement of damaged neural circuits, which might be used to treat trauma in adults and neurological defects in children (Gill, Smith, et al. 1989).

Heart Disease and Cancer

Heart disease and cancer are the first and second leading causes of death in America. Laboratory animals have been a critical tool for researchers struggling to find cures for these afflictions.

Much of our knowledge about cardiovascular disease, particularly atherosclerosis (narrowing of arteries), has been based on studies of its nature in animals. Primates, rabbits, dogs, mice, rats, pigs, pigeons, chickens, turkeys and quail have all been involved in heart disease research (Leader and Stark 1987), and as the focus of research has turned to metabolic aspects, primates have become more important than ever. Atherosclerosis develops in primates almost identically to the way it does in humans. The work done with primates confirms the hypothesis that people can reduce the risk of heart attack by reducing fat and cholesterol in their diets.

Work with transgenic animals has demonstrated the role of specific oncogenic viruses in cancer formation. One such virus is the hepatitis B virus (HBV), which is believed to cause the cancer hepatocellular carcinoma (HCC) in humans. One way to determine if HBV causes cancer is to infect an experimental animal with the virus and study its long-term development. This has been done using a number of species. Another way is to produce transgenic mice that overexpress portions of the HBV genome. When this experiment was conducted, by twelve months of age some of the mice had developed HCC, and by twenty months all mice had HCC, proving that the production of HBV protein was sufficient to cause liver cancer (Iannaccone and Scarpelli 1993). Another virus implicated in the onset of cancer is the human papilloma virus (HPV), which is hypothesized to contribute to human cervical cancer. Transgenic mice have also been engineered to overexpress this viral genome, and HPV RNA was recovered from the resulting tumors (Iannaccone and Scarpelli 1993). Years of research into HPV paid off when, in November of 2002, researchers announced the development of a vaccine against the virus.

In addition to determining the ability of viruses to cause cancer, animals have also been used to determine the carcinogenic effects of chemicals. Assessment of carcinogenicity involves the long-term dietary, parenteral, or topical application of a chemical to various species of test subjects. Using this method, dozens of chemicals have been implicated in causing various types of cancer, such as cancer of the bladder, lung, and prostrate (Rall 1979).

Proposed Method to Predict Costs and Benefits

I have argued that the significant improvements in human health justify the use of animals in biomedical research in at least some cases, but it may not always be apparent which. In anticipation of the response that the ends do not necessarily justify the means, I want to offer a method for determining just when the costs of biomedical research will outweigh the benefits, and when they will not.

Two features of the proposed calculation merit particular attention. First, it includes the costs and benefits to both humans and nonhuman animals. Humans are used in clinical trials at least as often as animals, and they too experience costs associated with research. On the other hand, animals frequently benefit from medical advances first developed for use in humans, a fact that is too often overlooked by overzealous animal rights activists. Significant advances have been made in veterinary medicine through the use of animal testing, such as vaccines for rabies and tetanus, treatment for parasites like heartworm, and cancer therapies (Hendee, Loeb, et al. 1988).

The second key feature of this calculation is that it is weighted according to the level of consciousness of beings involved. That is, costs and benefits accrued by humans count for more than costs and benefits accrued by organisms with a lower level of awareness.

To a first approximation, the morality of animal research could be evaluated using the following formula, which balances the suffering of research subjects against the alleviation of suffering in the associated beneficiary:

$$\frac{\sum_{s=1}^{n} C_s R_s P_s}{\sum_{s=1}^{n} C_s T_s B_s} < 1$$

The numerator quantifies the total costs of a research program and the denominator quantifies its benefits. C_s is the species-specific coefficient of consciousness, R_s is the number of individuals of a particular species used for research, T_s is the number of individuals that benefit from the treatment developed, P_s is the species-specific coefficient representing the level of pain experienced by a single individual participating in the research, and B_s is the species-specific coefficient representing the benefits received by a single individual receiving the treatment that is ultimately developed. This calculation gets summed over the total number n of species involved. If the sum of costs is less than the sum of benefits the inequality is true, and the research program is morally justified. While the measurements of these parameters are certainly far from trivial, they are, in principle, measurable and do represent a method of analyzing and quantifying otherwise elusive concepts.

Animal rights activists would argue that the benefits (human health benefits) never outweigh the costs (animal suffering). Their argument is based on two assertions: (1) that animal suffering should be weighed as equal to human suffering; and (2) that more animals suffer due to biomedical testing than humans are spared, and hence the costs of biomedical research always outweigh the benefits. These two assumptions are false. Animal suffering should not be weighed as equal to human suffering, because animals and humans are not equal, not in levels of suffering, consciousness, morality, or otherwise. As Cohen has argued,

> Between species of animate life . . . the morally relevant differences are enormous, and almost universally appreciated. Humans engage in moral reflection; humans are morally autonomous; humans are members of moral communities, recognizing just claims against their own interests. Human beings do have rights; theirs is a moral status very different from that of cats or rats (Cohen 1986).

The second assertion that animal rights activists make, that the costs of biomedical research always outweigh the benefits, is also incorrect. It would be impossible to quantify the cumulative costs and benefits of the entire field of biomedical research over the last 100 years, but if the statistics regarding the decline of smallpox and polio mentioned above are any indication, the benefits have been incredible.

If the proposed method is adopted, it would show animal welfare advocates that animal testing confers greater benefits to both animals and humans than it causes suffering, and thus the need for a law that protects animals from unnecessary suffering would no longer exist.

Conclusion

Biomedical research has been fundamentally important to human life. As Hendee et al. (1988) note, "had scientific research been restrained in the first decade of the 20th century as antivivisectionists and activists were then, and are today urging, many millions of Americans alive and healthy today would not have been born or would have suffered a premature death." Animals are critical to the maintenance of this research. As it is not possible to protect all laboratory animals against all possible suffering (the same is true of humans), the only alternatives are to eliminate this research and lose all the benefits it stands to bring to our society, or to replace animal subjects with human ones. Both of these alternatives would increase net suffering, and shift the majority of that suffering to our own species. These alternatives are not acceptable.

Ideally, biomedical researchers and animal welfare advocates should share the same ultimate goal: to decrease suffering. It is imperative to illustrate quantitatively that the only way suffering will be decreased is through the continuation of biomedical research, not the elimination of it. The proposed method would enable researchers to predict whether each prospective experiment would or would not lead to a net decrease in suffering through the benefits it stands to confer to both animals and humans. In determining the utilitarian benefit of each experiment, both researchers and activists could be satisfied that with each experiment, their mutual goal of decreasing suffering could be met.

References

Cohen, C. (1986). "The case for the use of animals in biomedical research." *New England Journal of Medicine* 315: 865–870.

Fan, J., M. Challah, et al. (1999). "Transgenic rabbit models for biomedical research: Current status, basic methods and future perspectives." *Pathology International* 49(7): 583–94.

Gill, T., G. Smith, et al. (1989). "The rat as an experimental animal." *Science* 245: 269–276.

Hendee, W., J. Loeb, et al. (1988). *Use of animals in biomedical research: The challenge and response.* Chicago, American Medical Association.

Iannaccone, P. M., and D. G. Scarpelli (1993). "Exploring pathogenetic mechanisms using transgenic animals." *Annals of Medicine* 25(2): 131–8.

Leader, R. W., and D. Stark (1987). "The importance of animals in biomedical research." *Perspectives in Biology and Medicine* 30(4): 470–85.

Rall, D. P. (1977). "The role of laboratory animal studies in estimating carcinogenic risks for man." *International Agency for Research on Cancer, Scientific Publications* (25): 179–89.

Animal Welfare and Biomedical Research

Andrew N. Rowan

One of the major themes in the controversy over the use of animals in biomedical research is the issue of the cost/benefit (utilitarian) ratio of such use. A second major theme is based on the deontological approach that animals have basic rights that should prevent them from being used (or regarded) as the property of humans. A third theme is that animal research produces no useful information for human health purposes. All three themes surface in the four papers (by Flombaum, Guttentag, Chen, and Vance) that stimulated this publication, but I plan to focus largely on the first. I also would like to discuss how we might make some sense of the many conflicting claims in the literature.

Table 1: Three major themes in animal research debate

Themes	Issue
1	Cost/benefit (utilitarian) analysis of laboratory animal use
2	Animals have rights that prevent use in the laboratory
3	Animal research is useless (and fraudulent) because it produces no information of value

Utilitarian arguments (theme 1) are widespread among both defenders and critics of animal use in research. Leading critics, such as Peter Singer, argue that the costs of animal research (in suffering and harm) are very great and that the benefits are meager. Leading supporters, such as Leader and Stark (cited by Vance), argue that the benefits (in new knowledge and medical therapies) are considerable and that the costs are minimal. In theory, it should be possible to evaluate the accuracy of these two contrasting claims by examining the empirical record and deciding which is correct, but in practice this has proved to be a remarkably difficult task. In her essay, Vance attempts to tackle this problem head-on with a mathematical model—I take a broader, more qualitative approach.

The challenge is not made any easier when the two opposing sides come at the issue from very different perspectives. For example, Greek and Greek (2000) base their arguments on the assumption that animal research has been mostly irrelevant (theme three), and sometimes even dangerously misleading, while Leader and Stark (1987) believed strongly in the importance and value of animal research (theme one) when they set out to look for evidence of its usefulness in Nobel Prize–winning research. It is, therefore, hardly a surprise that Greek and Greek (2000) concluded that animal research is largely or totally useless while Leader and Stark (1987) came to exactly the opposite conclusion.

When I was teaching at Tufts University, I usually approached the challenge of helping students understand the different themes and issues and leading them through the process of working out their own thoughts on the place and "necessity" of animal research and testing by examining relatively narrow cases in detail. In doing this, students need to develop an understanding of the prevailing thinking at the time (it is a critical error to assume that the scientists in 1940 or even 1960 know what we do today) and the process by which insight and knowledge was gained. The thalidomide story mentioned by Chen is one of the cases that I used and I detail it below.

Utility Issues—The Thalidomide Example

Chen repeats the widespread claim in the animal activist literature that thalidomide was properly tested on animals before it was marketed to the public. This claim goes back twenty-five to thirty years but it is false. Unfortunately, by getting this claim wrong, activists then go on to make the more damaging (to the animal advocacy cause) claim that the thalidomide disaster is a wonderful example of the disastrous errors we can fall into by relying on animal safety studies. Careful historical research and investigative reporting (particularly by The Sunday Times Insight Team in the 1970s) revealed that the drug was subjected to relatively superficial and sloppy safety tests prior to its being marketed in Germany, Great Britain and Australia. When enough evidence indicated that thalidomide was probably the cause of the rash of fetal deformities, drug authorities around the world demanded much more animal testing, not less! In the United States, the 1962 Kefauver Amendment greatly increased the amount of animal testing required for new drugs and reproductive toxicity testing became a standard requirement.

The time course of the thalidomide story is as follows (taken from Botting (2002) and The Sunday Times Insight Team (Deutsch 1979). The first paper describing thalidomide's pharmacology was published in 1956 by scientists from Chemie Grunenthal, a German pharmaceutical company. Thalidomide was described as a new sedative with remarkably low toxicity in animals (in acute and thirty-day subacute tests). Later on, it was demonstrated that thalidomide's "low toxicity" was mainly a consequence of its low solubility in water and in body fluids and hence its low bio-availability. When the drug was finely ground and suspended in a sugar solution (as was done in some dispensed forms of the drug), it was much more toxic. A later paper then reported on the clinical effects of thalidomide in humans and, based on such relatively superficial studies, the drug was launched in Germany by Chemie Grunenthal in November of 1957. Its sales increased through 1959, then the first signs of trouble appeared in October. The initial problem was a diagnosis of polyneuritis in three patients who had been on the drug for a year. There were other, earlier reports of similar neurological side effects, but Chemie Grunenthal brushed these reports aside. However, this effect on the peripheral nerves was in part responsible for Frances Kelsey of the FDA delaying approval of thalidomide in the United States despite significant pressure from the drug company who had received the U.S. marketing license to approve the drug.

The first case of fetal deformity caused by thalidomide appears to have been reported in Germany in 1959, although it was another six years before this clinician uncovered the fact that the mother had been prescribed a preparation containing thalidomide during the critical period of her pregnancy. By the beginning of 1961, it was clear that Germany was experiencing a rash of formerly very rare fetal abnormalities and Lenz, a German physician, became certain that a single cause was responsible. Thalidomide was considered as a possible culprit in August 1961 because, in a series of twenty cases, five of the mothers had taken thalidomide. On the other hand, other pregnant women who had taken thalidomide produced normal offspring. (As late as 1965, respected medical practitioners were still questioning whether thalidomide could have been the cause of the deformities. It was then demonstrated that there was a critical period early in pregnancy and that, if a woman took the drug after this period, there were no effects on fetal development.) In November, Lenz had enough cases linked to thalidomide to send an urgent letter to Chemie Grunenthal requesting the withdrawal of the drug from the market. During the same period in 1961, an Australian obstetrician also began to draw a link between thalidomide and fetal deformities and he published the first report in the medical literature (on December 16, 1961) describing his conclusions.

George Somers, the chief pharmacologist for Distillers (a British beverage company that wanted to get into the pharmaceutical business and took up the license to market thalidomide in Britain and Australia as one of its first products), launched what appear to have been the first properly conducted and controlled studies of the effects of thalidomide in animals in November 1961. Within five months, he produced the same fetal deformities in rabbits that were seen in humans. Subsequent studies on rats, mice and other laboratory animals produced mixed results. Botting (2002) speculates that many of the negative results were due to poor technique (teratogenicity testing was not a well-defined process at this time) and to ignorance of the fact that thalidomide breaks down rapidly to inactive metabolites when in alkaline solutions. Nonetheless, in the two years following the withdrawal of thalidomide from the market, approximately twenty papers were published reporting the adverse effects of thalidomide on rat fetuses. Admittedly the adverse effects were usually seen at higher doses, often much higher, than those prescribed for humans.

In summary, the thalidomide story (and teratogenicity testing in general) does provide plenty of evidence for significant differences in metabolism and fetal toxicity of drugs in different species. Chen is correct to argue in her essay that the utility of such animal testing is limited and that some drugs that may be safe in humans are rejected because they cause problems in animals. However, the thalidomide story does not support Chen's claim that animal testing was done on the drug prior to it being marketed and that animal testing is therefore useless.

The above description provides some sense of the complexities of the thalidomide story and the type of detail that is needed to begin to make an informed decision about the utility of animal studies in any particular case. Similar examples could be developed around insulin, polio vaccine, and other medical discoveries. Usually, the analysis produces a mixed outcome and it is not difficult for the critic to find narrow examples of sloppy or unnecessary animal studies. For example, in the insulin story (see the excellent history by Bliss (1982)), the studies done by Banting and Best on dogs were poorly performed (e.g., the record keeping and the experimental technique was sloppy) and the successful isolation of insulin owed little to these experiments. However, the development of a bioassay of insulin activity using rabbits and mice by Collip, the biochemist assigned by McLeod to help Banting and Best, was a critical step that permitted Collip to develop a protocol for the purification of insulin and get it to market. Guttentag and Vance describe some of the other success stories of animal testing in biomedical research.

In the above section, I have focused on the benefit side of the utilitarian equation and claim that even careful analysis produces mixed results. When we look at the other side of the utilitarian calculus—namely, the cost in animal suffering—we come up against another set of complexities and uncertainties.

Animal Pain and Suffering

Guttentag notes with approval, citing the 1991 annual report from the U.S. Department of Agriculture (USDA), that 61% of animal studies in the United States involved no pain or distress, 33 percent involved pain that was alleviated, and a mere 6 percent involved unalleviated pain and distress. However, these USDA reports are notoriously problematic. When one looks at data from other countries that also provide rough estimates of the animal pain and distress experienced during research and testing, one finds that The Netherlands reports that 45 percent of its animals experience moderate to severe pain and distress, while both Canada and Switzerland place 29 percent of their laboratory animals in these categories. While assessing pain and distress is difficult, all three countries make a considered and sincere effort to estimate the level of suffering of laboratory animals. The same cannot be said of the way the USDA annual reports are completed and compiled. Some of the problems with the USDA annual reports are detailed in the following paragraphs and these problems call into serious question the accuracy of the annual figures.

For starters, the USDA annual reports do not include mice and rats. These species account for 90 percent or more of all laboratory animals used in America. Second, the few studies that have looked carefully at how pain and distress are reported indicate that they are significantly underreported because they are either not looked for by researchers or because they are just not recognized. Furthermore, most people seem to focus only on "pain," whereas "distress" is probably much more common. (The Netherlands and Canada do take distress into account, while Switzerland uses some research exemplars to help those completing the reports to estimate the level of pain and distress experienced by the animals.) An animal with a bacterial disease may not experience pain, but it will be in distress because of general malaise and fever.

To date, thirty years after the USDA was required to report on pain and distress and their alleviation, the USDA has yet to provide a definition or any practical guidelines for assessing "distress." Finally, when one looks at the annual reports from individual institutions, one finds that, of the top 50 noncommercial research centers (in terms of government funding—corporations are not included), about 70 percent report that *none* of their laboratory animals experienced pain and distress that are not alleviated. On average, less than 1 percent of the animals used at these 50 institutions (far less than the 6 percent overall figure in the 1991 USDA report), experience unalleviated pain and distress. These institutions conduct a wide range of studies in surgery, pharmacology, physiology, immunology, cancer, pathogenic diseases, just to name a few areas, and it is not at all difficult to find published examples from these institutions of research that clearly involved animals in distress. In fact, for many studies, the mere living conditions cause distress, as social species are too often housed alone, or in remarkably small cages that provide little room for movement and normal behavioral repertoires.

Despite the claim by many in the research community that they are focused on detecting and alleviating animal pain and distress, there is remarkably little research on identifying animal pain, on developing better methods for alleviating it, or on identifying and assessing the level of distress and then developing ways of preventing that distress. The National Institutes of Health, the largest biomedical research entity in the world, with tens of billions of dollars disbursed to support research annually, has devoted almost no funding to assessing animal pain and distress and developing approaches to alleviate or prevent them. This is despite the fact that pain and distress introduce unwanted effects on the data collected from those studies. The few individuals who work on these issues around the world are reduced to scraping together a few small grants from veterinary and other foundations.

There is a lot more money available for farm animal welfare research and some of the ideas on assessing animal well-being and distress are extrapolated from the studies performed on farm and production animals. For example, Marian Dawkins has pioneered the use of preference testing to find out what an animal wants and how strongly motivated it is to perform certain behaviors. What definitions of well-being and distress we now have almost all come from farm animal studies.

The end result is that we know rather little about normal and abnormal behavior and physiology in laboratory animals. We have only crude assessment tools to detect pain and distress and these are only implemented in a haphazard and inconsistent way in laboratories across the country. In other words, we cannot even begin to develop a realistic evaluation of the costs of animal research—statistics of the type that Guttentag cites simply do not do the job. This means that the current "utilitarian" arguments about whether animal research is justified or not will continue merrily onwards, unencumbered by sound data and informed analysis.

Animals as Property and Implications for Their Laboratory Status

One of the arguments that has been advanced by animal activists is that the current sorry status of animals (e.g., leading to their use in harmful research) is largely the result of their being classified as property. The treatment of animals as property is probably an underlying reason for the relatively low status of animals in both laboratories and industrial agriculture, but it is not clear that providing animals with some new status as sentient beings (between mere chattels but not quite at the level of human persons), will necessarily remove them from being subjects of research. The European Union has added language to the treaty that underpins its functioning that acknowledges that animals are sentient beings that can suffer, but to date this new language has not resulted in any significant change in research animal oversight.

There are already some animals that have begun to move out of the category of being mere property—namely, our pet dogs and cats. Fifty percent of pet caregivers define their pets as members of the family and some courts have already suggested that pets are not mere property. Nonetheless, dogs and cats (and sometimes even current and past pets) are used in laboratories. Humans, who are not treated as property, are also used in research in rather large numbers. Admittedly, most of these human experimental subjects have given consent (that is not always as informed as it is meant to be) but some noncompetent humans also end up as research subjects (albeit in experiments that are not meant to place them at much risk of harm). Thus a change in the property status of animals might affect what we allow scientists to do to animals in the laboratory, but it would probably not end animal research.

Another area where the property issue looms large is the patenting of animals. Many animal advocates regard animal patenting as a very dangerous precedent—in part, because it tends to reinforce the notion that animals are mere mechanisms and property. Patents do not always reinforce the notion that an animal is mere property, however. Flombaum also proposes that the property status of animals may erode the rights of humans in the emerging field of gene patenting. The European Patent Office (EPO) now has a "public morality" criterion that it must consider when it weighs a possible patent on an animal. The EPO examiners tend to deal with this criterion using a utilitarian calculus. They awarded a patent for Oncomouse (a mouse model used in cancer research) but not for a hairless mouse that was proposed as a model to study baldness. Clearly, the EPO felt cancer was a serious issue and thus the human need for new knowledge trumped the animal's claim not to be harmed, while baldness did not rise to that level of seriousness.

The above are just a few thoughts on the animals as property issue. Anyone looking for a more detailed discussion should consult the papers and books by Gary Francione, Jerrold Tannenbaum, or Steven Wise for a range of views on the matter.

Conclusion

There is no question that animal research involves serious moral questions (theme two). Mostly these questions are phrased in terms of whether we should use animals or not. However, this is the wrong conflict. We all agree, even the rhetorical opponents of the animal protection movement in the animal research debate (e.g., the Foundation for Biomedical Research), that animals should not be used in research if it is not necessary. Some scientists are also on record as saying they also look for the day when animals are no longer used in research that causes them harm, and in 1969 Nobel Prize winner Sir Peter Medawar indicated that the day would come when we no longer would need to use animals.

Thus, the real debate facing us is not the false conflict about whether or not we should do animal research but rather differences of opinion about how much effort we should be putting into reaching the goal of no longer harming animals in the name of biological research.

Considerable strides have already been made in the past thirty years in reducing laboratory animal use (the numbers have been cut by 50 percent or more). Nonetheless, the new genetic technologies mean that many more mice are being housed in research facilities than was the case ten years ago. We need to address this upward tilt in animal use and put us back on the steady downward trend that we enjoyed from 1970 to 1990. Human ingenuity and the levels of concern we all have (both scientists and animal advocates—and sometimes they are one and the same) are certainly up to the challenge!

References

Bliss, M. (1982). *The discovery of insulin.* Chicago, University of Chicago Press.

Botting, J. (2002). "The history of thalidomide." *Drug News and Perspectives* 15(9): 604–611.

Deutsch, A. (1979). "Suffer the children: The story of thalidomide." *The Sunday Times Insight Team.* London.

Greek, C. R., and J. S. Greek (2000). *Sacred cows and golden geese: The human cost of experiments on animals.* New York, Continuum.

Leader, R. W., and D. Stark (1987). "The importance of animals in biomedical research." *Perspectives in Biology and Medicine* 30(4): 470–85.

Section 5—Animal Care

While many of the essays in this book present highly theoretical arguments, the issue of animal welfare is not simply an academic matter. Cognitive scientists and philosophers can discuss issues of animal welfare for eternity and the status of animals may never change. Likewise, if the laws regarding the legal standing of animals were to change tomorrow, such academic fields would remain unaffected. The essays in this section are therefore a necessary complement to the more abstract counterparts that precede them.

The perspectives offered in this section, veterinary medicine and animal farming, lay a foundation for thinking about issues in animal rights that other, more theoretical disciplines are unable to provide. In particular, they present evidence grounded in personal experience with both animals and an industry that is animal-centered. Whereas the other essays in this book focus on questions of cognitive ability, moral worth, and ethical obligation, these essays offer insight into questions of need and effect. The essays presented in this section assess, from the standpoint of entirely animal-oriented careers, both the necessity of an alteration in the legal standing of animals and the consequences of such an alteration.

From the animal farmers comes a strong word of caution about the drastic consequences of such a proposal for agriculture and food services, a cornerstone of the American economy. We are implored to view the question of the legal status of animals not only from the animal perspective but from the human one as well. From the veterinarians, on the other hand, comes a divided opinion. Both pro and con argue from the perspective of committed professionals, equally devoted to animal care and welfare, and yet, one finds the proposed legal change a necessity, while the other deems it unnecessary and even counterproductive. Finally, this section's professional contribution provides a comprehensive set of arguments that manages to integrate the diverse opinions of the students' essays. Temple Grandin, an expert in animal science who has approached the relevant problems from her unique perspective as someone with autism, explains that the legal issues may be subtle and the solutions unclear, but the intentions behind them are largely the same: to protect animal welfare.

Ethics . . . It's What's for Dinner

Animal Farmers against Moral Animals

Matt Kamen

Introduction

THOUGH THE ISSUE OF ANIMAL WELFARE and the plea of animal rights activists is hardly a new phenomenon, the nature of this controversy is quickly becoming both more controversial and more complex. This paper will address a recent proposal to move animals out of the realm of property and into a circumstance more akin to the status of children, considered as moral patients who require guardianship from human adults acting as moral agents. In this paper, I will argue against such a proposal from the perspective of an animal farmer. Though countless opinions can be offered on this proposal, many of which stand with a firm footing on a strongly theoretical and intellectual foundation that the farming industry may lack, the position of the animal farmer or stockperson deserves perhaps even greater consideration, for it is founded in personal livelihood. Thus, I will argue against the said proposal most adamantly on the basis of its potential to cripple the livelihood of an entire work force designed around the livestock industry.

My argument will be presented in three main sections. The first will focus on the economic factors revolving around the animal farming industry. This section will discuss the breadth and size of animal farming businesses, the income that such businesses draw from export and national sales, and a concluding comment on the widespread damage that the ending of such an industry would cause with reference to the countless other agricultural enterprises that are intimately involved with the production of meat products. The second section will address issues in animal welfare and will be designed specifically to point out that the proposal under consideration does not address issues of animal welfare and is motivated by a different purpose, so that the two should be clearly distinguished. Finally, the last section will consider two concluding lines of thought. First, it will address the issue of dealing with non-property animals. Second, it will question the effectiveness of such legislation to halt the use of animals as food products or even eliminate the practice of animal farming.

Economic Factors

Introduction

We must begin by acknowledging an initial truth: We are simply a consumer society, and the entire scope of our history has been spent cultivating exactly this type of consumer culture. We have always placed great priority on innovations, both technological and cultural, which feed the growth of such rampant consumerism and we inherently take for granted the extent to which we are entrenched in a world that has as its center the interaction between production and consumption. Supply and demand stands at the heart of such interactions; we do our best to get what we want and society develops in such a way that there are those who get it for us. Humans are mongers for paraphernalia, and in a time when nearly everything sits well above the line of necessity, that's exactly what things become; we like our toys, our cars, our clothes, our variety of little trinkets, and perhaps most of all (but perhaps the least acknowledged) we like our food. The narrative of human history twists and turns upon this last point—food. We have struggled since the beginning, as we must continue to do, to maintain, if not oversupply, ourselves with the food resources that are required to sustain an ever-expanding, ever-demanding way of life. But, thousands of years after this struggle began, things have gotten a little more complex.

The advent of evolutionary theory and cognitive science in recent history calls into question many previous assumptions about the categorical difference between humans and animals. As we reexamine our current treatment of animals, we realize that the gap between humans and nonhuman beings has become ominously narrow. And so we stand today looking ironically dismayed at the system of supply and demand that brought us here in the first place. Previously unhindered by evolutionary theory and moral angst, society has grown to supply an ever-increasing demand for animal products. If we turn our backs on this history we must realize that we are dealing with something of an inoperable tumor, which is to say, we can't simply take it out free of cost. We must ask ourselves what happens when, in a strong system of supply and demand, demand throws up its hands to say "I'm finished." Supply has a substantially greater inertia than demand and will most likely be carried forward into catastrophe. This represents the situation at hand with respect to the bill under discussion. If the bill is passed and the industry of animal farming comes to a halt, we must accept that countless managers, workers, and farm owners will be faced with the realization that they most likely cannot change their lives as fast as this bill says they must.

Thus, even if we begin this discussion by granting animals the necessary mental faculties to warrant this new legal status, we are still faced with a painfully difficult moral juxtaposition: us or them. Though it is often difficult to see economic factors as moral arguments, we must accept that in this situation they most certainly are. From the perspective of an animal farmer, the bill being proposed reads as follows: your livelihood will suddenly be taken away from you because your livestock are moral patients, kind of like kids. But we must not forget that animal farmers have moral claims in this situation as well. The decision then demands weighing the metaphorical moral scale, with the costs to farmers on one side and the benefit to animals on the other. This image, though extravagant, puts the difficulty of the situation in an appropriate perspective and offers due concern to the farmers involved. And though such a calculation is impossible, we can flesh out the metaphor even further, and clarify the situation with the relevant facts.

Statistics

In recent years, the U.S. animal farming industry has reached an unprecedented size, supporting both a growing national and an even more rapidly growing international market. In January 1, 2002, USDA Economics and Statistics System reports, in the U.S. there were 96.7 million head of cattle and calves alone, with beef cows totaling at 33.1 million head and milk cows at 9.11 million head. Furthermore, from the same summary, the USDA reports that there were 1.05 million cattle farm operations in the United States (USDA 2002d). In addition, red meat production, which includes—in addition to cattle—veal, lamb and mutton, and pork, reached record highs in 2000 of 45.7 billion pounds, and fell just slightly in 2001. Beef production accounted for 26.2 billion pounds, veal production totaled 204 million pounds, pork production was at 19.2 billion pounds, and lamb and mutton production totaled 228 million pounds (USDA 2002a). Looking at the current U.S. population, which totals (estimated value as of 9:29 EDT May 8, 2002) 286,996,929 people (Bureau 2002), this works out to approximately 259 pounds of red meat per person (including adults, children, etc.) per year. Even taking into account U.S. exports of 3,840,000,000 pounds of red meat in 2001, and per capita consumption of red meat therefore at 118.1 pounds per year (USDA 2002b), it seems fair to say that the animal farming industry is in high enough demand.

From a monetary perspective, the 2001 gross income from the slaughter and sale of red meat totaled $53.7 billion (which is the sum of cash receipts and home consumption, which refers to the total value of animals slaughtered and consumed on the farm where they were produced), with total cash receipts of $53.3 billion (USDA 2002c). Furthermore, according to the 1997 U.S. Census of Agriculture, approximately 1 million farms in the United States with cattle and calves alone generated $40.5 billion in sales, which accounted for 21 percent of the total market value of agricultural products sold in the United States and was ranked first among the sales of all commodities (Short 2002). Furthermore, according to the 1997 U.S. Census of Agriculture, there were 1,009,487 farms involved in the production of all animal products, with a total value of agricultural products sold totaling $99,139,731,000 (USDA 1997).

The industry is nothing less than enormous and hugely important to the U.S. economy. Furthermore, if we consider the human aspect of the industry, we find that there are approximately 1,066,944 farm managers and another 1,590,184 farm workers on farms involved in animal production (1997 Census of Agriculture).[1] The moral scales are not easily tipped toward animals when so many people's careers and a nation's economy are firmly held on one side. The repercussions of such a bill would stretch across this massive industry outlined above and such serious effects must be duly considered. Finally, though specific evidence is not presented here for the sake of maintaining a manageable presentation, it is important to note that the statistics provided here do not even begin to include the other agricultural products required for animal farming, including the tremendous amounts of grain feed needed as well as the farm machinery and landscape maintenance (workers and equipment) required to handle the 528,226,253 acres of land used for animal farming (USDA 1997).

Issues in Animal Welfare

Introduction

An important distinction must be made, with regard to the bill proposed here, between removing animals from the status of property and improving issues of animal welfare on farms. At best, this bill takes a highly assumptive stance towards the moral standing of nonhuman beings, a stance that current science cannot support or entirely deny, and it does so, as we have seen, at great cost. It is important to note that this bill does not in fact address issues of animal welfare. Animal welfare does not stem directly from a belief in animals as moral agents, but rather in humans as moral agents and their obligations to animals. Ensuring that animals are treated well and that all possible precautions are taken to minimize suffering and pain for animals is not the same as considering them moral patients and abandoning the enterprise of farming. Thus, it is important to discuss this confusion here so that this bill is not mistakenly supported.

Without doubt, animals respond in their own observable ways to pain, fear, stress, aversion, satisfaction, comfort, and a whole host of other emotions with which humans can surely sympathize. That there are countless instances of animal cruelty and abuse on farms today remains nothing less than tragic. It is certainly difficult, if not impossible, to deny a deeply emotional reaction to such abuses. While feelings of anger, sadness, and disgust, for example, are not unwarranted, we must ensure that they are not misguided. To act solely on emotion, no matter how real or even how decent, remains dangerous and is not how laws should be made.

The farming industry itself does not wish to cause undo torment to such animals. If only for selfish reasons, the farming industry has an inherent concern for animal welfare, because it directly affects animal productivity (Hemsworth and Coleman 1998). The government is already involved with controlling almost all aspects of farming in order to maintain standard practices of animal treatment and to maintain adequate conditions of animal welfare. But of course, there is still room to improve. Acknowledging this possibility for future improvement does not in any way require the termination of the animal farming industry by the change in animal status from the realm of property.

I will present here a few areas of animal farming which may present more readily accessible changes to the industry in hopes that they will point to compromises less drastic and more suitable to the times than the bill currently proposed.

The Problems

The first problematic area that I will consider refers to the production of specialty meat products. Certain food products that are in very high international demand require certain practices in animal treatment, feeding, and slaughter that raise specific issues for animal welfare, particularly the confinement of veal and the force-feeding of geese for foie gras. The techniques involved in the production of these specialty foods step far beyond the realm of simple meat production and are only practiced by very few farmers (Orlans 1998). A ban on the production of such specialty foods due to their excessive methods would satisfy a great number of animal rights activists by eliminating the more distasteful and cruel practices in the animal farming industry while not devastating the market or outlawing animal products altogether.

Other issues in farm animal welfare include branding/tagging, housing, transportation, castration, dehorning, and slaughter. Admittedly, there are numerous practices that occur on farms and are often unregulated by the government that bring up problems for animal welfare. However, with improved techniques for farming, possible government subsidization for the practice of such new techniques, and/or with new specific government regulations of farm practices, these welfare issues can be adequately addressed. Furthermore, in terms of the actual methods of slaughter, new techniques are being provided which are more effective and efficient and new scientific research is being employed to accurately test the effectiveness of such slaughter techniques. Thus, the animal farming industry is constantly improving to make animal welfare less a problematic issue and more of a sense of comfort that animals are being well taken care of and spared unnecessary pain and discomfort (Rollin 1995). Lastly, research into the effectiveness of human-animal interactions between farm animals and stockpeople to improve animal welfare has had great success. The importance of the stockperson has been largely ignored in the past, with farming practices discouraging contact with the animals. These beliefs are beginning to change such that people working on farms are beginning to have more contact with the animals and become educated as to how to treat them in ways that significantly reduce their stress and fear levels (Hemsworth and Coleman 1998).

Let us not be too drastic in our measures. Though the animal farming industry certainly has room to improve conditions of animal welfare—which may involve abandoning the production of specialty foods and the like—there are numerous improvements which can be made short of abolishing the system altogether. If only as a consideration, these changes to the system should be presented as options for compromise.

Concluding Questions

Will They Roam Wild?

If this proposal passes, and animals are released from the status of property and made, like children, moral patients requiring human guardianship, what then will become of them? What will become of millions of animals, capable of maintaining (if not increasing when on their own) their numbers? The modern world, without a livestock industry, is neither designed nor equipped to have that many animals, ones that require huge amounts of land to graze, roaming freely. Furthermore, we must ask, is it morally right on our part to expect a species that has been selectively bred for domestication to fend for itself and can we justify making it do so? Cattle that have been bred to be larger than before and have had their size maintained by supplied diets may be unable to graze enough on their own to support their physical needs. These are unanswered questions that must be considered. Likewise, the proposal explicitly mentions that these animals will require human guardians. On whom will this responsibility fall? Is the government prepared to support millions of animals with no income coming back from their guardianship?

Is This the End of Animal Farming?

As a concluding thought, I present the following question: Why does it seem an insufficient moral argument to claim that humans are predators and animals (particularly those being farmed) are simply the prey? The entire ecosystem of the planet is constructed with hierarchies of predator and prey relationships. We don't often think of a gazelle being morally indignant towards a lion for eating it, do we? Furthermore, it is common practice in many parts of the United States to get a hunting license and go hunting, which obviously involves killing an animal. However, this practice does not invoke any sense of ownership. Would removing animals from the status of property exempt them from the natural order of the food chain? Is it possible that farmers could simply claim that they are predators and the animals are the prey, with no sense of property or ownership? What would then be the difference between shooting a deer and keeping deer in a corral until ready for slaughter? Granted, this possibility depends entirely on the exact stipulations that this bill would contain. If the bill simply claims that animals cannot be considered property, I present here the idea that they may still be used as food. Numerous societies which have hunting and farming within the bounds of their culture do not consider animals as property, but rather as prey in the way this argument suggests. Furthermore, returning once again to the concept of the natural order of the food chain, it would be possible as well for such predators (farmers) to entrap their prey. There are countless natural species that have evolved highly intricate methods of trapping prey. Beavers, for example, build complex dams to keep fish contained for their source of food. Spiders, likewise, weave vast webs to trap their prey. This process is certainly not unknown in the natural world, and it is one into which we unavoidably factor. In truth, we know little about the expanse of our species' history. However, we know that for much of our existence we were predators, and we can be sure that for at least some time we were prey as well. Just think, if a lion could build a fence around a herd of deer, I bet it would.

An appeal to this style of argument carries with it the stigma of the naturalistic fallacy. Of course, we must always remind ourselves that just because something is natural or evolved it does not mean that it is right or good. But still, we must remind ourselves with equal consistency that just because we have reason and moral philosophy on our minds, we should not go around claiming that everything that is natural need be overcome.

Conclusion

Primarily, this bill threatens the way of life of countless farm workers across the country, as well as numerous other individuals employed in related fields, including grain supply for feed and farm machinery. While we may continue to pursue the issue of animal rights and animal welfare, as we should, we must here recognize the difference between animal welfare and animals as moral patients. Finally, we must ask ourselves why with our capacity for reason we suddenly insist on applying moral philosophy to what may simply be an advanced predator-prey relationship. In summation, we must simply continue to be leery of a proposal of this sort, for its simple assumptions may lead to drastic conclusions that we are hardly prepared to handle.

Note

1. Telephone interview with U.S. Census Bureau, Massachusetts Office (2002).

References

Bureau, U.S. Census (2002). Demographic Profile Population Clock, U.S. Census Bureau, United States Department of Commerce. 2002.

Hemsworth, P. H., and G. J. Coleman (1998). *Human-livestock interactions: The stockperson and the productivity and welfare of intensively farmed animals.* New York, CAB International.

Orlans, F. B. (1998). *The human use of animals: Case studies in ethical choice.* New York, Oxford University Press.

Rollin, B. E. (1995). *Farm animal welfare: Social, bioethical, and research issues.* Ames, Iowa State University Press.

Short, S. D. (2002). Characteristics and production costs of U.S. cow-calf operations, United States Department of Agriculture.

USDA (1997). Table 18: Selected characteristics of farms by North American Industry Classification System: 1997, United States Census of Agriculture-United States Data, from USDA, National Agricultural Statistics Service.

USDA (2002a). Livestock slaughter: 2001 report, National Agricultural Statistics Service, United States Department of Agriculture.

USDA (2002b). WASDE-385: World agricultural supply and demand estimates, United States Department of Agriculture.

USDA (2002c). Meat animals production, disposition, and income 2001 summary, National Agricultural Statistics Service and United States Department of Agriculture.

USDA (2002d). National Agricultural Statistics Service (NASS), Agricultural Statistics Board, and U.S. Department of Agriculture.

Treating Animals Humanely

Veterinary Medicine's Defense to the Law

Rianna Stefanakis

> "People of other genders, races and even age groups were once treated as property in this country. Now, it is time for 'people' of other species to be accorded the same simple dignity of being recognized not as someone else's property but as beings in their own right."
>
> —Michael Mountain, Best Friends Sanctuary

ANIMALS ARE PROPERTY in the eyes of the law, severely limiting the type of legal protections they enjoy. This status allows for abuse, exploitation, needless subjugation to cruelty, and infliction of unnecessary pain by humans and human environments. The current treatment of animals is antithetical to the principles of veterinary medicine.

A veterinarian's professional commitment is to provide physical and psychological health and disease control to animals. The Association of Veterinarians for Animal Rights endorses "the premise that all non-human animals have value and interests independent of the values and interests of other animals, including human beings. As physicians protect the interests and needs of their patients, so should veterinarians." I begin with this simple notion, common to veterinarians: that animals have value and interests that merit rights. From this follows the crux of my argument, that the striking and critical similarities between many animals and humans justify a particular kind of right, the right to legal personhood, protected by human guardianship.

In the process of working towards the health of animals, veterinarians grow to gain a better understanding of animals' medical and behavioral needs, characteristics, and very distinct personalities. In recognition of these qualities, the American Veterinary Medical Association (AVMA) chooses the language not of animal welfare, but of animal rights. Animal welfare theories accept that animals have interests but allow these interests to be traded away as long as there are some human benefits that are thought to justify that sacrifice. Alternatively, animal rights means that animals, like humans, have interests that cannot be sacrificed or relinquished so that they might benefit others.

Giving animals rights does not hold that rights are absolute; an animal's rights, just like those of humans, must be limited, and rights can certainly conflict. As Bernard Rollin states, rights are "moral notions that grow out of respect for the individual. They build protective fences around the individual. They establish areas where the individual is entitled to be protected against the state and majority even where a price is paid by the general welfare" (Rollin 1983). Animals have the right to equal consideration of their interests. For instance, a dog most certainly has an interest in avoiding the infliction of avoidable pain on him or her. We therefore are obliged to take that interest into consideration and respect the dog's right not to have pain unnecessarily inflicted upon him or her.

Animal rights are widely accepted as fact in the veterinary community, but it is not always apparent precisely what those rights entail. One way to approach this question is to ask what rights animals share with humans. Though a veterinarian may not always adopt such a moral stance, daily interactions with animals often lead to the realization of their startling similarities to human infants and young children.

Many studies of primate vocalizations are focused on identifying the evolutionary foundations of language, based on the observation that human language has ancestral homologs in primate vocalization. These tend to focus on aspects of the vocalization that have implications for the evolution of linguistics, such as the distinction between categorical and graded signals, and the presence of referentiality. Despite a lack of human language, animals seem to be able to categorize, just as pre-linguistic infants do, and some primate vocalizations also contain specific referential content that is learned, not innate. Primates also seem to possess some of the fundamental adaptive mechanisms to discern intentionality and critical aspects of agent-like behavior (Wasserman and Rovee-Collier 2001). Finally, some researchers study facial and vocal expressions as ways to convey the emotional and/or motivational aspects of the behavior. Crying in chimpanzee infants is well-documented—these animals seem to display human characteristics of behavior in their daily affairs (Bard 2000).

Though we cannot anthropomorphize animals, there is no denial that animals feel pain on a comparable level to that of humans. Animals respond to subtle changes in environment, have intentions and motivations, and produce facial expressions and body language that often communicate a sophisticated, emotionally enhanced life. Bees "dance," vervet monkeys make complex alarm calls, and chimpanzees, beyond maintaining a 99 percent genetic similarity to humans, also share a fundamental facet of human consciousness, theory of mind. Companion animals form life-enhancing relationships and are critical to the daily survival of a multitude of elderly or handicap human beings. Substantial evidence for psychological disorders in animals implies that symptoms of anxiety, depression, and even schizophrenia contribute to a complex animal psyche comparable to that of a human.

Psychological theories of attachment suggest that infants are biologically predisposed to form strong emotional bonds with their primary caregivers early in development. These bonds help secure infants with a base for subsequent social relationships they will develop and any exploration of their environment. Disrupted mother-child relations occurring during the early years of life may pose long-term effects on personality development (Bowlby 1976). Comparative research with nonhuman primates, as well as cross-cultural literature, all create a compelling set of evidence in support of the evolutionary basis for attachment (Suomi 1995). Proper rearing of human and nonhuman animals seems critical to healthy development. However, the emotional and intellectual interests and needs liken animals to human children as well.

In recognition of the mental and cognitive capabilities shared between animals and young humans, we must admit the intrinsic worth of animal lives beyond their utility to humans. These living beings should not be reduced to human commodities, but rather they should be perceived as maintaining the status and rights of a human child—a moral agent. Attaining a status of "child" may help set a premise for what sort of animal treatment is ethically acceptable.

Animals' fundamental needs for proper shelter, food, and medical treatment give rise to the need for a provider. For infants, adult humans assume this role—why should humans of greater cognitive abilities not assume this parental role for animals? Animals ought to be adopted by humans under legal guardianship. It must be understood that, just as we do not own other people, such as our children, we do not "own" animals; we are guardians, caretakers, and family members (In Defense of Animals-IDA) Guardianship would automatically create a legal constraint on the permissible treatment of animals, whereas ownership permits no such right to legal defense.

The American Veterinary Medical Association's animal welfare and animal rights policy is notable for its insistence that "Animal welfare is a human responsibility that encompasses all aspects of animal well-being, from proper housing and nutrition to preventive care, treatment of disease, and when necessary, humane euthanasia. The AVMA's commitment to animal welfare is unsurpassed." The key aspect is the necessary humane treatment. Under a status of guardianship, the above care-facilitating factors are manageable; the permissibility of maintaining animals in inhumane cages, subjecting them to inhumane cosmetic and pharmacological testing in laboratories, and inhumanely murdering them for educational purposes all violate the moral notion of animal rights.

Nor is guardianship over animals an entirely foreign concept today. Veterinarians attend to three types of animals; these are domesticated animals (including companion animals), farm animals (food), and caged animals exploited for research or entertainment purposes. The majority of those subjected to consistent veterinary care are in the first category. Privately owned pets or companion animals are intimately connected to their "owners," usually in a deep and valuable reciprocal relationship. Even though pets are bought and sold, indicating their clear status as property, any owner would consider his or her companion pet as part of the family and not as a mere commodity.

Those who would maintain animals under the status of property inevitably fall into a speciesist argument, invoking an unjustified bias towards their own species. The human bias towards in-group favoritism is easily explained by evoking the adaptive history under which moral intuitions evolved; indeed, similar explanations are frequently employed to explain racial biases. Such interests will prevail in normative ethical debates when theorists are guided by intuition rather than reason. However, the inherent flaw lies in the distinction between "is" versus "ought." It is a fact that humans are more likely to consider their ethical obligations to each other, raising these above identical obligations to animals, but that does not imply that it ought to be so.

In separating an animal from its species, removing it from its natural environment and relatives to be brought up alone amongst humans, we unethically create a speciesist justification to enslave creatures that have the right to an equal status to that of human infants. Though nonhuman animals lack a sophisticated human-compatible communication system, have no concept of free will, and thereby lack the ability to make rational decisions, this does not justify euthanasia of healthy animals, cosmetic castration, and unnecessary spay-neutering procedures, among other abuses inherent under ownership status. When seeking to resolve a perceived human-animal conflict, it may be appropriate to balance the human benefits to be derived against the interests of the animals that will be sacrificed in the process. The limiting principles of this balancing process, however, are that we treat animals humanely, that we not subject them to unnecessary suffering, and that we respect their rights. For this reason, animals' right to have active precautionary protection of these rights legally must be supported with a release from their current property status.

> Our dream: To have every person, young or old, see and treat companion animals, not as property to be exploited, abandoned or killed, but as individuals who deserve consideration for their needs . . . their quality of life.

This dream is fast becoming a reality as thousands upon thousands of compassionate people are throwing off the mantle of "ownership" in favor of the caring mantle of "guardianship."

The benefits of choosing guardianship over ownership—of convincing millions of people never to buy, but always adopt and rescue animals—are far reaching. From helping end the deaths of millions of animals in our nation's shelters, to helping end the horrors and abuse of the puppy mill trade, to helping put real teeth in laws that would truly punish and deter animal abusers, to raising children to respect animals . . . to treat them with dignity . . . will be but a few of the benefits that accrue to millions of animals around the world. I thank everyone who is helping make this dream become a reality.

—Elliot M. Katz, DVM, President, IDA

References

Bard, K. (2000). "Crying in infant primates: Insights into the development of crying in chimpanzees." In B. Hopkins (ed), *Crying as a sign, a symptom, and a signal: Clinical emotional and developmental aspects of infant and toddler crying,* 157–175. New York, Cambridge University Press.

Bowlby, J. (1976). "Human personality development in an ethological light." In A. Kling (ed.), *Animal models in human psychobiology*, 27–36, 297. New York, Plenum Press.

In Defense of Animals-IDA. http//www.idausa.org/.

Rollin, B. E. (1983). "The legal and moral bases of animal rights." In H. B. Miller and W. H. Williams (eds.), *Ethics and animals.* Clifton, N.J., Humana Press.

Suomi, S. J. (1995). "Influence of attachment theory on ethological studies of biobehavioral development in nonhuman primates." In S. Goldberg, R. Muir, and J. Kerr (eds.), *Attachment theory: Social, developmental, and clinical perspectives,* 185–201. Hillsdale, N.J., Analytic Press.

Wasserman, E. A., and C. Rovee-Collier (2001). "Pick the flowers and mind your As and 2s! Categorization by pigeons and infants." In M. E. Carroll and J. B. Overmier (eds.), *Animal research and human health: Advancing human welfare through behavioral science,* 263–279. Washington, D.C., American Psychological Association

Veterinarians and the Case against Legal Personhood for Animals

Allen Yancy

> "To label something property, is, for all intents and purposes, to conclude that the entity so labeled possesses no interests that merit protection and that the entity is solely a means to the end determined by the property owner" (Gary Francione quoted in St. Pierre 1998).
>
> ". . . without legal personhood, one is invisible to civil law. One has no civil rights. One might as well be dead" (Wise 2000).

GARY FRANCIONE AND STEVEN WISE are arguably the two leading legal voices in the movement to remove animals[1] from the status of property and place them in the category of legal persons. Francione and Wise argue that without legal personhood animals have no legal protections that guarantee their interests. In other words, the property status of animals offers them no protection from harm and suffering. As a profession, veterinary medicine is deeply concerned with the health and well-being of animals. Most American veterinarians take the oath of the American Veterinary Medical Association, in which they swear to protect the health of animals and relieve their suffering (Fox 1990).

Although veterinarians are committed to promoting the health and reducing the suffering of animals, they should not support the redefinition of animals as legal persons. Legal personhood is an unnecessary and possibly deleterious means to ensure the well-being of animals. It is unnecessary because, contrary to Francione and

Wise, the property status of animals is not incompatible with their having rights that protect their interests.[2] There are deficiencies in the current laws that allow for needless animal suffering, but these may be corrected without recourse to legal personhood. Secondly, legal personhood should be avoided because it has ramifications that are potentially deleterious to the welfare of animals. Legal personhood for animals would end biomedical research on animals. This research has not only benefited humans, it has also produced many medicines which have eliminated or alleviated many of the diseases that cause harm and suffering in animals. Lastly, legal personhood would create "rights" for animals that could greatly hinder the practice of veterinary medicine.

Legal personhood for animals is not the only option that a veterinarian concerned with promoting animal welfare may pursue, for although animals are currently considered property, the law grants them rights. All fifty states and the federal government have passed laws that seek to protect the well-being of animals. There is great variation in the specific provisions of the various state laws, but in general all have provisions against the following: (1) unnecessary or cruel torture, mutilation, beating, or killing of an animal; (2) deprivation of food and water for an impounded animal; (3) the use of animals in fighting and baiting; (4) overworking animals; and (5) abandonment of sick, maimed, infirmed, or disabled animals (Madeline 2000).

There are also federal statutes that protect the well-being of animals. For example, the Animal Welfare Act of 1970 (AWA) establishes "standards to govern the humane handling, care, treatment, and transportation" of animals in the charge of dealers, research facilities, and exhibitors. It also creates minimum standards for "handling, housing, feeding, watering, sanitation, ventilation . . . and adequate veterinary care" (Sunstein 2000). The AWA requires the use of pain-relieving drugs, veterinary care, and euthanasia for all animals used in experimentation (Hendee, Loeb, et al. 1988). The law even has provisions that aim to satisfy the psychological well-being of primates. It necessitates that owners of primates address their needs for "social grouping," environmental enrichment such as swings, perches, and mirrors, and that great apes over 110 pounds must have opportunities for "species-typical behavior" (Kolber 2001). The AWA demonstrates that some laws have begun to address what many veterinarians already know, that animal welfare encompasses more than the mere prevention of suffering. Although the AWA still recognizes animals as property, it clearly recognizes that animals have interests, which need to be protected. Rather than being solely a means to the ends of the owner, these laws significantly circumscribe how an owner may use his property, and they impose constraints on the welfare of the owner.[3]

The preceding survey of the current federal and state laws regarding animals demonstrates that animals enjoy legal rights even though they are classified as property. These laws not only establish negative obligations (one cannot torture animals), they also create positive obligations (great apes must be allowed opportunities for species-typical behavior). The analysis presented here suggests that animals occupy an intermediary space between property and legal personhood in which, contrary to Francione and Wise, their interests are protected by legal rights.

There is no clearer expression of this intermediate status than in *Corso v. Crawford Dog and Cat Hosp. Inc.* (1979). The majority wrote, "This court now overrules prior precedent and holds that a pet is not just a thing but occupies a special place somewhere in between a person and a piece of personal property"(Kelch 1998). The *Corso* decision refers specifically to household pets, but the state and federal statutes suggest that other animals occupy an elevated status as well. This analysis undermines the argument for legal personhood because it demonstrates that legal personhood is not necessary for animals to enjoy legal rights that protect their health and well-being.

Although state and federal law establishes legal rights for animals, advocates of legal personhood may still point to loopholes and limitations that diminish the ability of these laws to prevent suffering and promote the well-being of animals. The penalties established by these laws are often not severe enough to discourage cruelty. For instance, killing, maiming, or poisoning an animal is a misdemeanor and not a felony in many states (Dryden 2001). More seriously, state animal welfare and anti-cruelty laws often exempt animals used in medical and scientific experiments, agriculture, and in forms of entertainment such as rodeos and horse races (Dryden 2001, Chandola 2002).[4] Additionally, some veterinarians may object that many state laws ignore important aspects of an animal's health and welfare by adopting too narrow an understanding of animal interests by focusing almost solely on the prevention of cruelty.

Lastly, these laws are difficult to enforce because the U.S. Department of Agriculture, which oversees compliance with federal statutes, lacks funding and relies on public prosecution. Public prosecutors tend to pursue only the most egregious cases of abuse. Currently, private third parties interested in animal welfare, such as People for the Ethical Treatment of Animals and the Humane Society of the United States, are not allowed to sue on behalf of animals (Sunstein 2000).

While these loopholes and limitations are troubling, legal personhood is not the proper remedy. Shortcomings, such as small penalties and broad exemptions, do not need legal personhood in order to be redressed. Some states, Michigan for example, have already made cruelty to animals a felony (Madeline 2000). Some states have laws that qualify the exemptions. For instance, Maryland law covers most exempted activities, such as research, with the caveat that these activities are done humanely (Dryden 2001).

It may be objected that it would be prohibitively difficult to regulate the exemptions in the other states because the farming, racing, and research industries would use their power and influence to lobby against such changes. This is really no objection at all, for these industries would likely lobby even harder against legal personhood for animals, which would outlaw these industries outright. Rather than advocate for legal personhood for animals, veterinarians concerned with relieving animal suffering should attempt to get more states to follow the examples of Michigan and Maryland. Too often, state laws simply focus on preventing the grossest cruelties such as the maiming of animals. However, from a veterinary perspective it is clear that animals have interests beyond the prevention of suffering. For example, studies have shown that "pigs need to root in soil . . . hens need to dust-bathe, and both of these species need to build a nest before giving birth or laying eggs" (Broom 1981).

The AWA, a federal law, provides a model for how state statutes may be expanded to include a broader conception of animal well-being. The AWA, which requires that great apes have the ability to engage in species-typical behavior, demonstrated that a broad conception of animal interests is not incompatible with their status as property.[5] As we have seen, property status and legal rights are compatible; therefore, it is possible to pass a law that required young calves to be stored in crates large enough for them to groom themselves. Thus, veterinarians may support measures to increase the health and well-being of animals without supporting legal personhood for animals.

One of the most powerful arguments in favor of redefining animals from property to legal persons is that it would allow for better enforcement and prosecution of laws designed to protect animals. Animal welfare and protection laws allow only public prosecutors—who typically lack the funding and the desire to pursue only but the most egregious cases of abuse—the right to sue on behalf of animals. Some legal scholars believe that allowing private third parties that are interested in animal welfare to sue on behalf of animals would greatly increase the enforcement of animal welfare laws (Sunstein 2000, Kolber 2001). Private parties cannot bring suit because they lack standing, the technical legal term for whether a litigant is entitled to have the court decide on the merits of her dispute. Standing requires that a plaintiff demonstrate (1) injury-in-fact that was (2) caused by the defendant and (3) that a favorable ruling in favor of the plaintiff would redress the injury (Kolber 2001). In most cases, the courts dismiss most third party suits brought on behalf of animals because humans cannot show that they suffered an injury-in-fact from the violation of an animal welfare law (Kolber 2001).

Advocates of legal personhood for animals often point to the important need to enable third parties to sue on behalf of animals (St. Pierre 1998). However, the current property status of animals is not incompatible with allowing private third parties to sue on their behalf. In other words, standing does not require legal personhood. As the legal scholar Cass Sunstein has noted, "plaintiffs need not be or be expressly labeled persons" for suits may be brought on behalf of "trusts, municipalities, partnerships, and even ships" (Sunstein 2000). Historically, slaves were allowed to challenge unjust servitude in courts through a white guardian or "next friend" even though they were considered property in the eyes of the law (Sunstein 2000). These examples demonstrate that Congress *can* and *has* granted third parties the right to sue on behalf of non-legal persons, including those considered property. The best course of action would be to lobby Congress to grant standing to private third parties for animals, not legal personhood. Additionally, many environmental laws have citizen-suit provisions that allow private parties to bring suit against violators. Coupled with standing, these provisions would give animal welfare laws the bite that they currently lack.

I have thus far argued against granting legal personhood to animals on the grounds that it is unnecessary for their protection and well-being. Current laws regarding animals already grant them substantive legal rights. Furthermore, we have seen that the scope of these laws may be broadened and that they may be given greater enforcement power without recourse to legal personhood. Contrary to Francione and Wise, a being is not invisible to civil law without legal personhood. I have sought to establish that legal personhood is an unnecessary legal maneuver for ensuring the welfare of animals, but one may still ask why veterinarians should diligently oppose it.

Veterinarians should resist legal personhood for animals because it could prove disastrous for animal health and well-being. The proposal could have these deleterious effects because it would eliminate all biomedical research on animals. Advocates for legal personhood believe that it would eliminate the use of animals for human ends (St. Pierre 1998), but this view ignores the fact that biomedical research also directly benefits animals. Research on animals has led to immunizations against distemper, rabies, parvovirus, infectious hepatitis, anthrax, and tetanus. It has also led to treatments for feline leukemia, the prevention of brucellosis and tuberculosis in cattle, and immunotherapy for cancer in dogs. This is only a partial listing of the many ways that animal experimentation has been used to relieve suffering and improve the health of animals (Hendee, Loeb, et al. 1988).

Some animal liberation advocates believe that we can do away with animal experimentation because in vitro research and computer modeling are viable substitutes. The Congressional Office of Technology Assessment reported, "isolated systems (cultures) give isolated results" (Hendee, Loeb, et al. 1988). In other words, isolated cells do not behave the same as cells in intact systems. Computer models cannot fully replicate biological systems because many of the finer details and interactions of these systems are unknown. With an incomplete model, computer simulations will not yield true-to-life results. The end of animal experimentation would mean that progress in veterinary medicine would be greatly slowed and in some areas perhaps blocked altogether. Such a consequence does not bode well for the health and well-being of animals.[6]

An alternative to the analysis presented here is the suggestion that animal experimentation would be allowed if the experiments benefited the species experimented upon. Presumably, all precautions to prevent pain and suffering would also have to be taken. From the perspective of the animal liberationist, however, allowing animal experimentation for the benefit of animals is self-defeating because it would reopen the door to animal experimentation for the sake of humans. The animal experimented upon would be used as a means to an end. Whereas the animal liberation movement creates a moral community between humans and animals by asserting that the interests of all sentient beings should be given equal consideration (Preece and Chamberlain 1993), once it is allowed that a creature may be used as a means to an end, why should that creature not be used as a means to benefit any member of the moral community? There would seem to be no reason why chickens should only be used for chicken ends, dogs for dog ends, etc. Cats could be used for chimpanzee ends, pigs for human ends, and humans for dog ends. As the preceding examples suggest, the logic that would allow animal experimentation only if it benefited animals would actually open the door to both animal experimentation for human ends—a scenario unacceptable to the animal liberationist—and human experimentation for animal ends.

Legal personhood would also needlessly create legally unclear situations that have implications for veterinarians. For example, could a veterinarian be sued for feeding a mouse to a snake as she attempts to nourish it back to health? Whose "rights" would triumph? The mouse's "right" to life or the snake's "right" to nourishment? These examples suggest that legal personhood would create a series of conflicting "rights" that could hinder the practice of sound veterinary medicine. Animal liberationists often use babies and the mentally incompetent as moral analogues for the treatment of animals, but these examples show that there is a fundamental difference between babies, the mentally incompetent, and animals. Unlike babies and the mentally incompetent, some animals must infringe upon the "rights" of other animals in order to survive. Secondly, legal personhood for animals would limit, if not nullify, the utilitarian considerations that are an integral part of veterinary medicine. What if a veterinarian had to kill one member of an animal herd in order to save the rest from an infectious disease? What if it is necessary to exterminate a disease-carrying animal that threatens a human population? In these situations it seems appropriate to kill the animals in question, but we certainly do not kill babies or the mentally incompetent in such scenarios. These utilitarian considerations point to another important difference between babies, the mentally incompetent, and animals. The creation of conflicting "rights" and the abrogation of the utilitarian considerations that veterinarians must make represent two salient examples of the kinds of unintended consequences that would arise from legal personhood for animals. The unintended consequences would have the effect of greatly hindering the practice of sounder veterinary medicine.

This essay has argued that veterinarians concerned about fulfilling their oath to protect the health of animals and to relieve them from suffering need not support legal personhood for animals. In fact, veterinarians should oppose it, for legal personhood is both legally unnecessary and potentially harmful to the practice of veterinary medicine. Contrary to the assertions of Francione and Wise, the property status of animals is not incompatible with their having rights. At present, these rights are from far from perfect, but they can be strengthened and made more extensive within the framework of animals as property. Veterinarians should perhaps be most concerned with legal personhood for animals because it would ultimately prove harmful to animal welfare. Legal personhood would end biomedical research on animals, which has yielded many medicines to cure or alleviate the diseases that plague animals. Furthermore, legal personhood might unintentionally create conflicts between the "rights" of various animals and it might limit the options available to veterinarians. These unintended consequences would hinder the practice of veterinary medicine. Thus, if veterinarians are truly concerned with protecting the health of animals and relieving them from suffering, they would be wise to advocate for more expansive laws and better enforcement of those laws within the existing framework of animals as property.

Notes

1. All references to animals in this essay refer to nonhuman animals. "Animal" will also be used only to refer to sentient beings, in other words, those animals that can experience pain. I have chosen this distinction because it is the one most often used by supporters of legal personhood.
2. This essay deals primarily with veterinary and legal perspectives, and not philosophical ones. Thus any discussion of rights herein refers to legal rights as opposed to moral rights. Broadly defined, legal rights are an entity's interests that are protected by the law. Legal rights may not necessarily encompass moral rights and vice versa.
3. In fact, these provisions are imposing a severe burden on the owners of animals. The American Medical Association estimates that it would cost half a billion dollars for every lab to come into compliance with the law Hendee, W., J. Loeb, et al. (1988).
4. Recall that animals used in labs with federal funding are not exempt from welfare regulations.
5. The AWA is, of course, not perfect. It too could be expanded to included provisions for the well-being of animals other than dogs (it requires that they get exercise), primates, and great apes.
6. Animal experimentation for cosmetic reasons can and should be phased out. This is already beginning to happen as scientists are looking for alternatives to the Draize test, which sprays chemicals and other substances into the eyes of rabbits for toxic effects in chemicals and household cleaners. This reform could also be accomplished without resort to legal personhood.

References

Broom, D. M. (1981). *Biology of behavior: Mechanisms, functions, and applications.* New York, Cambridge University Press.

Chandola, M. V. (2002). "Dissecting American animal protection law: Healing the wounds with animal rights and Eastern enlightenment." *Wisconsin Law Review,* Winter.

Dryden, A. J. (2001). "Overcoming the inadequacies of animal cruelty statutes and the property-based view of animals." *Idaho Law Review* 38.

Fox, M. W. (1990). *Inhumane society: The American way of exploiting animals.* New York, St. Martin's Press.

Hendee, W., J. Loeb, et al. (1988). *Use of animals in biomedical research: The challenge and response.* Chicago, American Medical Association.

Kelch, T. (1998). "Toward a non-property status for animals." *NYU Environmental Law Journal 6.*

Kolber, A. (2001). "Standing upright: The moral and legal standing of humans and other apes." *Stanford Law Review* 54: 163–204.

Madeline, B. A. (2000). "Cruelty to animals: Recognizing violence against nonhuman victims." *University of Hawaii Law Review.*

Preece, R., and L. Chamberlain (1993). *Animal welfare & human values.* Waterloo, Wilfrid Laurier University Press.

St. Pierre, D. S. (1998). "The transition from property to people: The road to the recognition of rights for non-human animals." *Hastings Women's Law Journal* 9: 255.

Sunstein, C. R. (2000). "Standing for animals." *UCLA Law Review* 47: 1333.

Wise, S. M. (2000). *Rattling the cage: Toward legal rights for animals.* Cambridge, Mass., Perseus Books,

Animals Are Not Things

Temple Grandin

SINCE I AM AUTISTIC I do not understand purely abstract concepts that are based only in language. To understand a word, I have to make a picture in my imagination and define words with concrete examples. When I think of the phrase "buy a car," I immediately get images of past experiences of buying cars. Some purely philosophical arguments I do not understand because I cannot visualize them.

I am going to approach the subject of animals as property in a very concrete manner that is based more on neuroscience instead of philosophical concepts. First of all, an animal does not understand an abstract concept such as being property or non-property. It is going to experience an environment that humans can manipulate to the animal's detriment or well-being. The student essay that I could relate to the most was the one by Allen Yancy on "Veterinarians and the Case Against Legal Personhood for Animals." Yancy states that "although animals are currently considered property, the law grants them rights."

To discuss whether or not animals should be property, I first have to define what the word "property" means in a concrete manner. I will limit my discussion to the framework of the U.S. legal system and culture. When I own an item as property, I am allowed to do certain things with it. If I own a cow and a screwdriver I can sell them, give them away, destroy them, experiment on them, eat them, put them in my will, profit from them, or use them in my business. I am also allowed to buy another cow or screwdriver. For example, I am allowed to slaughter the cow or destroy the screwdriver in a stamping press. Although absurd, I could even eat the screwdriver if I ground it into very fine powder. Both the cow and the screwdriver can be used in my business and I can put them in my will. I am allowed to modify cattle by selective breeding and I can modify my screwdriver by painting its handle green.

However, both the laws in the U.S. and our culture put severe restrictions on the kinds of things I can do to the cow but place no restrictions on the things I can do to the screwdriver. I could be punished for felony animal abuse if I stabbed the cow in the eye with the screwdriver, but there would be no penalty for mangling the screwdriver and slowly destroying it by hitting it with my hammer. In his essay, Allen Yancy offers a thorough discussion on the current legislation regarding this issue, discussing both its strengths and weaknesses.

Animals Feel Pain

There is a fundamental difference between cows and screwdrivers. Cows feel pain and screwdrivers do not. In her essay, Rianna Stefanakis argues that "animals feel pain on a comparable level to that of humans." I am allowed to kill the cow for food but she must be killed in a manner that will not cause pain. Allen Yancy discusses the current requirements for the use of pain-relieving methods in the treatment of animals. From many hours of observing the behavior of cattle at slaughter plants and feedlots, I have learned that cattle do not understand that they will be slaughtered. During handling they behave the same way at both a slaughter plant and in a feedlot veterinary chute. If they knew they were going to die they should be wilder and more agitated during handling at a slaughter plant (Grandin 2001).

A reviewer of this paper asked me to address the possibility that the observation that the animal's behavior is the same in both places is learned helplessness. It is not learned helplessness because in both the slaughter plant and the feedlot, cattle sometimes make active attempts to jump fences or run away from people. Active escape attempts occur more frequently when cattle are shocked with electric prods. The way people handle the cattle has a much greater effect on their behavior than the location where handling occurred. This point is addressed by Matt Kamen, who writes that "people working on farms are beginning to have more contact with the animals and [are becoming] educated as to how to treat them in ways that significantly reduce their stress and fear levels."

Measurements of cortisol also indicate that stress levels are similar at both the slaughter plant and handling in the veterinary chute at a feedlot. A review of these studies is in Grandin (1997). If cattle knew they were going to die it would be reasonable to assume that cortisol levels would be much higher in the slaughter plant.

U.S. law and culture require that even though the cow is property, I have certain responsibilities for the cow and no moral responsibilities for the screwdriver. I can be charged with animal abuse and punished if I beat or starve my cow. These laws are designed to prevent the animal from suffering. As Allen Yancy also mentions, laws for protecting research animals require keeping them in social groups so they have the company of their own kind. As scientists learn more about animal behavior, additional protections may be needed. I am not required to keep a pair of screwdrivers in my toolbox so that they can socialize with other screwdrivers.

The cow has legal protections that a screwdriver does not have. These legal protections only apply to live animals that have a well-developed nervous system.

Science has shown that animals such as mammals and birds feel pain in a manner similar to humans. Insects, viruses, and microbes are not able to feel pain or suffer. More research is needed to determine the extent that fishes and amphibians feel pain. Current research shows that they do experience fear. Fear is very aversive and animals should be shielded from situations that cause great fear. Fear will cause a great rise in stress hormones. Kamen discusses the importance and the effectiveness of methods of fear reduction at feed lots and slaughter facilities. Animals such as dogs also need to have environmental enrichments. Melzack (1954) and Burns (1955) found that puppies kept in barren kennels became hyperexcitable and had abnormal EEG patterns which indicated extreme arousal.

When the structure of the brain and nervous system is studied, there is no black-and-white line between people and higher mammals such as chimps, dogs, or cows. The genome project has shown that humans and mice share many genes (Gunter and Dhand 2002). In mammals 30 to 40 percent of all genes are involved in nervous system development and function. The basic design of the nervous system and the neural mechanisms that process fear and pain are similar in humans and other mammals (Rogan and LeDoux 1996). Colpaert et al. (2001) reported that rats will self-medicate themselves with pain killers to relieve pain in arthritic joints. Stefanakis makes a similar reference to more complex cognitive abilities and psychological mechanisms seen in animals. Pain and fear both cause suffering. As nervous system and brain complexity increases, the welfare needs of the animal increase and become more complex, but all animals that have sufficient nervous system complexity to suffer from either pain or fear need basic welfare protections. Animals with complex brains also have greater social needs and a need for greater environmental enrichment.

My logic falls apart in two areas. Human babies are given full legal protection even though a newborn's cognitive abilities are less than the abilities of mature farm animals. They are given this protection because they will grow and develop into cognizant people. A mentally retarded child and a cow may have the same cognitive abilities. I can sell or kill the cow but I am not allowed to do this with a retarded child. Why should the retarded child or human newborn have more protection than a cow? One reason is that the child is our own species and we protect our own species. Even lions do not usually dine on lion for dinner. A further discussion of arguments for or against speciesism is beyond the scope of this essay. However, biologically I think there is an instinct to protect one's own kind.

The cows have legal protection from pain and suffering but they have less legal protection than a retarded child. I would be sent to prison for killing or selling a retarded child and I would not be allowed to do invasive research on the child. Human children are legally not property. Legally, a major distinction between property and non-property is that I can buy, modify, sell, give away or destroy items that I own.

In Boulder, Colorado, dog owners are now called "guardians," but the dog "guardians" still have the same property rights. Legally they can still sell or kill their dogs. Changing the dog owner's designation to "guardian" may help improve people's attitudes towards dogs, but legally they are still property. Even though they are still property, their welfare may be improved if people's attitudes are changed. Improving attitudes towards animals can greatly improve how people treat animals. Hemsworth et al. (1989) did studies that showed when people had positive attitudes towards farm animals they treated them better and the pigs were less fearful of people.

Nervous System Complexity

With the framework outlined above, I can argue that animals can be property and still have a high standard of welfare. However, I will argue very strongly that animals need many protections because they are not things like a screwdriver. As the phylogenetic tree of animal species is climbed, protection from suffering must be increased. Chimps would require more protection and need different kinds of protection than frogs to ensure that they would not suffer. Chimps have a more complex brain than frogs and a rich social life. As nervous system complexity increases, the animal needs increasing amounts of protection from society to ensure that it does not suffer from pain, fear, or a lack of environmental and social stimulation. Even though the phylogenetic tree is not linear, it moves along its various branches from less complex nervous systems to more complex. Comparative physiology and psychology have shown that there is a broad range of nervous system complexity. As complexity increases, a brain forms in the head of the animal that becomes increasingly complex. Different animals can be ranked in order of brain complexity. For example, ranking from less complex to more complex would be clams, lobsters, fish, birds, mice, dogs, apes, chimpanzees, and people. There are some animals that are approximately equal in nervous system complexity such as dogs and pigs. Both rats and chimps should have equal protection from pain and fear, but the chimp may need additional protection to ensure that it has adequate social stimulation. Chimps have a greater need for social and environmental stimulation than rats, but recent research indicates that even mice need social stimulation to prevent abnormal stereotypic behavior (Bohannon 2002). Simple environmental enrichments such as materials to burrow in and several companions are probably adequate for a rat, but a chimp needs much more. Yancy points out that primates need opportunities for "social grouping" and "species-typical behaviors."

As one travels back in evolutionary time, there is a point where an organism did not have sufficient central nervous system capacity to experience fear or pain. The brain circuits that process fear are more primitive than the circuits that process pain. For example, fish experience fear but their pain perception may be limited. They may need protection to primarily reduce fear. Research is needed to determine the points on the hierarchy of nervous system complexity where conscious perception of pain and fear is lost. It is likely that pain perception will cease at a higher level of nervous system complexity than fear perception. As the phylogenetic tree is ascended and nervous system complexity increases, animals will have other needs, such as social interaction, in addition to protection from pain and fear. My basic principle is that development of the nervous system is a major determinant of the welfare needs of the animal.

Animals are not things, but there is probably a point where legally protecting an organism from pain and fear should cease. From my knowledge of neuroscience, I can be reasonably sure that oysters, flu viruses, and bacteria do not need legal protection to prevent people from being cruel by inflicting pain and fear. Advocating for the rights of oysters is something I think is silly.

The key is, does the animal have sufficient nervous system complexity to experience pain and fear and actually suffer? Simple reflexes are not reliable indications of suffering. Removing the cortex of the brain leaves reflexes intact and the decerebrate animal will not feel pain (Woolf 1983). To suffer, the animal must have sufficient associative circuits in the brain to process pain or fear. This is discussed in a review by Grandin (2002).

It is obvious to me that intelligent animals such as elephants experience emotions that are more complex than simple pain or fear. They will need different legal protections than animals with simpler nervous systems. The degree of protection and environmental and social enrichment an animal will require will be dependent on the level of complexity of its nervous system. Brain development is the key, and more research is needed to make logical decisions about protecting fish or worms. Fish experience fear and worms are probably too primitive to suffer.

Property is a legal term and a language-based concept that animals do not fully understand. Monkeys have a sense that they own certain things (Kummer 1991). Even the family dog may growl if you attempt to take away his bone. Animals guard both their territories and their food. To put it simply, animals have a sense that certain places or food items are theirs. However, animals do not understand that they themselves may be the property of a human being. Property is a legal term and a language-based concept that gives the owners of property certain legal rights above and beyond physical possession. For example, if my prize bull is stolen, the insurance company will pay for him. I can also transfer ownership by selling my bull. Animals deserve the same protections from society whether or not they are property.

How can I justify eating meat when I say that animals deserve the same protections whether they are property or non-property? The cattle I have eaten would have never lived at all if we had not raised them. Another viewpoint from a reviewer is that this does not justify eating them because that perpetuates more cattle and more care. It is my opinion that having more cattle is justified provided we take care of their welfare. I feel very strongly that we owe agricultural animals a decent life and I will be the first to admit that some agricultural practices need to be changed. If I were in total agreement with this reviewer, the extreme outcome of this statement would be to let animals become extinct so they would not suffer. I would not want this to happen. Ironically, ownership of animals on the African plains may motivate the local people to take care of them and improve their welfare.

There is another issue of the value of different animals and plants. The above discussion only applies to welfare and protection from pain, suffering, or boredom. It does not imply that more primitive living organisms such as oysters or insects have less value than the animals with more complex nervous systems and social lives. Biological and genetic diversity in the animal and plant kingdoms is of great value. Preserving the organisms that are not capable of suffering is important. When a species becomes extinct, it is lost. To formalize my agreement, I will give some concrete definitions of value and how it differs from property. Some examples of value in the animal world would be: bees pollinating flowers, worms maintaining the soil ecosystem, a species that becomes extinct that may have provided a cure for cancer, natural ecosystems that are beautiful, and the valuable genetic information in all species. Our society also has laws to protect animals and plants from becoming extinct. In many cases, this value concept overrides property rights. Even if I own the land, I am not allowed to completely destroy a unique wildlife habitat.

In conclusion, animals can be property and still have many laws and other protections to ensure their welfare. Changing language-based concepts like property are only important to animals if changes in rhetoric cause people to treat animals better. The student essays in this section do a good job of acknowledging this point. All three clearly state that animal welfare is the top priority. I have little interest in rhetoric unless it provides actual changes where the animals live. All my life I have worked to make concrete improvements out in the field.

References

Bohannon, J. (2002). "Animal models: Can a mouse be standardized?" *Science* 298 (5602): 2320–1.

Colpaert, F. C., J. P. Tarayre, et al. (2001). "Opiate self-administration as a measure of chronic nociceptive pain in arthritic rats." *Pain* 91 (1–2): 33–45.

Grandin, T. (1997). "Assessment of stress during handling and transport." *Journal of Animal Science* 75(1): 249–57.

Grandin, T. (2001). "Welfare of cattle during slaughter and the prevention of nonambulatory (downer) cattle." *Journal of the American Veterinary Medical Association* 219 (10): 1377–82.

Grandin, T. (2002). "Distress in animals: Is it fear, pain or physical stress?" American Board of Veterinary Practitioners—Symposium 2002. May 17, 2002, Special Session, Pain Stress and Fear, Manhattan Beach, CA.

Gunter, C., and R. Dhand (2002). "Human biology by proxy." *Nature* 420: 509.

Hemsworth, P. H., and G. J. Coleman. (1998). *Human-livestock interactions: The stockperson and the productivity and welfare of intensively farmed animals.* New York, CAB International.

Kummer, H. E. a. C., M. (1991). "Cues of ownership in Macaca fasicularis." *Animal Behavior* 42: 529–549.

Melzack, R. (1954). "The genesis of emotional behavior: An experimental study of the dog." *Journal of Comparative and Physiological Psychology* 47 (166–188).

Melzack R., and Burns, S. K. (1955). "Neuropsychological effects of early sensory restriction." *Experimental Neurology* 13: 163–175.

Rogan, M. T., and J. E. LeDoux (1996). "Emotion: Systems, cells, synaptic plasticity." *Cell* 85 (4): 469–75.

Woolf, C. J. (1983). "Evidence for a central component of post-injury pain hypersensitivity." *Nature* 306 (5944): 686–8.

Conclusion

Fiery Cushman and Matt Kamen

For a project designed with debate at its heart, a remarkable consensus circulates through the pages of *People, Property, or Pets?* Humans, agree the authors, ought to respect the interests of nonhumans. This common intuition quickly breeds divergent conclusions and fierce debate—and the essays in this volume are no exception. But it would be a shame for the areas of conflict to overshadow the very substantial points of agreement. Our shared instincts towards animal welfare can begin to bridge the gap between the disciplines represented in this book, as well as between academic debate and real-world progress.

As described in the preface, students were assigned to argue either for or against a proposition granting animals legal personhood, a structure similar to the guardianship of young children by competent adults. With few exceptions, students sought to undermine the connection between property and rights. Those assigned to support the proposal argued that legal personhood is requisite for basic animal welfare, but does not imply an extreme version of animal rights. Those assigned to oppose the proposal, on the other hand, argued that legal personhood implies a very extreme version of animal rights, and that animal welfare can adequately be protected even if animals are legally categorized as property. Either one of these opinions can be justified, and the contributions of the student authors, while impressive, are hardly as comprehensive as the relevant professional experts. The real point of interest is that nearly all students shared a common intuition about what we owe animals—some welfare protections, but not the full slate of human rights—regardless of their allegiance to the specific legal proposition.

While students supporting the proposition typically emphasized the complex cognitive and social behavior of the primate species most closely related to humans, and students opposing the proposition instead voiced doubt about the capacity of an oyster for pain, a chicken for self-reflection, or a cow for ethical evaluation, at least both sides agree on the sorts of cognitive capacities that count in a moral calculus. At the most basic level, pain matters and ought to be avoided. Higher levels of rights depend on consciousness, reflection, abstraction, and, ultimately, the ability to engage as a moral agent. In this regard, cognitive science has an important role in ethics. At the same time, as the argument from marginal cases illustrates, no single cognitive criterion will ever suffice to admit or deny rights. Nor is the animal welfare debate disconnected from human needs; practical considerations weighed heavily in many of the essays. Fiercely contested issues included whether animal testing models have an important impact on biomedical science, and whether modern cultures and economies rely on the ownership of animals. In the end, however, most authors agreed that some human interests are strong enough to void the rights that animals would enjoy under ideal circumstances.

The importance of core intuitions is underscored by the contribution of the experts involved in this project. Although much more knowledgeable about the subject, and presumably more personally committed to the debate, their essays are both less academic and less polemical than the students'. Whereas the student essays steer clear of highlighting points of agreement and concession so as to remain unquestionably committed to their position, the professionals exhibit no such qualms. Their arguments rely not on nuanced details or intellectual acrobatics, but rather on reasonable claims, concrete examples, and straightforward analysis. The expert essays also speak to the importance of building ethics up from common assumptions and offer encouragement that such common assumptions regarding animal welfare actually exist. Indeed, philosophers like Peter Singer arrive at shocking conclusions by preying upon our more moderate moral intuitions—logic, unlike some intuitions, can be carried to extremes.

As a result of these pervasive intuitions, the most effective arguments for and against animal welfare focus less on philosophical justification of what ought to be, and more on exposing the current state of what is. Purely intellectual arguments founded in philosophical principles do little to sway public opinion. A poignant description of the inhumane treatment of animals, however, can capture powerful emotions. For these reasons, the legal question motivating these essays was ripe for the exposure of our underlying intuitions. Ideally, it is on such fundamental similarities that legal systems are built. The law must aim to capture the domain of ethical beliefs shared by every citizen. The challenge for lawmakers, therefore, is not to derive animal rights from abstract principles, but to bring policy in accord with public sentiment.

Contributors

Editors

Marc Hauser's research sits at the interface between evolutionary biology and cognitive neuroscience and is aimed at understanding how the minds of human and nonhuman animals evolved. By studying monkeys and apes in both the wild and in captivity, as well as human infants and adults, Hauser's work has unlocked some of the mysteries of language evolution, conceptual representation, social cooperation, communication, and morality. He is a Harvard College Professor, Professor in the Departments of Psychology, Organismic & Evolutionary Biology, and Biological Anthropology, Co-Director of the Mind, Brain and Behavior Program, Director of the Primate Cognitive Neuroscience Laboratory, and the author of more than 200 papers and five books, including *The Evolution of Communication* (1996), *Wild Minds* (2000), and the forthcoming *Moral Minds: The Unconscious Voice of Right and Wrong.* He is currently working on a book about the mind with Noam Chomsky.

Prof. Hauser received a BS from Bucknell University and a PhD from UCLA. He has taught at Makerere University, Uganda, University of California, Davis, and Harvard University. He is the recipient of a National Science Foundation Young Investigator Award and Guggenheim Fellowship, as several awards from Harvard for his teaching.

Fiery Cushman is a doctoral candidate in cognitive psychology at Harvard University. His primary research focus is moral psychology. Working at Harvard's Primate Cognitive Neuroscience Laboratory, he synthesizes research on the mechanisms of moral psychology in humans with research on the evolutionary history of those mechanisms in non-human primates. Together with several collaborators, Mr. Cushman maintains *The Moral Sense Test,* an online psychological test of moral judgment (moral.wjh.harvard.edu). As an undergraduate at Harvard, where he received his BA in biology, he also studied psychology and moral philosophy. He gained first-hand experience with animal care and the use of non-human primates in science as a research assistant at the Primate Cognitive Neuroscience Laboratory. *People, Property or Pets?* is Cushman's first co-edited volume.

Matt Kamen studied cognitive neuroscience at Harvard University and received a BA in Psychology in 2003. As an undergraduate he began working with non-human primates at Harvard's Primate Cognitive Neuroscience Laboratory. After graduation, Mr. Kamen continued his work at the Primate Cognitive Neuroscience Laboratory, as a research assistant and teaching fellow. He concentrated his research on primate vocal communication, specifically analyzing the acoustic components used to encode information in non-human primate vocalizations. Today he works as a software developer in New York. This book is his first co-edited volume.

Students

People, Property, or Pets? is a volume principally populated by a lucky group of undergraduates at Harvard University who participated in a springtime seminar on evolutionary ethics led by Marc Hauser. A central aim of the seminar was to promote crosstalk between diverse academic disciplines, and the students majored in fields ranging from psychology to neuroscience, biology, the history of science, philosophy, religion, government, and economics. This heterogeneity was also reflected in the seminar's structure. Each week a visiting lecturer assigned readings and led discussion from the perspective of a different academic discipline. Guests lecturers included defense lawyer and law professor Alan Derschowitz, evolutionary biologist Steven Jay Gould, psychologist Steven Pinker, and the Reverend Peter Gomes.

The students who participated in Evolutionary Ethics remember it as one of their most intellectually engaging experiences at Harvard. The arguments in each three-hour meeting spanned centuries of philosophy and wide swaths of scientific research. They also probed some of the most deep and enduring intellectual enigmas: What is the source of morality? What are the fundamental differences between humans and animals? How can we reconcile spiritual and material world views? What is the interaction between learned and innate knowledge?

In an attempt to weave these disparate threads into a single pursuit, Hauser assigned his students to write essays on a hypothetical proposition: to raise the legal status of animals from property to a sort of personhood, akin to the status of a child who is overseen by appointed guardians. In went the creative energy of a handful of sharp and engaged students, and out came the essays that form the heart of this book. Students worked hard to edit their contributions into a publishable form and eagerly awaited the feedback of the professional contributors to the volume. They share the hope that *People, Property or Pets?* and the seminar from which it was born will be a model to students and other academics who wish to reach out across disciplinary divides, grapple with big questions, and share their new perspective with the world.

Commentators

Gary Francione is Professor of Law and Nicholas deB. Katzenbach Distinguished Scholar of Law and Philosophy at Rutgers University School of Law in Newark, New Jersey. Professor Francione is the author of several books on animal rights and animal law, including *Introduction to Animal Rights: Your Child or the Dog?* (2000) (foreword by Alan Watson), *Animals, Property, and the Law* (1995) (foreword by William M. Kunstler), *Rain Without Thunder: The Ideology of the Animal Rights Movement* (1996), and *Vivisection and Dissection in the Classroom: A Guide to Conscientious Objection* (with Anna E. Charlton) (1992). He is also the author of numerous articles on animal rights, animal law, law and science, and intellectual property.

Professors Francione and Charlton started the Rutgers Animal Rights Law Clinic in 1990, making Rutgers the first law school in the United States to have animal rights law as part of the regular academic curriculum, and to award students academic credit not only for classroom work, but also for work on actual cases involving animal issues.

Temple Grandin earned her PhD in animal science from the University of Illinois and is an associate professor at Colorado State University. For thirty years she has worked on designing facilities for handling cattle and pigs on ranches, farms, feedlots and slaughter plants. Half the cattle in the U.S. and Canada are handled in facilities she has designed. She is also the author of the welfare auditing system developed for the American Meat Institute. This system is used by restaurant companies, such as McDonald's Corporation and Wendy's International, to audit animal welfare.

Dr. Grandin provides a unique insight into animal behavior because she has autism and wrote two books on autism, including the seminal *Thinking in Pictures.* She is the author of three books on animal behavior and welfare—*Livestock Handling and Transport; Genetics and the Behavior of Domestic Animals;* and *Animals in Translation*—and has been featured widely in the media, including *48 Hours* and *The New York Times.* She is a sought-after speaker on autism and animal rights, and is considered one of the world's leading academic theoreticians in her field.

Lewis Petrinovich began his undergraduate academic life at the University of Idaho as a music major. Soon the seduction of academic analysis and argumentation swept him away, and he switched to what resulted in a career in comparative and physiological psychology—although always keeping an active hand in musical (jazz) performance. After several years of research on the effects of drugs and brain lesions on the development and recovery of learned responses, he concentrated on factors influencing the normal development of behavior, such as the study of the development of language in humans. For many years, he conducted laboratory and field research on a simple analogue of human language development—song in a dialectical bird species, the white-crowned sparrow. To understand the development and function of communication it is necessary to invoke the principles of evolutionary biology.

Each year he taught animal behavior at both the undergraduate and graduate levels. These courses ended with a discussion of the applicability of evolutionary principles to understand human behavior. Another question—often raised by students—concerned the permissibility of experimentation using animals. He convened a graduate seminar to address this issue in a proactive manner, which made it necessary to consider the niceties of argumentation in moral philosophy, and his studies led to several papers investigating the organization and universality of human moral intuitions.

In 1990, Petrinovich took an early retirement and began to write a book on the evolutionary bases of human morality. That decision resulted in two books discussing the permissible use of humans by humans, one on the permissible use of animals by humans, and one on an evolutionary view of human cannibalism. Now he is doing a book on health care in a just society. He has also come full circle in his musical explorations—playing baritone saxophone in three jazz big bands in the San Francisco Bay Area.

Bernard E. Rollin is University Distinguished Professor, Professor of Philosophy, Professor of Biomedical Sciences, Professor of Animal Sciences, and University Bioethicist at Colorado State University.

Rollin taught the first course ever done in the world in veterinary medical ethics, which has been a required part of the veterinary curriculum at CSU since 1978, and was a pioneer in reforming animal use in surgery teaching and laboratory exercises in veterinary colleges. He is a principal architect of recent (1985) federal legislation dealing with the welfare of experimental animals, and has testified before Congress on animal experimentation. He has consulted for various agencies of the governments of the U.S., Canada, Australia, the Netherlands, New Zealand, and South Africa on many aspects of animal research, for the Office of Technology Assessment of the U.S. Congress on genetic engineering of animals, for NIH on animal pain, and for the World Health Organization on using antimicrobials in food animals. He has consulted for the USDA/CSRS on farm animal welfare research, for APHIS on future planning, and for numerous multinational corporations on a variety of animal issues.

Rollin has lectured extensively on animal ethics, genetic engineering, animal pain, animal research, animal agriculture, veterinary ethics and other topics in bioethics and philosophy to audiences of medical researchers, attorneys, psychologists, philosophers, veterinarians, animal advocates, ranchers, farmers, government officials, students and lay people in more than a dozen countries. He is the author of over 200 papers and fourteen books, of which the best known is *Animal Rights and Human Morality*, which won an Outstanding Book of the Year Award from the

American Association of University Libraries. Rollin's most recent books include *Veterinary Ethics: Theory and Cases* (1999), *Complementary and Alternative Veterinary Medicine Considered* (2003, with David Ramey), and *The Well-Being of Farm Animals: Challenges and Solutions* (2004, with John Benson). Rollin is general editor of the Issues in Animal Bioethics Series for Blackwell.

Rollin is designated as state animal welfare extension specialist by CSU dairy extension. He was elected to the National Western Stock Show Association and founded their animal welfare committee. He is also founder and chairman of the Guide Dogs for the Blind animal care and use committee, as well as a competition-level weight lifter and a Harley rider.

Index

active rights, 72–73
AIDS, 166
American Animal Welfare Act of 1911, 78
American Humane Slaughter Act, 78
American Quarter Horse Association, 38
American Veterinary Medical Association (AVMA), 192, 193–194
animal cruelty, 141. *See also* anticruelty laws
animal deficits, 4
animal experimentation. *See* biomedical research; research animals
animal farmers
  and animal rights, 181, 184–186, 188–189
  concern for animal welfare, 187–188
  factory farming by, 79
  versus hunters, 188–189
  income of, 185–186
  laborers under, 186
  methods of slaughter, 187
  statistics on, 185–186
animal legal rights
  active versus passive, 72–73
  alternatives for, 51
  and American legal traditions, 60, 61–62
  anticruelty laws (*see* anticruelty laws)
  approaches to, 60–63
  arguments against, 66–69
  binding nature of, 56
  and biomedical research, 143, 160
  and cognitive science, 127–132
  considerations of, 47
  distinctions between animals deserving, 67
  by equal consideration principle, 84
  goals of, 141
  through Humane Slaughter Act, 60
  by humane treatment principle, 84
  versus human rights, 66
  hypothetical situation for, 57
  implications of, 160, 165, 202, 203
  inconsistent with U.S. Constitution, 60
  through Laboratory Animal Welfare Act of 1966, 60
  and moral agency, 62–63
  and property status, 71–72, 141, 191, 198–199, 200
  protections of, 56
  standard for, 52–53
  and suffering, 60–61
  and theories of rights, 68–69
  utilitarian approach to, 61
  and veterinarians, 197–203
  and welfare laws, 55–56, 78–79, 80–82
animal patenting, 179
animal rights
  actualization of, 33–35
  and animal interests, 56 (*see also* interests)
  versus animal welfare, 65
  anticruelty laws (*see* anticruelty laws)
  argument from marginal cases for, 20–21, 68–69, 100–101
  arguments against, 18–23, 49

animal rights *(continued)*
arguments for increasing, 59, 90–91
avoiding generalization in, 7
basic, 35, 134–135
beginnings of, 25
and biomedical research, 173–174
in Canada, 42–43
and constitutional amendment, 37
deontological approach to, 60–62
deserving versus non-deserving animals for, 63
economical concerns with, 181, 184–186
effecting change for, 33–35
effect on farmers, 184–186
and equality of consideration principle, 11–12, 84
equivalent to children's rights, 35
establishment of, 35–37
and evolutionary theory, 133–142
ex ante experiment for, 52
and farming, 188–189
and humane treatment principle, 84
and human jurisdiction, 72–73
and human rights, 14–15, 50, 192
implications of, 17–18, 30, 67–68, 88, 92–95, 181, 184–186, 188, 198, 202
interest in, 38
versus interests, 18–19
justification for, 59, 90–91
and legal codes, 6
through legal rights (*see* animal legal rights)
legislative conferral, 37
and linguistic abilities, 36
and marginal humans (*see* marginal cases argument; marginal humans)
and neonatal rationality, 135–136
and nervous system complexity, 208–210
and plant life, 63
and preference autonomy, 20
and property status, 30–31, 71–74, 194–195 (*see also* property debate; property status)
regulation difficulties for, 199–200
and sentience, 14
shortcomings of, 199–201
situational, 214
and social bonds, 135–136
social concern for, 35, 214
and species-specific behaviors, 136–137
and spread of disease, 202
and suffering, 28, 105–106 (*see also* suffering)
in Sweden, 38
utilitarian approach to, 61
through welfare laws, 55–56
See also animal legal rights; animal welfare laws
animals
amoral treatment of, 139–140
autonomy of, 19–20, 163
benefits from biomedical research, 169
benefits of property status of, 29–30
categorization of, 7–8, 100, 194
changing status of, 43 (*see also* property debate; property status)
cognitive abilities of, 21, 50, 62, 88–89, 90, 103, 119–124, 194, 213–214 (*see also* cognitive science)
communicative abilities of, 119–120, 122–124, 131–132
as companions, 39–40
complexity of, 208–210
consciousness of, 119–120, 122, 128, 162–163
and consent, 6
core consciousness of, 89
criteria for moral status of, 14–15
criteria for treatment as property, 3–6 (*see also* property debate; property status)
and Darwin (*see* evolutionary theory)
decision-making skills of, 120–121
equality with humans, 25, 43 (*see also* animal rights)
fear in, 207
feelings of, 119–124
and food chain, 189
as food source (*see* food supply)
goal-oriented behavior of, 120–122
guardianship of, 38–40, 193–194
and hard labor, 29
versus humans, 9–11, 27, 60–61, 88–89, 90–92, 157
individual treatment of, 10–11
interests of (*see* interests)

and language, 27
legal protection for (*see* animal welfare laws; anticruelty laws)
legal status of (*see* animal legal rights; animal rights)
and mandatory vegetarianism, 76
memory of, 121
versus mentally challenged humans, 10–11, 12 (*see also* marginal humans)
and moral agency, 19–20, 43–44, 62–63, 140–141
moral behavior of, 90
moral equivalence with humans, 7
moral faculty of, 108–114
as moral patients, 7, 20, 37, 38–40, 183, 193–194
nervous system of, 208–210
pain of, 192–193, 206–208
pain versus suffering in, 176–178
parenting of, 193
as pets, 137–138, 199, 208
as pleasure for humans, 5–6
with preference autonomy, 101–102
as property (*see* property status)
protection of, 30–31, 65, 71–74, 88 (*see also* animal welfare laws; anticruelty laws; suffering)
public policy for, 47
questions for legal status of, ix
and rationality, 3–4
reflective consciousness in, 129–131
rights versus interests of, 18–19
secular approach to, 61–62
self-awareness of, 25–27, 44, 89, 99–100, 108
self-recognition in, 107–108, 124
sentience of, 14
social interactions between, 112
suffering of (*see* animal suffering)
sympathetic abilities of, 88–89
thoughts of, 119–124
tool use by, 122
value of, 210
welfare of (*see* animal welfare)
Western views of, 41
and worse-off principle, 18
Animals Act of Britain, 160
animal shelters, 40
animal suffering, 28, 44, 92–93, 146–147, 169–170
and anticruelty laws (*see* anticruelty laws)
causes of, 78–79
and property status, 81–82
See also suffering
animal testing. *See* biomedical research
animal welfare, 55
and animal legal rights, 201
versus animal rights, 65, 192
basis for, 186
concern for, 187–188, 213–214
disagreement in, 56
and factory farming, 79
farmers' concern for, 187–188
in food farming, 98, 209–210
Humane Slaughter Act, 60
and humane treatment principle, 78–79, 84, 95–96
issues in, 186–188
legal protection for, 55–56, 61, 208
and legal status, 56–57, 203
and nervous system complexity, 208–210
philosophy of (*see* philosophy)
through property status, 65–66, 71–74, 198–199, 206–207
rights-based approach to (*see* animal legal rights)
and specialty meat products, 187
and suffering (*see* animal suffering; suffering)
by veterinarians, 193–194
Animal Welfare Act of 1970 (AWA), 80–81, 198, 200, 203
animal welfare laws, 78, 92, 198, 200, 203
compared to slave welfare laws, 85–87
shortcomings of, 80–83, 92, 192
success of, 82–83
tests for cruelty through, 141
anticruelty laws, 41–42, 78
Animal Welfare Act of 1970 (AWA), 198, 200
against dehorning, 97
and research animals, 83
shortcomings of, 81
success of, 82–83
tests for cruelty through, 141
in United States, 198

Association of Veterinarians for Animal Rights, 191
atherosclerosis, 168
autonomy, 19–20

behavioral sciences, 105
Bentham, Jeremy, 76, 105–106
biomedical research
 alternatives to, 150–151, 161, 201
 and animal legal rights, 159–164
 animal pain in, 159–164
 and animal property status, 143
 benefits of, 201–202
 and cancer, 168
 changing approach to, 145–146, 151
 costs and benefits of, 168–170, 173
 effects of eliminating, 18
 ethics in, 145
 failure of, 148–150, 174–176
 health advances due to, 18
 history of, 145
 on humans, 99, 159–160, 178–179
 importance of, 165–170
 justification for, 94, 161–162
 legislative regulation of, 160
 moral issues in, 146
 numbers of animals in, 145, 161
 organ transplants, 167
 policies for, 160–161
 and property status, 178–179, 198
 and surgery, 167
 tests in, 150
 thalidomide example, 149-150, 174–176
 utilitarianism in, 170, 173
 vaccines from, 165–167
British Animals (Scientific Procedures) Act of 1986, 78
British Cruelty to Animals Act, 78

cancer, 168
Carruthers, Peter, 27, 44
cattle
 as food supply, 185
 handling of, 206
 legal protections of, 206–207
 versus marginal humans, 207
 pain of, 206
Chen, Frances, 145
chimpanzees
 and AIDS research, 166–167
 American Sign Language by, 123
 cognitive abilities of, 119, 120
 learned behaviors of, 109–110
 as moral agents, 140
 protection of, 208
 social grouping of, 208
 theory of mind in, 110–112, 114, 193
 See also primates
cognition, 103
cognitive science
 and animal legal rights, 127–132
 and animal suffering, 129
 and animal welfare, 103
 and communicative abilities, 131–132
 on consciousness (*see* consciousness)
 effects of, 184
 influential writings in, 106
 mental self-awareness, 108 (*see also* consciousness)
 on moral faculty, 108–114
 questions of, 103
 role of, 214
 self-recognition, 107–108
 on suffering, 106–108, 129
 and taught behaviors, 109–110
 theory of mind tests, 110–112, 114
 See also animals, cognitive abilities of
communication
 between animals, 122–124
 and cognitive science, 131–132
 human versus animal, 28–29
 See also language
companion animals, 39–40
conferral, 37
consciousness
 of animals, 89, 120, 162–163
 core, 89
 defined, 128, 133
 determining, 122
 evidence of, 163–164
 extended, 89–90
 language as evidence of, 163–164
 as moral standard, 162
 perceptual, 128
 reflective, 128
consent, 6
core consciousness, 89
Corso v. Crawford Dog and Cat Hosp. Inc., 199
Cushman, Fiery, 105, 213

Damasio, Antonio, 89
Darwin, Charles, 9, 105, 114–115
Dawkins, Richard, 154–155
Declaration of Helsinki, 159
Dershowitz, Alan, viii, 10, 154
Descent of Man, The, 114–115
diseases
  AIDS, 166
  cancer, 168
  of heart, 168
  HIV, 166
  malaria, 166
  poliomyelitis, 166
  smallpox, 166
  stopping spread of, 202
  vaccinations for, 166
dogs, 39–40
dolphins, 148
Dombrowski, Daniel, 12
domesticated animals, 30
Dowling, John, 129–130
Draize test, 150, 203
Dworkin, Ronald, 66

equality of consideration principle, 11–12, 84, 85–87, 98, 101
European Center for the Validation of Alternative Methods (EVCAM), 161
European Patent Office (EPO), 179
European Union, 178
evolutionary theory, 9–10
  and animal morality, 109
  and animal rights, 133–142
  on cognitive abilities, 88–89
  effects of, 184
  and genetics, 154–155
  and morality, 142
  and Scopes trial, 36
  shortcomings of, 62
  and speciesism, 142
ex ante experiment, 52
extended consciousness, 89–90
externalist theory of rights, 69–70

factory farming, 79
fallacy of semantic symmetry, 71, 75
family, and human rights, 135–136
farm animals
  cattle, 185, 206–207
  protections for, 40–41
  welfare research for, 178
  See also animal farmers; food supply
farming industry
  versus hunting, 188–189
  statistics on, 9, 79, 185–186
  See also animal farmers; food supply
fear, 207, 208
Flombaum, Jonathan, 153
food supply
  and animal population, 209–210
  and animal welfare, 98
  and anticruelty laws, 81
  cattle as, 185
  and economy, 184–186
  and evolutionary theory, 9–10
  and factory farming, 79
  and human tastes, 96
  income from, 185–186
  justification for, 9, 79
  and mandatory vegetarianism, 17–18
  numbers of animals for, 9, 79
  protection for animals as, 60
  specialty meat products, 187
  and welfare laws, 78
Fox, Michael W., 74
Francione, Gary, viii, 47, 77, 141, 160, 197–198

Gallup, Gordon, 44, 107–108
genetics, 154–158
Goodall, Jane, 26
Grandin, Temple, ix, 205
Great Ape Project, 37, 38, 100
Griffin, Donald, 89, 128
guardianship, 193–194
Guttentag, Lisa, 159

Hambrick, David, 55
Hass, Derek, 9
Hauser, Marc D., vii, 111–112, 113
heart disease, 168
hepatitis B virus (HBV), 168
hepatocellular carcinoma (HCC), 168
HIV, 166
honeybees, 163
horses, 38
Humane Slaughter Act, 60
humane treatment principle, 78–79, 84, 95–96
human experimentation, 99

human papilloma virus (HPV), 168
human rights, 134
  and animal rights, 50–51, 80
  and animal welfare, 71
  basis of, 62–63
  beginning point of, 11, 49
  and biomedical research, 18
  and cognitive ability, 10–13, 14, 21
  correlation to animal rights, 14–15
  and equality of consideration principle, 11–12
  for individuals, 10–12
  for marginal humans, 10–11, 50–52, 63 (*see also* marginal humans)
  regarding consumption of meat, 17–18
  relation to humanness, 56–57
  and social bonds, 135–136
  source of, 25–26
  and suffering, 129
  universality of, 49–50, 51
  versus utilitarian reasoning, 49–50
  and veil of ignorance, 52
humans
  versus animals, 27, 60–61, 88–89, 90–92, 157
  benefits of owning animals, 29–30
  in biomedical research, 178–179
  cognitive abilities of, 88–89, 103 (*see also* cognitive science)
  core consciousness of, 89
  and economic fairness, 113
  empathy in, 164
  and food chain, 189
  genetics of, 155–157
  health issues and animal testing, 151
  and language (*see* language)
  marginal cases of (*see* marginal humans)
  mentally challenged, 10–11, 12 (*see also* marginal humans)
  as moral agents, 19, 20, 25–26, 43–44, 62, 108, 112–113, 139
  as moral patients, 108–109 (*see also* marginal humans)
  obligation to protect animals, 71
  parenting of, 193
  responsibility to animals, 213
  suffering of, 169–170
  temporal consciousness of, 44–45
  treatment of pets by, 137–138
  vaccines for, 165–167
  and worse-off principle, 18
human slavery
  and animal rights, 98–99
  and animals' property status, 92
  and law suits, 200–201
  and property status, 85–87
hunting, 188–189

interests
  of animals, 13–14, 72, 186
  determination of, 72
  difficulty in knowing, 56
  of estates, 56
  human versus animal, 28–29
  and property debate, 52, 77, 198
  versus rights, 18–19
internalist theory of rights, 68–69

Jadeja, Neha, 17
Johns Hopkins Center for Alternatives to Animal Testing, 161
Junge, Justin, 127

Kamen, Matt, 183, 213
Kant, Immanuel, 19–20, 99, 106
Kefauver Amendment, 174
knockout mouse, 155–156
Köhler, Wolfgang, 131

laboratory animals. *See* research animals
Laboratory Animal Welfare Act of 1966, 60
Landemore, Hélène, 65
language
  and conscious experience, 27, 163
  and higher order thoughts, 27–28
  moral significance of, 36
  in primates, 192
LD50 tests, 150, 161
legal rights
  active, 72–73
  for animals versus humans, 59, 61–62
  basis of, 62–63
  benefits of, 55
  defined, 66, 87
  deontological approach to, 60–62
  flawed standing of animals with, 66–69

and moral community, 69–70
passive, 73, 74
protections of, 87
relation to humanness, 56–57
theories of, 68–69
utilitarian approach to, 61
See also animal legal rights
legislative conferral, 37
livestock industry. *See* animal farmers; food supply
Locke, John, 99
Lomansky, Loren, 68–71

major histocompatibility complex (MHC), 167
malaria, 166
malnutrition, 17–18
marginal cases argument, 20–21, 50–52, 68–69, 91, 100–101
marginal humans
and animal rights, 68–69
and human-animal relationships, 139
human rights for, 10–11, 50–52, 63
legal protection of, 73, 207
in moral community, 70, 108–109, 164
and pain, 164
and property debate, 91
and social bonds, 135–136, 164
and suffering, 129, 147
McDonald's, 98
memory, 121
mentally handicapped
versus animals, 10–11, 12
and experimentation, 22–23
moral obligations to, 21
moral value of, 22
and property status, 88
rational defense of rights of, 22–23
and speciesism, 22
and suffering, 88
See also marginal humans
morality
agents versus patients of, 30–31, 108–109
of animals, 90
animals versus humans, 29
and autonomy, 19–20, 25–26
in biomedical research, 146–148, 169
boundaries for, 159
and cognitive science, 108–114
as community-based, 69–70
and consciousness, 162–163
Darwin on, 114–115
defined, 111–112
duties within, 140
and evolutionary theory, 142
full standing in, 140–141
as human institution, 132
human intuition as, 1
and human rights, 10
and language, 27–28, 36
and marginal humans, 65
and mental abilities, 62
philosophy of, 1
and reflective consciousness, 130
and relationship, 70
and self-consciousness, 19–20, 25–26
social contract in, 140
versus social response, 113
and speciesism, 21–22, 137–138
and suffering (*see* suffering)
and theories of rights, 69
and theory of mind tests, 110–112, 114
and treatment of animals, 206
moral patients. *See* animals, as moral patients; marginal humans
multivalent theory of rights, 69–70

National Institutes of Health, 177–178
naturalistic fallacy, 189
neonatal rationality, 135–136
nervous systems, 208–210
neurobiology, 122
New Zealand, 57
nociception, 107
no-kill animal shelters, 40
Nozick, Robert, 5

Oncomouse, 179
organ transplants, 167
Orlans, Barbara, 146

pain, 107
of animals, 192–193
in biomedical research, 159–164
and consciousness, 162
and fear, 208–209
and humane treatment principle, 95–96

pain *(continued)*
in humans versus animals, 163, 207
importance of, 214
and property status, 206–208
in research animals, 146–147
versus suffering, 127–128, 129, 176–178
See also suffering
painism, 61
passive rights, 73, 74
patenting, 179
People for the Ethical Treatment of Animals (PETA), 60
perceptual consciousness, 128
Petrinovich, Lewis, ix, 103, 133
pets
legal protection for, 199, 208
and speciesism, 137–138
philosophy
against animal rights, 18–23
beginning point of, 1
and behavioral sciences, 105
and human intuition, 1
poliomyelitis, 166
Pollen, Alex, 49
preference autonomy, 19–20, 101–102
primates
abstract thought by, 131
and AIDS research, 166–167
animal rights legislation for, 38
cognitive abilities of, 119, 120
inhibitions of, 111–112
language ability of, 192
learned behaviors of, 109–110
mental self-awareness in, 108, 109–110
as moral agents, 140, 192
and number theory, 120
protection of, 57
protective legislation for, 198
self-recognition in, 108
theory of mind tests for, 110–112, 114
tool use by, 122, 131
principle of equal consideration, 11–12, 84, 85–87, 98, 101
Principles of Humane Experimental Technique, The, 161
project pursuit, 69
property debate
and animal interests, 52
animal legal rights in, 71–72
against animals as non-property, 65
against animals as property, 90–92
and animal welfare, 55
and anticruelty laws, 41–42
basic tenants in, 25
and biomedical research, 18
categorization of animals in, 7–8
and community support, 59–60
consent of animals in, 6
consequences of changing animals' legal status, 17–18
contradictions in, 55–56
and experimentation issues, 22–23 (*see also* biomedical research; research animals)
and guardianship, 38–40
and language, 27–28
legal approach to, 60–63
mandatory vegetarianism in, 17–18
marginal cases argument, 20–21, 50–52, 68–69, 91, 100–101
and moral autonomy, 19–20
philosophical considerations in, 17–23
pleasure in, 5–6
and protective legislation, 60
and rationality, 3–4
reconceptualizing ideas of property in, 30
responsibilities of humans in, 72–73
and self-consciousness, 25–31
shortcomings of existing criteria in, 3–6
and speciesism, 21–22
property status
and animal interests, 77, 84, 88
and animal legal rights, 191
and animal pain, 206–208
and animal rights, 194–195
and animal welfare, 71–74
arguments for and against (*see* property debate)
and biomedical research, 143, 178
compared with human slavery, 85–87
compatibility with animal legal rights, 200
consequences of, 78–80
and criminal liability, 82
criteria for, 3–6

defined, 205
and gene ownership, 154–158
history of, 96
and humane treatment, 78
implications of, 5–6, 93–95, 153–154, 188–189, 191, 197
legal approach to, 60–63, 80–83
legal protection through, 206–207
moral considerations with, 83
negative denotations of, 29
popular support for, 60
power of legal right over, 87
protections offered by, 65, 66, 198–199, 206–207
reconceptualizing, 30
and research animals, 151–152
responsibilities with, 209
restrictions of, 205–206
as speciesism, 194
and suffering, 81–82, 84
types of, 141
Protection of Animals Act of 1911, 78

rationality, 3–4
Rawls, John, 52
reflective consciousness, 128, 129–131, 147
Regan, Tom, 10, 18–20, 66–67, 72, 101–102
research animals
and anti-cruelty laws, 42, 83
benefits from, 169, 201–202
and cancer, 168
conditions of, 160
conflict over, 179–180
for cosmetics, 203
determining situations for use of, 168–170
and *ex ante* experiment, 52
failed use of, 148–150
and heart disease, 168
history of, 145
importance of, 94, 165–170
legal protection of, 34–35, 37–38, 40–41, 60
legislative regulation of, 160
necessity of, 179
numbers of, 145, 161
pain of, 159–164
pain versus suffering in, 176–178
and property status, 151–152, 178–179
reductions in, 201
suffering of, 79–80, 146–147
and surgery, 167
tests on, 150
and thalidomide, 149-150, 174–176
and utilitarianism, 173–174
and vaccines, 165–167
welfare laws for, 78, 80–81
rights, 18–19
Rollin, Bernard, viii-ix, 33, 74
Rowan, Andrew, ix, 143, 173
rule utilitarianism, 161–162
Ryder, Richard, 148

Scopes trial, 36–37
self-awareness, 99–100
self-consciousness, 25–27, 89
self-recognition, 124
sentient beings
defined, 14, 89
duties towards animals as, 18–19
as moral criteria, 21, 100
Silverman, Robbie, 119
Simon, Ariel, 3
Singer, Peter, 10–11, 13–14, 28
as animal liberationist, 74
on animal research, 173
influence of, 33
on marginal humans, 29
and principle of equal consideration, 101
on speciesism, 66
on suffering, 106
slaughter methods, 187
slavery. *See* human slavery
slave welfare laws, 92
smallpox, 166
specialty meat products, 187
speciesism, 4, 66
basis of, 137
defined, 21
irrelevance of, 137
justification of, 139, 142
and morality, 21–22, 162
motivations for, 147
property status as, 194
versus racism, 137–138, 147
versus sexism, 138

Stammbach, Eduard, 111
Stefanakis, Rianna, 191
suffering
  of animals, 28, 44, 92–93, 146–147, 169–170
  and biomedical research, 165, 169
  causes of, 207
  and childbirth, 128
  and consciousness, 128
  as criteria for animal rights, 106–108
  as criteria for animal welfare, 105–106
  defined, 127
  examples of, 128
  and human rights, 129
  human versus animal, 28–29, 169–170
  justified by property status, 81–82
  legal protection from, 208
  levels of, 107–108
  by marginal humans, 147
  minimizing, 19
  and morality, 129
  versus pain, 127–128, 129, 176–178
  questions on, 106
  and reflective consciousness, 147
  of research animals, 146–147
surgery, 167
thalidomide, 149–150, 174–176
theory of mind, 27, 193
theory of mind tests, 110–112, 114
theory of rights, 68–71
Tomb, Ian, 59
tool use, 122
torture, 99
transplantation research, 167

univalent theory of rights, 68–69
USDA annual reports, 177

vaccines, 165–167
Vance, Virginia, 165
vegetarianism
  and health concerns, 17–18
  mandatory, 17–18, 76
veil of ignorance, 52
vervet monkeys, 131–132
veterinarians
  animal categorizations by, 194
  and animal legal rights, 201–203
  and animal rights, 181, 191–195
  and animal welfare, 193–194, 200
  oath of, 197
  responsibility of, 191

de Waal, Frans, 90
welfare laws. *See* animal welfare laws
Wise, Steven, 63, 66, 75, 163, 197–198
worse-off principle, 18

Yancy, Allen, 197